Rebellion or Revolution?

England 1640–1660

G. E. AYLMER

Oxford   New York

OXFORD UNIVERSITY PRESS

1986

Oxford University Press, Walton Street, Oxford OX2 6DP

Oxford New York Toronto
Delhi Bombay Calcutta Madras Karachi
Kuala Lumpur Singapore Hong Kong Tokyo
Nairobi Dar es Salaam Cape Town
Melbourne Auckland
and associated companies in
Beirut Berlin Ibadan Nicosia

Oxford is a trade mark of Oxford University Press

British Library Cataloguing in Publication Data
Aylmer, G. E.
Rebellion or revolution?: England 1640–1660.
— (OPUS)
1. Great Britain—History—Charles I, 1625–1649
2. Great Britain—History—Commonwealth and
Protectorate, 1649–1660
I. Title   II. Series
942.06'2   DA405
ISBN 0–19–219179–9

Library of Congress Cataloging in Publication Data
Aylmer, G. E.
Rebellion or revolution?
(OPUS)
Bibliography: p.   Includes index.
1. Great Britain—History—Puritan Revolution,
1640–1660. I. Title.   II. Series.
DA405.A95 1986   942.06'2   85–15578
ISBN 0–19–219179–9

Set by Grove Graphics
Printed in Great Britain by
Biddles Ltd.
Guildford and King's Lynn

Preface

This book is intended both to serve as a short history of mid-seventeenth-century England, and to provide a survey of current historical interpretations. I have been interested in the English Civil War ever since I was a schoolboy, and a full list of acknowledgements would turn into an intellectual auto-biography. Besides what I owe to my own teachers, I am indebted to numerous historians among my elders, my own contemporaries, and those of a younger generation, as well as to many of my undergraduate and graduate pupils over the years. I will not embarrass them with a list of names, particularly since I owe much to those with whom I disagree. I am especially grateful to Mr Keith Thomas, the Editor of this series, for the challenge provided by an invitation to contribute this volume for OPUS and for much editorial help. I am grateful to Miss C. McMillan and Mrs M. F. Aldworth for having retyped my drafts. The Governing Body of St Peter's College has kindly given me a term's leave which has speeded completion. As with all the other books which I have written, my wife has helped me immeasurably at all stages. I hope to live long enough to see this book superseded in its turn.

G. E. AYLMER

St Peter's College, Oxford
and Llangrove, Herefordshire
1984

Contents

Introduction

Contemporaries who lived through the events of 1640–60 found them amazing and controversial. Not surprisingly, so have historians ever since. It would be very strange if there were agreement, or 'consensus' as the fashionable term now is, on the causes and origins, the nature and significance, the consequences and effects of those events. What happened can be, and has been, written about from many different points of view: theological, moral, ecclesiastical, political, military, social, economic, cultural, and so on.[1] In this book I shall try to present what happened primarily as a political and religious upheaval, or rather series of upheavals, with a decisive military dimension to them and with economic and social aspects of great interest and importance but which were decisive only in negative ways, in helping to ensure what did not happen.

Some historians believe that the facts speak for themselves, that one has only to tell a clear, balanced story in an unpretentious, unfictitious way, and what happened in the past will all become plain and evident. Others believe the problems of explaining to be so important and so difficult that they spend almost all their time on the interpretation, not only of 'facts' but of factors, origins, causes, trends, developments, movements, etc. Any author may fairly be expected to put at least some of his or her cards on the table. I do not believe that the facts speak for themselves. Too often historians cannot even agree what they are or were, still less on which ones mattered—then and now. So explanation and interpretation, however risky and intellectually over-ambitious, cannot be avoided, indeed are essential. On the other hand: without straw, no bricks, and without facts, no interpretation. So the structure of this book is mainly chronological, with some excursions along the way to review particular aspects which help to explain what was happening. In order not to overload the text with too many details and dates, a comparative table of events is provided (see pp. 212–48 below) to help put these in context and to relate them to each other.

In spite of all the cruelties, blunders, and injustices which were committed, moral condemnation is not the historian's business. And beside the crimes and follies, can be set heroism, endurance, charity, and creative achievement. How then did it all come about?

1

Reform

In the spring of 1640 King Charles I had been reigning for fifteen years over England, Scotland, and Ireland. For the last eleven of these he had been ruling in England without having called a parliament. The King had had more than his fill of parliaments in the first four years of his reign. The longest previous intervals between parliaments had been six and a half years under his father and just on seven under Henry VIII and Wolsey. Although some MPs in the early seventeenth century had argued that, by the terms of a statute passed two and a half centuries earlier, there should be annual parliaments, very few people seem to have taken this seriously. There was a sense in which parliaments were still only periodic rather than regular parts of the country's government. The 1620s had seen five parliaments called, and the overall experience of them must have been disillusioning both for the kings and their ministers and for those peers and MPs who felt that Parliament should act as the great council of the realm, advise the monarch, and exercise some influence over his policies. The Commons had neither provided adequate supply for the military intervention which they demanded the King should undertake, calling on him to enter the European War on the Protestant side, nor did they deflect the Crown from its unpopular policies. This was especially true after the conscientious, self-righteous Charles had succeeded the more cautious, if sometimes lazy and choleric James. None the less, the behaviour of the Commons at the end of the second session of his third parliament in March 1629 had shown them up as factious and irresponsible, and had given Charles a sound justification for seeing whether he could manage without Parliament at least for a time.

Historians continue to disagree about which of the policies pursued during the eleven years 'Personal Rule' aroused most opposition. Almost all agree about the unpopularity of the Arminian, or High-Church, trend followed in matters ecclesiastical. Its name came from the early seventeenth-century

Dutch theologian, Jacobus Arminius, who had tried to revise
Calvin's doctrine. As its alternative name, Laudian, suggests,
this policy was intensified after the promotion of William Laud
to the archbishopric of Canterbury in 1633. Laud's zeal and
assiduity were in fact matched by the activity of Richard Neile
at York (1631–40), who was actually Laud's senior as a diocesan
bishop and had come independently to his High-Church
convictions. It is less easy to be sure about the unpopularity of
the particular measures taken at a local, parish level: for
example, turning communion tables placed in the naves of
churches back into altars at the east end, beautifying churches
with glass, carvings, hangings, etc., introducing more ritual into
services, the wearing of more elaborate vestments by the
officiating clergy. Where a strongly Protestant, even a Puritan,
tradition had grown up since the Elizabethan church settlement,
especially in cases where an anti-Arminian or Low-Church
minister was popular and esteemed by his parishioners, we may
be sure that Laudian innovations were much resented. But this
was far from being universally the case. And the notion of the
whole country boiling with hatred for Laud and the Laudians,
and terrified of the incipient restoration of Popery, is a little far-
fetched. Ironically Laud, like the King himself, was blamed for
the favour enjoyed by Catholics at Court; in fact the Archbishop
disapproved of the Catholic Queen's political influence and
wanted stricter controls over Catholics at Court and in foreign
embassies. Paradoxically it was easier for men known themselves to be strongly Protestant, even Puritan in their religious
sympathies, to be political allies of the Queen and yet to escape
any taint of crypto-popery than it was for a sincere Anglo-
Catholic like Laud to distance himself from such associations.
Twentieth-century parallels will easily come to mind.

Likewise the use of the prerogative courts, particularly Star
Chamber, the High Commission, and the Council in the North,
had come to have a bad name by 1640. This seems mainly to
have arisen from the proceedings against the three anti-episcopal
Puritan pamphleteers—William Prynne, Henry Burton, and
John Bastwick—who between them represented the three
learned professions of law, divinity, and medicine. It is less
clear how much resentment had been aroused by the savage
punishment of Alexander Leighton (in 1630), by the proceedings

against a separatist congregation in Surrey (described in a letter by Laud as if they were stags to be hunted down), or even by the first trial and mutilation of Prynne for his attack on the stage and his alleged libelling of the Queen (in 1634). There seems no doubt that the use made by Thomas, Viscount Wentworth, of the Court at York in his capacity as Lord President of the North and then of the Court of Castle Chamber in Dublin as Lord Deputy, to harass his personal opponents and force through his policies, had a polarizing effect. Both in Yorkshire and in Ireland he made mortal enemies who subsequently joined with others at the national level to help bring about his downfall and destruction.

It is hard to estimate how much resentment was generated by the King's financial policies. An attempted campaign of resistance to the payment of customs duties which had not been authorized by Parliament, on the part of some merchants mainly in London, had collapsed by 1631. The fines imposed on landowners worth more than a modest amount in yearly revenue for not having come forward to be knighted at the King's coronation back in 1626, while it was the epitome of an archaic, obsolete law suddenly being reintroduced as a fiscal device, may indeed have been resented but was hardly the stuff of which rebellions are made. The reintroduction of monopolies in concealed guises and in such ways as to circumvent rather than to defy the act against them passed in 1624 was vexatious to other business interests, but only in the cases of salt and soap did it threaten to establish the equivalent of a regular indirect tax on the consumer. Charles I's passion for incorporating and regulating people and their activities, and his Privy Council's zealous oversight of local officials, first in the enforcement of the poor laws, then in reforming the militia, may have been resented by those most affected as tedious and interfering but scarcely more. The raising of ship money in time of peace to pay for a naval rearmament programme (1634), then its extension from the seaboard towns and counties to the whole of England and Wales (1635), and finally its apparent establishment as a semi-permanent addition to the royal revenues (1636–7) was potentially much more serious. Because there was a strict censorship and because correspondents knew that their letters were liable to be opened by royal postal officials, the surviving written evidence cannot be taken as a true measure of the discontent. If the Crown were to become financially independent of Parliament for the indefinite future, then the extension and increase of the customs duties on exports and imports, monopolies on semi-necessities, and ship money were among the pillars upon which such an achievement would have to rest. Use of the King's feudal prerogatives to raise the equivalent of a tax from wardship and other feudal dues and purveyance for the royal household were useful but of secondary importance. The remuneration of officials largely through fees and gratuities received from those requiring their services can be thought of as a valuable substitute for the much larger wages and salaries bill which the Crown would otherwise have had to meet. Whether it was an efficient administrative system was doubted even by some contemporaries. The King attempted to regulate fees by a royal commission, but this body did little more than take penal composition fines from some of the most notorious exacters of excessive fees: a characteristic example of how an apparent reforming instrument became another minor fiscal device. Charles seems to have stopped the sale of offices and titles by the Crown from 1629 to 1639, but even in his father's time this had never been a major source of royal income as it was in France. What the Crown needed was a regular tax on landed wealth, to balance the customs as a tax on trade. And for this local officials or commissioners, willing and able to collect and account for it, would also be necessary. The King and his Council used the sheriffs, local landed gentry appointed annually in each county, for the collection of ship money. Some sheriffs got behind, either because the taxpayers dragged their feet or because they were dilatory. A few individuals refused to pay, but almost all the tax levied was actually collected and paid in for the use of the navy from 1634 to 1638. Whether that would have continued indefinitely is a matter of guesswork. Less was asked for in 1638 for 1639, more again in 1639 for 1640. By the time that resistance and outright refusal to pay became widespread in 1639–40, contributions were also being levied for the payment of soldiers, including local militiamen, to be moved across the country. 'Coat and Conduct Money', as it was called, was thus being levied simultaneously with ship money, which had not happened since England's last involvement in foreign was during the 1620s; and even then ship money had not been raised from the inland counties.

So there is a general problem of evidence in relation to the policies of the Personal Rule. How far did the prominence given to the different grievances—ecclesiastical, fiscal, and others—when criticism, indeed opposition, could once more be openly expressed, correspond to the intensity and the scale with which particular grievances had in fact been experienced during the preceding years? And we might also ask: experienced by whom? For there may well have been a distinction, if only we had the evidence to draw it, between those who had an articulate voice in Parliament, the pulpit, and the press, and the population at large. Some of these questions are unanswerable; others in a sense will answer themselves as we follow developments foward after the end of the so-called 'Eleven Years Tyranny'. Even if propagandists for the King and the royal cause generally were later to exaggerate the prosperity and happiness of the people during these years, the country was at peace, without foreign war or internal disturbance of any seriousness. The Crown lacked the means, even if it had wished, to inaugurate any kind of 'police state'; the number of political and religious prisoners was barely into double figures; there was not a single execution for treason or other crimes of state during more than a decade. We need not indulge in any absurd mythology about merry England or the good old days to perceive that, by the standards of the time, there were discontents but things could all too easily have been much worse. All this bears very directly on the question: were the events of 1639–40 the cause or only the occasion of that regime's collapse? In short, how far was Charles I along the road to establishing a monarchy which, if not in the fullest sense absolute, was viable without the help or interference of parliament?

We have in fact no means of telling whether or not the King had ever intended to rule without Parliament indefinitely. But by 1639–40 this option was no longer open to him, or only so on conditions which he found it impossible to accept. For he could only, it seems, have done so at the cost of letting his Scottish subjects go their own rebellious, anti-episcopal way. More surprising even than the hole into which the King had thereby manœuvred himself is the way in which he and his chief

minister (Thomas Wentworth, now Earl of Strafford) seem to
have thought that the Crown could—as it were—take up with
Parliament where it had left off in the 1620s; they appear to have
hoped for, even to have expected, a 'good', that is a tractable,
parliament like that of 1624 (although even then an unwilling
King had had to sacrifice his Lord Treasurer as the price of
amity and supply). Alternatively they may have supposed that,
as had happened in 1629, given enough rope the opposition
leaders, the trouble-makers in the Commons, would hang themselves. But any of these assumptions grossly underrated the
Crown's weakness due to its involvement with the Scots and its
unpopularity in England, at least with those who could express
their views in Parliament.

The Scottish troubles

It may seem strange that it was Scotland, the home country of
the Stuarts, who had only come to England in 1603, that was the
first to rebel against them. As with the Crown's troubles in
England, the issues were both religious and secular. James I had
succeeded in modifying the extreme or 'Melvillian' presbyterianism of the Scottish Church, by restoring bishops in reality
as well as in name, and by reintroducing elements of ceremony
and ritual into the church services. But he had not replaced the
existing liturgy wholesale, and he seems in his last years to have
sensed that he had gone about as far as he could go without
arousing more opposition than the game was worth. Charles had
hardly succeeded to the throne when he persuaded the Court's
supporters in the Scottish Parliament to pass a bill which
appeared to threaten the title of virtually everyone who held any
ex-church (that is monastic and other) lands which had been
secularized at any time since the beginning of the Scottish
Reformation a century or so earlier. It was the fear of resumption, which would now have a legal basis, rather than the
fact of such a policy taking place that aroused alarm. This was
much the same as in the case of Laud's supposed threat to lay
tithe owners, 'impropriators' as they were known, in England.
However the Scottish Resumption Act must have seemed all the
more menacing coupled with other aspects of royal policy.
Bishops were appointed to the royal Council and to some of the
major secular offices; leading members of the nobility were

slighted; after Charles's visit to Edinburgh for a belated coronation in 1633, one peer who was charged with conspiracy on dubious evidence was condemned to death and his subsequent pardon does not seem to have undone the damage.

In 1637 came the scheme for a new Prayer Book. It is a fallacy propagated by some nineteenth-century textbooks that Laud imposed this on the Scottish Church, though it is true that he approved of the new liturgy and supported its enforcement. It was in fact the creation of a few Scottish Episcopalians—bishops and others—who were more Laudian, perhaps we should rather say more Arminian, than Laud himself, in the way that members of small minorities often are extremist because of their very isolation. Popular opposition in some of the Edinburgh churches and elsewhere may have seemed to presage some kind of radical social upheaval; alternatively the nobility and gentry (or lairds as they were known) may merely have been waiting for such an opportunity to present itself. Sincere commitment to the church settlement of eighty years before, if not to its theocratic extravagances, was more broadly based in Scotland than support for any one denominational standpoint was in England. The movement which led to the drafting and then the mass subscription of the National Covenant was so widespread, being both highly organized and genuinely spontaneous, that for once the adjective 'national' does not seem out of place. With the notable exceptions of the Catholic Gordons in Aberdeenshire and the anti-Campbell clans of the western Highlands and Islands, almost all the major families and their respective followings, whether clansmen or tenants and dependants, adhered and were at least in the technical sense Covenanters. They included the King's subsequent military champion, the hero of many romantic novels and popular biographies, James Graham, Marquis of Montrose. The King's ministers in Scotland were and felt themselves to be isolated and vulnerable, and their morale cracked. Perhaps even more serious, Charles allowed himself to be advised on Scottish matters, especially to do with the Church and the Covenant, by a small informal committee, not even fully representative of the English Privy Council, let alone of its Scottish counterpart. Besides Archbishop Laud, whose ignorance of Scotland seems to have been remarkable in someone of his intellectual capacity, its most influential member was the King's remote cousin, the Marquis of Hamilton (who had been made Earl of Cambridge and March in the English peerage—a fact used to justify his trial and execution for treason some ten years later). Hamilton was a politically equivocal character. At worst it was believed that he saw himself as an alternative monarch to the main Stuart line; at best he counselled concessions but then failed to conciliate the leading Covenanters or to build any kind of trust between them and the King; he seems to have been one of those unfortunate people who generate mistrust, others fearing the worst of them even when it is not intended.

In the summer of 1638 Charles decided that he would coerce his Scottish subjects into obedience, even if this meant the use of armed force and involved temporary concessions while the military measures were being prepared. As had been the case with the foreign expeditions of the 1620s, the probable cost of such an undertaking was grossly underestimated. The King's financial advisers were able to report that he had a modest revenue surplus, thanks to the financial policies and the economies in royal spending (in spite of the King's marvellous collection of Italian paintings and the costly Court masques of the 1630s). If this had not been the case, even the most obstinate and unrealistic of monarchs could hardly have envisaged suppressing the Covenanters by armed force. But the financial resources, reserves of cash, and credit available to the King would have needed to be far greater than they were for such a policy to have carried through successfully.

The first of the so-called 'Bishops' Wars', that of 1639, involved no actual fighting between English and Scots. Inside Scotland it was not really a civil war; except in the remoter areas, the anti-Covenanter forces and those loyal to the King were virtually obliterated or else driven into quiescence; this was only to change with the emergence of Montrose as their leader some four years later. An English army, consisting partly of militia units almost all unwillingly drafted from the northern counties, together with some Court volunteers and professional soldiers of fortune, was assembled in Yorkshire and then marched up to the Tweed. Both sides relied on officers who had been trained in various of the Continental armies, mainly those of the Dutch, the Swedes, and the German Protestants. The English found themselves confronting a superior number of Scots whose enthusiasm for the Covenant and for their supposed national rights probably made them readier to sustain the hardships of campaigning in the field without adequate provisions and other facilities. By twentieth-century standards, seventeenth-century armies travelled light. But it was still a major feat to equip, supply, and support thousands of men and animals hundreds of miles from home, especially in the bleaker, poorer parts of the country. Disease, usually due to bad sanitation and consequent contamination of food and water, was normally a worse enemy than any hostile army. As it was, neither side proved keen to begin a real shooting war. Face-saving negotiations led to a truce called the Pacification of Berwick, since it was by no means a real peace treaty. The King conceded more than the Covenanters. Both armies withdrew, a large part of the royal forces melting away. Just as Charles had made temporary concessions to the National Assembly of the Church of Scotland and to the Scottish Parliament in 1638–9 but had planned to revoke these when he was strong enough to do so, this was his intention again after the first Bishops' War. The Pacification was soon followed by renewed military preparations, this time involving the militias of the midland and southern counties and a larger contingent of regular paid troops.

A decisive new element in the situation was the increased prominence of Wentworth in the King's councils. Soon to be created Earl of Strafford as a reward for his services, he made three disastrous miscalculations, two large and one apparently trivial, which together demonstrate how a combination of semi-absolute power and absenteeism can warp the political judgement even of a very able, highly intelligent person.[1] On the wider political scene, he seems to have regarded religion as no more than a smokescreen for the secular ambitions of the Marquis of Argyll (the head of the Campbells) and the other aristocratic Covenanting leaders, their aim being to take the country over and turn it into an oligarchy. As we have seen, a wide section of the Scottish nobility did indeed disapprove of Charles's policies and resented their own exclusion from influence; the notion that even Argyll, let alone the others, was planning some kind of constitutional revolution has no basis in fact, beyond the actions of the Scottish Parliament in 1639 and again in 1640, which did pass various acts some of which anticipated the measures which we shall find taken in England during 1641, aimed at reversing the policies of the Personal Rule and making a repetition impossible. It was however true that some of the noble and laird leaders were more devout than others: Argyll and Johnston of Warriston could fairly be called enthusiasts, what their enemies would have called fanatics.

Secondly, Wentworth's relative success with the Irish Parliament in 1634 had apparently led him to suppose that an English parliament could be handled in the same sort of way, be effectively browbeaten, outwitted, or both. This was a curious error for someone to have made who had himself sat in every parliament but one from 1614 to 1628 and had taken a leading role in at least three of them. Lastly, on the narrower stage of private and family pride, he deliberately took the Barony of Raby (in county Durham) as a subsidiary to his new title as Earl of Strafford, when the King's newly appointed Secretary of State (who had been the Queen's, not Laud's or Wentworth's choice for the post), the elder Sir Henry Vane, had a house and estate there and may well have aspired to end his days as Lord Raby. Vane's son, the younger Sir Henry, was one of the most talented but also most extreme members of the Puritan opposition, closely linked with the future parliamentary leadership. Of such seeming trifles are major political disasters sometimes partly composed.

The Short Parliament

So our curtain goes up in the early part of 1640 on parliamentary elections in England and Wales, the first which had taken place for some twelve years. As was usual until the eighteenth century, the elections were spaced out over several weeks in different counties and boroughs. What sort of Parliament was it that was to assemble after so long an interval? Thanks to Stuart creations of new peers, the House of Lords was potentially nearly twice as large as it had been at the accession of James I. The Commons was somewhat larger too, more boroughs having been enfranchised plus the two universities. As was usual in the seventeenth century, many seats were not contested, that is there were no elections with a counting of votes. But the significance of this can easily be misunderstood. It does not mean because there was no election in our sense that there was no interest, no controversy, above all no discontent with the way things were. It might simply mean that one family or one electoral patron, or a broader alliance of influential people, normally landed gentry perhaps also peers, had decided who should represent the county or more often the borough in question. The real political process therefore took place behind the scenes before the day when the sheriff or other returning officer declared the outwardly unopposed candidate to be duly elected. Whether more con-stituencies (the word was not used then) were becoming less controllable by patrons, more liable to genuine contests with larger, wider electorates, remains at present open to debate. But it was true then, as it was to remain until at least the first Reform Act of 1832, that there was no real correlation between the 'openness' of the franchise or contestability of a seat and the degree of political commitment to court or opposition of the member returned.

Many histories of the seventeenth century take the failure of the first Parliament held in 1640 too readily for granted.[2] It gets swept off-stage too cursorily; for it need not have been so short as to have become known as the 'Short Parliament'. The King's spokesmen asked for massive financial support in order to renew his campaign against the Scots, so that the new Prayer Book could be imposed and royal authority together with episcopal control be restored more generally. The Commons' spokesmen, notably John Pym, a veteran from the 1610s and 1620s who had himself been a royal revenue official for over twenty years, John Hampden, hero of the ship-money case of 1637–8, and Sir Robert Holborne, one of Hampden's counsel in that case but in fact a future royalist, called for the fullest consideration of grievances under three main headings: religious, civil, and parliamentary. Perhaps because ship money bulked large in the second, it was agreed that Hampden's other counsel, Oliver St John, should take charge of that heading and Holborne of the third—the long interruption of parliaments and breach of privilege of members. If the King's spokesmen had taken the initiative by proposing a bill to make ship money into an exclusively parliamentary tax in future, and had also made some immediate concessions under the other two headings, he might well have got, if not all the twelve subsidies for which he was asking, at least a very substantial grant of funds. More important still, a general atmosphere of co-operation, goodwill, and mutual trust might have brought Country and Court, Commons and Crown together again, away from what has in later twentieth-century Britain been aptly called the politics of 'us' and 'them'. Once off the sensitive topic of taxation, where the Commons showed an acute resentment of any pressure from the Lords (so much for the lately revived view that peers controlled MPs in these years), the King's natural supporters in the Upper House could have voted down or refused to proceed with extremist attacks on the Bishops or on the Crown's own constitutional prerogatives.

It was not only the King's and his advisers' loss of patience and the consequent summary dissolution but what followed this that proved so damaging to the regime. Arrests were made, studies searched, papers seized; above all there was an immediate resort to non-parliamentary means of raising money. The Convocation of clergy from the southern ecclesiastical province of Canterbury remained in session after the Parliament had ended. Not content with voting additional clerical taxes to the King, this body passed a new set of canons (the first since 1604), which seemed more Catholic than those they replaced and which intensified opposition to the Crown's religious policies and the leadership of the Church. A serious riot in south London aimed at the Archbishop was suppressed and two ringleaders executed. Parallel with all this, renewed military preparations went forward, and a second campaign was mounted against the Covenanters, effectively led by Strafford, who thus increasingly together with Laud became the joint focus of popular fear and hatred. The second Bishops' War of 1640 involved a little more actual fighting than the first and resulted in an ignominious English defeat, the loss of Newcastle-upon-Tyne, and Scottish occupation of the extreme north-east of the country.

To wage an unpopular war and then lose it is indeed to have the worst of almost every world for any government. Charles I resorted to yet one more characteristically archaic political device in summoning the peers to York as the King's 'Great Council'. No monarch had tried to transact important public business with the Lords (or the Commons) alone since the fourteenth century. And in any case the pressures on the King to call another parliament were growing all the time. Twelve peers, all but two of them future parliamentarians, petitioned him to this effect just before the summons to York. And at some time between the summons to the peers and his opening speech later in September, Charles had evidently decided to do so. Therefore, even if the Great Council was originally intended as a substitute for another parliament, it did not actually serve as such. The King indeed tried to keep peace negotiations with the Covenanters in the hands of peers and other privy councillors, but even this did him little good. The resulting Treaty of Ripon merely ensured that he would meet his new Parliament in a position of extreme weakness and vulnerability, having undertaken in effect to pay for the Scottish army's maintenance, so that it did not simply live off the country, that is until there was a more permanent settlement and it could be paid off and sent home. Again there is some doubt about whether more seats than usual were contested in the October elections for a new House of Commons. As has already been explained, the level of political awareness and the extent of feeling against the Court and its policies cannot safely be measured by the number of constituency contests. The actual shift in the membership of the House between the two sets of elections in eight months was numerically large but not overwhelming; but, as was later observed, the temper of the House was now very different.[3] And because there were now two unpaid armies in the north of England—the King's and the Scots'—for both of which supply must be found, the Crown's bargaining position was much more fragile, and the royal policies and ministers more unpopular and at risk than in April.

The Long Parliament

If there had been some justification then for the King's expectation of a tractable parliament, there was surely none in November on any rational calculation. Why should the Commons have voted supply without exacting very stiff terms, major concessions, and the punishment of scapegoats? Both parties, or 'sides' as we may almost call them, had been bitten too often for a sensible, moderate compromise to be possible. Once more, however, what happened was not the only logical possibility. Strafford might have done what some of his enemies feared or alleged that he meant to do: namely to have some of the Country leaders in both Houses arrested and charged with treason, for having incited the Scots to rebel, even for having encouraged them to invade England, and for seditious correspondence with the French government. This was the more plausible in that Queen Henrietta Maria, so influential with her husband, was on notoriously bad terms with Cardinal Richelieu, her brother's chief minister and the manager of French foreign policy. Precisely who had gone how far in which of these negotiations is obscure, and in any case this does not really affect the issue. Some of the Country leaders, 'the faction' or 'the factious party', as they were to be named, had undoubtedly been in touch with the Covenanting leaders; and the substance, if not the detail, of such a charge would not have been wholly implausible. Alternatively, failing this kind of bold, perhaps admittedly reckless, pre-emptive blow, the King could at once have offered generous concessions, have played for the support of the Lords, and—as in 1629—have given the Commons enough rope with which to hang themselves.

But we need not pursue these possibilities any further. Charles did none of these things. A week after the Parliament met, the Commons impeached Strafford; by refusing to hear his defence and by having him sent to the Tower, the Lords conceded that there was a case to be met. The Commons purged itself of monopolists, thereby weakening even more the Court element in its membership. Attacks on other unpopular ministers, churchmen, and judges soon followed; some of these fled abroad, others were imprisoned, in Archbishop Laud's case for over four years, after which he was finally tried and executed long after he had ceased to be a threat to anyone but simply in order to appease the Puritan zealots.

In the winter of 1640–1 the King's councillors and ministers were utterly demoralized, and government was almost at a standstill. In Parliament so many different committees were processing so many different grievances, including the very detailed preparation of the case against Strafford, that there too there was little to show. Concessions were bound to be extorted from the King sooner or later, unless he went once more for a summary dissolution, but the risk of large-scale disorder, perhaps of an armed uprising in London and in the north, would then have been very great. Instead the King spoke passionately against a bill for three-yearly parliaments as being incompatible with his essential prerogatives, but later gave way and accepted it without major amendments. He gave Strafford what moral and legal support he could during the long-drawn-out impeachment trial. In spite of key evidence which the younger Vane had abstracted from his father's papers, showing that Strafford had apparently advised the King to use the Irish army against his English not his Scottish subjects and to govern by emergency means after the Short Parliament, it seemed unlikely that the Lords would vote the fallen minister guilty of treason; so much of what Strafford had done was either an accumulation of minor misdemeanours and acts of high-handedness or else the faithful execution of his royal master's own chosen policies. This artificial separation of the guilt of minister from the real responsibility of monarch shows the strength of royalist feeling and the essential intellectual and political conservatism of the great majority in both Houses. When the Commons switched, in an atmosphere of plots and threats to their own safety, to an attainder against Strafford, a legislative rather than a judicial way of destroying someone, Charles promised him protection as to life and estate. In the face of angry crowds, mass demonstrations by large numbers of Londoners, first the House of Lords, then the King, gave way to the Commons and passed the Attainder Act; and the King, fearing for the safety of his wife and children, eventually signed the death warrant, an action for which he was to reproach himself all the rest of his life. At the same time, the Triennial Act having already been passed partly to satisfy the Scots as well as to procure votes of taxation and shore up royal credit, the King acceded to another bill intended to satisfy those lending money to the Crown on the security of future parliamentary grants. This laid down that the existing Parliament was not to be dissolved, prorogued, or even more than briefly adjourned except by its own consent. A whole series of other bills then went forward during the rest of the summer, and was passed into law, demolishing the prerogative courts, banning the various financial devices used during the years of non-parliamentary rule, and rectifying other abuses real and alleged.

Legislation

It seems not to be of much consequence, indeed perhaps only to be a matter of taste among historians, whether the Long Parliament's measures in 1641 are called constructive or destructive. The Triennial Act was an attempt to provide for a regular sequence of future parliaments by prescribing the means by which elections should be held and a new parliament meet at least once every three years for a minimum session of fifty days, unless deferred or shortened by mutual agreement of the King and both Houses. This act, therefore, only became operative in 1660, and was repealed a few years later, being replaced by an innocuous substitute without enforcement clauses, which Charles II happily broke for the last year of his life. A third and last Triennial Act, somewhat more like that of 1641, though less slighting to the monarch's prerogatives, was grudgingly accepted by King William III in the 1690s and remained in force until replaced by the Septennial Act of 1716. It seems fair to infer that an effective measure of this kind was regarded as a genuine constraint on the freedom of action of monarch and ministers. The statute against the dissolution, prorogation, and adjournment of the Long Parliament itself save by its own consent, called the act for a 'perpetual parliament' by the neutralist antiquarian scholar Sir Roger Twysden, was a far graver encroachment on the royal prerogative. It tied Charles I's hands in a way that has no parallel even with the constitutional monarchs of the nineteenth and twentieth centuries; and, as it turned out, this act was not to lapse for nearly another nineteen years. The Tonnage and Poundage, or Customs Grant Act, made the collection of these duties conditional on frequent parliamentary authorization; the first in a series of such measures allowed their collection for only some seven and a half weeks (May to July 1641). This was far more drastic than the one-year grant of Tonnage and Poundage offered by the Commons to Charles in both his first two parliaments of the 1620s. The abolition of Star Chamber and the High Commission and the emasculation of the judicial powers of the Privy Council and the other prerogative courts, leading to the disappearance of the Council in the North, proved that, in order to rectify what were seen as the abuses of the 1630s and render them impossible

for the future, it was necessary to abolish instruments of royal
government which long antedated Charles's Personal Rule or
even the accession of his father. The ending of all business in
Star Chamber, in the Court at York and (so far as can be seen)
in the Court of Requests, probably contributed to the over-
loading of Chancery and the common law courts, and thus
unintentionally intensified the later demands for law reform.

It can be plausibly argued that the political attitudes of the
common-law judges were of more consequence to the Crown.
James and Charles I had dismissed three senior judges in under
twenty years. The justices of King's Bench and Common Pleas
and the barons of the Exchequer had consistently given verdicts
favourable to the royal prerogative in test cases over the legality
of non-parliamentary customs duties, the Council's powers of
arrest and detention without trial, and finally the right to use the
Crown's emergency powers in levying ship money. None the less
the way in which the judges had been lobbied about the legality
of ship money before Hampden's case arose had clearly been
much resented, as was perhaps shown in the narrowness of the
actual verdict (only seven to five in the King's favour). The
appointment of judges who would decide cases with political
implications on their legal merits without fear or favour, and
their enjoyment of a secure tenure to protect them against
arbitrary dismissal, were of at least equal moment even with Star
Chamber, let alone the Council in the Marches of Wales or the
Court of Requests. The Long Parliament did try to obtain a
parliamentary veto on judicial appointments and to gain security
of tenure for judges once they were appointed, but not until it
was too late for such measures to be agreed. This was left
unresolved and was still an issue under the later Stuarts and
William III.

The act ruling ship money to be illegal and prohibiting it in
the future did not of course exclude extraordinary grants of
parliamentary taxes for naval and military expenditure. The
Long Parliament itself voted the equivalent of at least ten
subsidies in 1640–2. The grants might take the form of
traditional subsidies, a rate of so much in the pound on real and
so much on movable property, or the allocation of a fixed lump
sum which had to be found either by the requisite number of
subsidies or by 'Tenths and Fifteenths' (the previous direct tax

on wealth which was still in use); an alternative, used in 1641 and again in 1660–1, was to levy a poll tax graded according to wealth and social rank. Ship money had in fact been a more equitable as well as a more efficient tax than the subsidy because it was based on a far more accurate assessment of people's wealth and property holdings; somewhat ironically the assessment used for ship money was applied in raising the various weekly and then monthly 'Assessments', as they came to be called, which were to be the staple form of direct tax between 1643 and 1660. Some of these levies were to rest on as dubious a legal basis as ship money had; in fact no regular, constitutionally acceptable direct tax on property was to be established until the Land Tax of the 1690s. Other statutes passed in 1641 prohibited other revenue measures or substitutes for normal taxation which had been in use during the 1620s and 1630s: these included penal fines on landowners who were alleged to have encroached on the ancient boundaries of royal forests, fines for not taking up knighthood, and the imposition of punitive or penal fines in the law courts. By the late summer of 1641 enough money had been raised, either in taxes collected, or in loans on the security of taxes voted but not yet collected, for the paying off and dispersal of the two armies in the north of England—the Scottish Covenanters' and the King's. But constitutionally speaking all still rested on the present Parliament and its relations with the King; politically a condition of near vacuum continued.

Worsening relations

The death of Francis Russell, fourth Earl of Bedford, just before the Attainder and Perpetual Parliament Acts in May 1641, is believed by some historians to have destroyed any possibility of a lasting compromise between Charles I and the controlling figures in the two Houses. This would have involved some kind of package, with Bedford heading a government of national unity and reconstruction, and with places in it for other leading critics of the Crown among peers and MPs. Certainly Bedford was John Pym's electoral patron, Pym the Earl's client and family 'man of business'. But it does not follow from this that every important move made by Pym in the Commons was cleared in advance with Bedford; nor was it Pym who initiated all the most radical steps in the Commons. Still it is possible that there had been close consultation between them more often than not. That is not quite the same as making Bedford's death a decisive turning-point. For that to be so, we have to suppose that Charles I would have radically reconstructed his government, indeed was about to do so, and would then have governed on the advice and with the consent of his new ministers. The King did indeed admit, or readmit, several Country, 'opposition' peers to the Council at the beginning of 1641, and in the following months he appointed some of them to offices, likewise St John, another associate of the Earl of Bedford, who was made Solicitor-General. But he made no further move to give Bedford himself a major office, nor was anything done for any of the other leading figures in the Commons. Futhermore, none of those who were so appointed was effectively won over to the King's side in the most serious of the controversies which followed. True, those admitted to the King's councils and rewarded with office from the autumn of 1641 onwards did include some who later became royalist leaders; but by then much else had happened too, and this fact is not evidence about Bedford and the political situation in the summer of that year. Already before the end of June the Commons had passed and presented to the Lords a set of Ten Propositions which, if they had become operative, would have involved a very considerable further encroachment on the powers of the Crown: for example, that the King should accept parliamentary advice about controlling his wife and bringing up his children. Meanwhile Charles seems to have toyed intermittently with the idea of a counter-coup—to seize the opposition leaders and forcibly dissolve the Parliament. Some of the officers from his 1639 and 1640 armies were involved. There were two of these so-called 'army plots' in 1641; the King probably did not know about the first of them, but was almost certainly implicated in the second. In addition to all this—the bitterness aroused by Strafford's attainder and execution and the unexpected death of Bedford—there were other reasons why no lasting settlement proved possible.

The King decided to go to Scotland, to try to restore relations with his recent enemies there, perhaps also to create an effective royal party out of ex-Covenanters and others. When he announced his intention, Parliament began to put almost every possible obstacle in his way. It was understandably keen that he should pass the numerous bills, many of them already mentioned, which were designed to dismantle the regime of the 1630s and make any repetition of it impossible. When he eventually did set off for the north, a kind of small watch committee of both Houses was appointed to go with him and to report back; after the two Houses' self-adjournment for a belated summer break in September, its members were to report to a large standing committee of both Houses which was given unprecedented powers during the recess. Again these steps implied lack of trust and yet more restraints on the sovereign's freedom of action as ruler of the country. In addition, although the King failed to make a constitutional issue out of it as he was to do the following spring, the two Houses began to legislate by ordinance during August, although admittedly only on matters of secondary importance; and it is not clear that peers and MPs yet regarded these ordinances as having the same force and solemn binding quality at law as statutes which had the royal assent. But even if they were seen as executive orders, more like royal proclamations by the King and his Council, this was still a virtually unprecedented encroachment on the monarch's normal and proper sphere of government. It was his name appearing at the foot of an order issued by the adjournment committee which led to the royalist wisecrack that only the initial R (for Rex) was lacking after Pym's signature, and hence the nickname 'King Pym'. The fifty-seven-year-old Somerset gentleman was an unlikely candidate for the role of uncrowned king; nor were his personal ascendancy and political control over the two Houses ever nearly as complete as this might suggest.

2
Rebellion

The problems of Ireland

Two further developments finally blasted any hope of a peaceful compromise settlement. These were the attack on episcopacy and the Prayer Book and the Irish Rebellion. To take the second of these first, Ireland had been at peace except for local disturbances since O'Neill, Earl of Tyrone's surrender to Elizabeth's viceroy at the time of the Queen's death in 1603. The biggest change that had come about since then was the Anglo-Scottish settlement of Ulster in the 1610s and 1620s under James I's active patronage; this had followed the 'flight of the earls' (Tyrone, Tyrconnel, and their respective retinues), fearing charges of treasonable conspiracy, in 1607. The colonization was proportionately denser than previous English 'plantation', to use the Elizabethan word for it, which had mainly affected the eastern and southern parts of the island; and it was both urban and rural. The religion of the incomers was either strongly Protestant Church of England or Presbyterian Church of Scotland. The existing indigenous population was suppressed rather than being annihilated or driven out. Thus was created the first stage of the 'Northern Ireland problem' as we still know it today. Within the country as a whole certain clearly distinguishable sectional or communal interests had established distinct identities between the time of Elizabeth's Irish Wars and the early part of the seventeenth century.

The overwhelmingly Roman Catholic and ethnically Celtic-cum-aboriginal Gaelic-speaking Old Irish formed a large numerical majority. And in much of Ireland, except Ulster and the historic 'Pale' around Dublin, they still provided a large proportion of the landholding social élite. In the seaboard towns many of them were in fact at least partly of Viking (Norse) descent. Except for a very few who had ties of marriage or other Court connections, they were virtually excluded from government, even at the local level; and their religion, if not yet actually driven underground, had none of the privileges or

advantages of an established church, although there could be
no question of treating the Irish like the English Catholic
recusants—there were simply too many of them.

The Anglo-Irish or Old English were the descendants, in
varying proportions genetically speaking, of the Norman-
French, Welsh, and English settlers who had gone over in the
Middle Ages, many of whom had intermarried with the native
Irish. Since the populations of most countries in the world are
ethnic mixtures and racial purity is a myth, it may be asked why
students of Irish history in particular should be concerned with
such considerations. The answer is their interconnection with
almost every other aspect of life in Ireland: religious, political,
cultural, social, and economic. Since the successive religious
reformations during the reigns of Henry VIII, Edward VI, and
Elizabeth I, some of the Old English had been converted to
Protestantism, many others remained Catholic; often the
divisions cut through families. The greatest such family, the
FitzGeralds, Earls of Kildare and Desmond, were by the time of
Charles I extinct in both their main male lines. Since the end of
the O'Neills and the O'Donnells in the north, or at least the
disappearance of their leading representatives, no single family
enjoyed a clear primacy among either the Old English or the
Old Irish, although there were several with strong regional
followings and some with national pretensions. The current
head of the Butlers, Earls (later Marquises and then Dukes) of
Ormonde, had been converted to Protestantism; he was beginning to emerge as a national figure.

The New English were the settlers of the mid-sixteenth to early
seventeenth centuries, other than the Ulster Scots. They were
100 per cent Protestant, almost all of an aggressively 'Low-
Church' or Puritan inclination. They tended to regard the
Dublin Government as their natural and rightful preserve and as
the proper instrument of their personal and sectional interests.
Richard Boyle, the first or 'great' Earl of Cork, who had arrived
in Ireland with a few pounds in his pocket at the time of the
Spanish Armada, was the wealthiest of them (indeed probably
one of the richest individuals in the British Isles by 1640) and one
of the most ambitious. He had quarrelled sharply and, as it
turned out, irrevocably with Lord Deputy Wentworth about his
titles to various ex-church estates, which he had acquired at far

below market prices, and more personally over the positioning of his first wife's funeral monument in St Patrick's cathedral in Dublin. As with Vane and the barony of Raby, Wentworth liked the symbols as well as the substance of victory over his opponents; and in this case too it cost him dear. In the English House of Commons, Sir John Clotworthy acted as a kind of unofficial agent for the New English in Ireland, sitting for a borough in the partial gift of the Puritan Earl of Warwick.

The Irish Parliament had been subordinated to the English Privy Council and in effect to the English Parliament also since the late fifteenth century. The main issue in the early seventeenth century concerned the position of the Catholic Old English: could they sit as peers or MPs, and would the Crown honour its concessions, known as 'the Graces', which they claimed had been promised them as the price of their loyalty earlier in James's reign? Control of the executive was the particular prize of the New English. Their ideal was an indefinite intermission between lord deputies (or lord-lieutenants) when the deputy's powers were normally exercised by two or more lords justices drawn from their own ranks. Failing this, a weak and compliant lord deputy or an absentee lieutenant without a deputy would also suit their interests. It was thus almost inevitable that a strong viceroy like Wentworth should have come into collision with them. This was, however, intensified by his conversion to Laudianism under the influence of his friend, political ally, and religious mentor. He had also contrived to alienate important families and individuals among the Old English and Irish through his plantation policy, and was on predictably bad terms with the Ulster Scots. On the other hand, he had played off the different groups among his potential opponents against each other, and had got the best of handling the only Parliament of his deputyship prior to 1640. Outwardly all was calm; so much so that he offered to aid the King by transporting troops across from Ireland to help suppress the Covenanters in Scotland.

When he was summoned to take charge of the King's affairs in England during the winter of 1639–40, Strafford—by then Lord-Lieutenant—had appointed his cousin and close associate Christopher Wandesford as his Deputy. Wandesford was an able and honest man without his chief's gift of making enemies; and in normal times he might well have made an acceptable head of government. But the times were not normal. The Old English and others got out of hand in the Irish Parliament which met in 1640, and the Deputy died later in that year after less than twelve months in office. He was succeeded by lords justices in the usual way, as a stopgap until the King could persuade the newly appointed Lord-Lieutenant, the Earl of Leicester—an acceptable choice to the English Parliament—to cross over and take up his duties. As it turned out, Leicester never got to Ireland at all, although his son (a future Cromwellian councillor) was to serve there briefly twice during the 1640s. The Dublin Government was now more obviously linked to the interests of the New English than at any time sine 1632; moreover, it was closely associated with what looked to the Irish like the ultra-Puritan parliamentary leadership in London. There is no certain means of telling whether those who planned to seize Dublin and overthrow the pro-settler regime saw this as a desperate pre-emptive strike to prevent the destruction of their religion and themselves, or whether they were merely taking the opportunity to have their revenge for earlier events, especially in the north. The likeliest answer would seem to be a bit of both. Those at first involved were mostly Old Irish from Ulster with a scattering from the other three provinces; their planning must have begun in the summer or even the spring of 1641. Again it is not clear at what stage they decided to act in the name of King Charles, in modern terminology to be for home rule rather than a fully independent Ireland. The forgery of a letter purportedly from the King giving approval for their action was almost certainly the brainchild of one person only. As with most groups of conspirators their aims were mixed, and it is not surprising that the plan to seize Dublin Castle was betrayed and thus frustrated. But, this apart, the rising spread very fast into the rest of the country, even into the long-Anglicized Pale, and was joined by many of those Old English who were still Catholics. Not all Gaelic Irish or all Catholics supported the rising, just as not all Anglo-Irish or even all New English opposed it. Atrocities were certainly committed, although whether they were begun by the Irish or by the Ulster Scots or by both simultaneously is unclear. Beyond doubt is the impact which news of these, in grossly exaggerated form, was to make in England from November 1641 on. In Ireland it was overwhelmingly an ethnic and religious conflict: an abortive war of national liberation. In England it was seen as a bloody papistical rebellion, a horrifying manifestation of the work of Antichrist.

The armed forces

Control over the armed forces, and in particular over the trained bands of the county and city militias, was already beginning to be a constitutional issue between Charles I and the Long Parliament in the summer of 1641. But the uprising in Ireland and the effect which this had on people's outlook in England brought it to the forefront and made it into the central political issue. Although they often seem to have been confused in the minds of contemporaries, and were perhaps deliberately merged together for propaganda purposes, there were two distinct aspects to the problem. To assuage English fury against the Irish and match their apparently wellnigh universal determination to crush the rebellion and subdue the Irish for all time, would require the dispatch of a large, well-organized professional army. This was bound to be very expensive; and the question of who was to command it, highly controversial, although this would on precedent have fallen to the Earl of Leicester if he had taken up his position as Lieutenant. At the same time, fears—however ill-founded—of an Irish invasion of England, timed to coincide with a Catholic rising inside the country and perhaps with a foreign attack too, together with the acute mistrust of the King and his advisers, made control over the trained bands appear vital to national security. King and Parliament eventually agreed on how the reconquest of Ireland was to be financed. This was mainly to be done by borrowing on the security of lands which were to be confiscated from the Irish rebels after their defeat; in this way a large number of creditors, called the 'Adventurers', came to have a vested interest in the reconquest. Many members of both Houses subscribed, not all of them future parliamentarians. Command of the militia in England and Wales was normally in the hands of lord-lieutenants appointed by the Crown who then nominated their own deputy lieutenants (over whose appointment the Crown in turn had a kind of veto). Agreement over this proved impossible, at least within the bounds of constitutional legality. But it was a slow process, not

irreversible until March 1642, and by then there were other
reasons for the breakdown of relations between King and
Parliament.

The religious issue

A petition for the abolition of episcopacy 'with all its dependencies, roots and branches' had been presented by the
Puritan clergy of London only some five weeks after the
Parliament had opened, back in December 1640. It is impossible
to do more than guess what proportion of their parishioners,
that is the population of the capital, was positively committed
to a totally non-episcopal, presbyterian or congregationalist
structure of church government and all that went with it. There
was a strong element of popular anti-ecclesiastical iconoclasm
in London. Politically the petition worked something like a
delayed-action bomb. At first very little action was taken in
Parliament, though, as will be seen, there was more of a reaction
in the Lords than the Commons. During the spring of 1641 work
proceeded on two rival schemes for reformed and modified
episcopacy or some sort of mixed system of church government.
Neither was ever completed and formally submitted. Perhaps
Bedford and Pym really did favour a kind of limited episcopacy,
though not so strongly as to risk endangering their political
hegemony; and then, after the former's death, the latter lost
control over his 'Root and Branch' allies. That is surmise, but
it seems not to conflict with the known evidence. The MP who
eventually, in June, introduced a bill for the total replacement
of church government by bishops, more or less along the lines
of the petition, was far from being a political extremist; indeed
he was to change sides twice between the autumn of 1641 and his
own death in 1644, but he may of course have been a mere
'front-man' for the younger Vane, and other radicals. Again the
bill was not at all actively pursued. Shortly before the September
recess the Commons passed a series of resolutions against what
they called 'innovations in or about the worship of God'. Then,
as now, there was room for disagreement as to what constituted
Arminian–Laudian innovations and what had been the general
practice in the English Church since later Elizabethan times. The
Lords did not go along with the Commons on this. They had
carried a resolution back in January for the observation of

church services as laid down by statute, by which they must have meant primarily the Uniformity Act of 1559; and this resolution was now ordered to be printed and published. So there was clearly a pro-episcopalian, or, as we should say, 'Anglican' majority in the Upper House, though to what extent it depended on the bishops' votes is open to argument. Thus even by the autumn of 1641 it was the threat rather than the reality of 'Root and Branch' which was to act as a political catalyst.

In the early weeks of the Parliament yet another of its many committees had been appointed to consider the state of the kingdom. This was over and above the five 'grand committees' on religion, trade, grievances, Ireland, and courts of justice. Once more nothing came of it for a long time. Then in November 1641, after the Commons had taken further unilateral action by sending its own instructions to the committee attending on the King in Edinburgh, including an implicit threat that it would if necessary take steps to deal with the Irish rebels, the committee produced the fruits of its labours, a long and varied catalogue of grievances, styled 'the Remonstrance of the Kingdom', better known as the Grand Remonstrance. It recited almost everything that had gone wrong since the 1620s, what had been done to put things right, and what remained to be done. In places its tone is apocalyptic more than reforming: 'The root of all this mischief we find to be a malignant and pernicious design of subverting the fundamental laws and principles of government upon which the religion and justice of this kingdom are firmly established.' The authors, clearly speaking on behalf of the Commons, defended themselves vigorously from the charge of being religious anarchists; 'Root and Branch', though not mentioned by name, is taken for granted. In spite of last-minute insertions referring to the Irish Rebellion, of which only the first news had yet come in, there is no mention of the militia or command of the armed forces as such. The Commons proved to be bitterly and evenly divided on whether or not to adopt the Remonstrance and present it to the King with a covering petition, and then, when that had been carried by only eleven votes in a sitting of over three hundred, with comparable strength of feeling on whether or not to have it printed and published; this too was narrowly agreed. There was never any question of the Lords concurring in the Grand Remonstrance, and its true status is that of a party declaration by a bare numerical majority in one House. During the last weeks of 1641, control of the armed forces, including the Tower garrison in London and the guard for Parliament itself, together with the position of the bishops as members of the Lords emerged as the most urgent and divisive issues.

By the time that the King returned from Scotland and re-entered London in late November, a swing of opinion in his favour was generally evident. Whether, if we had the evidence, this would be found to have been true of popular opinion in the country, it was certainly true in political circles and the City. Charles enjoyed more popularity then than at any time since his coronation. But the speed with which much of this support was to be dissipated over the following weeks, particularly in London, suggests that cheering crowds are a poor measure of true loyalty and that public opinion then as now was a volatile fickle thing. Increasingly bad news from Ireland heightened suspicions if not of the King personally then of the Queen and other Catholics in his entourage, as fear and suspicion intensified that a great popish conspiracy was unfolding. How far Pym and his associates believed in the reported scale of the Irish massacres and other atrocities will always be unclear. (Standard and widely accepted versions had the Irish murdering more than the total English and Scottish settler population!) The same is true of the belief in a vast, all-embracing, and measurelessly menacing Catholic plot. Certainly they did nothing to restrain their propagandists—editors, publishers, preachers—from inflating the atrocities against the Protestants of Ireland and magnifying the dangers at home. Like all successful statesmen, Pym was up to a point an opportunist but he was not a cynic; and self-delusion seems the likeliest explanation of this and his supporters' obsession. That there was a real international Catholic campaign against Protestantism, a continuing determination to see heresy destroyed, is beyond dispute; it is likewise undeniable that there had been a Laudian–Arminian attack on some aspects of Puritanism in the 1630s.

During the last twenty years or so historians seem to have moved towards a somewhat negative consensus about the place of religion in the events of 1641–2. Those whom we call

Puritans and many other strongly committed Protestants were
so obsessed by fear of an international papist conspiracy, so
convinced that Archbishop Laud and the King were respectively
the secret protagonist and the willing dupe of this design,
that their otherwise instinctively moderate and intellectually
conservative political preferences were compelled into an
altogether more radical direction than would otherwise have
happened. This was the decisive factor in the breach between
Crown and Parliament and in maintaining the momentum of
rebellion following that breakdown. On the other side, religious
and political moderates who had been extremely unhappy with
the policies pursued in Church and State before 1640, many of
whom had helped to dismantle the structure of the Personal
Rule and to limit the King's freedom of action for the future,
now became convinced that the radical Puritan sects were bent
on destroying the Church. To them this foreboded democracy
and even anarchy, social as well as political subversion, so that
they rallied to the cause of the King and the hierarchy. For some
indeed love of the Anglican liturgy and its pattern of worship,
as well as loyalty to the Church as an institution, turned them
into royalists, but in defence of the Church primarily and of the
monarchy only incidentally.

There is some truth in these stereotypes. On both sides
political moderates can be found whose commitment to one side
or the other, and certainly their actual participation in civil war
when it came, arose directly from their religious standpoint. But
many contemporaries reacted in other ways too, and this we
cannot disregard. For all the zealous Episcopalians or Anglicans
in the royalist ranks, there were also a disproportionate number
of Catholics, especially among the officers of the King's armies,
and there were a good many others who wore their religious
convictions lightly to say the least of it: such as the King's
Calvinist-bred nephews, Rupert and Maurice, Sir George
Goring, Lord George Digby, even Montrose. And those
royalists whose sincerity and religious commitment is beyond
question represented every shade of ecclesiastical opinion from
ultramontane Catholic to non-episcopalian Calvinist. For many
royalists political loyalty came first, and their attitude towards
their enemies, at least towards the leaders of those opposing the
King, was to regard them as men using religion as a cover

for fundamentally secular ambitions—namely to seize power and turn the country into an oligarchy under their own control. Likewise on the other side, some of the Long Parliament's firmest supporters believed that the design for absolutism by the King and his councillors was the underlying problem they had to tackle and that the Arminian and pro-Catholic church policies were secondary or even incidental. And for many of those who did put religion first, it was as much a positive crusade for what they called godly reformation as a war against popish Antichrist. What form this reformation should take provoked wide and ultimately irreconcilable disagreement, already apparent by 1641. Only partially related to their holders' political and social outlooks, there rapidly appeared an extraordinary range of differing, even conflicting, viewpoints from the adherents of Low-Church limited episcopacy to those against any state church at all and likewise against any separate clerical profession. As we shall see, some of these issues remained unresolved right through the 1640s and 1650s; already by 1641 the gap between the supporters of a more or less Presbyterian state church and the more radical Puritan sects seemed likely to prove unbridgeable. They may all have been united in their determination to root out popery, open and concealed, and to overthrow Antichrist, but they were agreed on little else.

The Five Members

Just as Charles I had worsened his position by waging a second unsuccessful war against the Scots in 1640, so, when he did at last attempt a coup against his chief enemies, it failed ignominiously and left him weaker than before. Encouraged by the divisions over the Grand Remonstrance and by his apparent recovery of support in Parliament and in the City, enraged by the impeachment of twelve more bishops as part of a campaign to have them all excluded from the House of Lords, and alarmed by rumours of a forthcoming attack by impeachment or otherwise on the Queen herself, the King got his Attorney-General to prepare an indictment for high treason against one peer and five MPs. The choice of Lord Mandeville (heir to the Lord Privy Seal, the moderate Puritan Earl of Manchester) was a strange one: Edward Montague, shortly to succeed his father and better known therefore by his later title, was neither so radical as Lord Brooke, a champion of the sectaries, nor so influential as Viscount Saye and Sele and the Earls of Warwick and Essex; it is just possible that he had been less discreet and that there was more evidence against him. In the Lower House the choice of Hampden and Pym was obvious; Sir Arthur Hesilrige and William Strode were certainly what contemporaries called 'incendiaries', that is, extremists, but less dangerous than St John or the younger Vane; Denzil Holles was among the most active and prominent of the Court's critics but not really an extremist even in 1641. Unless there was evidence which was never to be tested in court, implicating these six in a particular conspiracy, it was an odd tactic. However, if it had come off—if they had been imprisoned and later charged with capital offences—it is just possible that the radical cause might have collapsed through demoralization and lack of alternative leadership. As it was, the six had two days' notice of the King's intention to have them charged. When the two Houses refused to co-operate and stood on the privilege of members, the King decided to come and take them by force. A warning was sent just in time, it was generally believed by the Earl of Northumberland's sister, the widowed Countess of Carlisle, whom malicious gossip portrayed as having been the lover successively of Wentworth and then of Pym; a handsome and witty lady, then in her forties, she was more like a modern political hostess, presiding over a salon of distinguished and entertaining individuals. At any rate the five had enough warning to escape from Westminster by boat and take refuge downstream in the City. The King came into the chamber of the House of Commons attended only by his eldest nephew, the Elector Palatine. But if the five had still been there and had refused to surrender themselves to the King and come out quietly, the large posse of armed courtiers and soldiers in the lobby would obviously have burst in and there would have been a fight, if not a massacre. After a bizarre exchange between himself and the Speaker, Charles withdrew; no attempt was made to fetch Mandeville out of the Lords. Like most unsuccessful resorts to direct action, the consequences were catastrophically damaging. The parliamentarian leaders' propaganda about a popish plot and a design for absolutism seemed to have taken on the character of a self-fulfilling prophecy. The King was virtually forced to leave London, fearing for his own and his family's safety. Certainly his enemies in Parliament now seemed to have a firm basis of support in the capital; the government of the City had already shifted in a more radical direction with the Common Council elections of December. Whether the King's personal safety was really at risk is unclear; it may well have been yet another of Charles's blunders to leave London, but he was surely not compelled to move again from Kent to the north of England on a kind of winter progress-cum-recruiting drive. If experts on regional history are correct, the Kentish gentry, though pro-Country in their opposition to many policies of the Personal Rule, were potentially royalist and Episcopalian rather than Puritan or parliamentarian; and, if so, they might presumably have been rallied by a continuing royal presence.[1]

The country divided

Once the King had begun his journey to the north and then to the west from February onwards, the divisions in the country began to assume a partially geographical character—the north and west versus the south and east—which it might not otherwise have had. A bill to put the militia in the charge of lord-lieutenants acceptable to the parliamentary majority passed both Houses but was vetoed by the King, or rather he simply refused to sign it. The Commons then redrafted the bill as an ordinance, modelled on those of the previous summer, to make it law without the royal assent; but their problem now was with the Lords who at first would not pass it. Only by a combination of factors—the renewed threat of direct action, of physical violence against them by the Londoners, cajoling by the Commons' leaders, and the withdrawal of more peers who supported the King to join him in the north—did the ordinance go through. Ironically the King gave his assent to the Act excluding bishops from the Lords and all clerics from holding civil offices; the absence of the bishops must also have eased the passage of the Militia Ordinance. Although it was different in degree perhaps more than in kind from what Parliament had already done, sticklers for legal and constitutional propriety, then and now, have correctly fastened upon the passage of the

Militia Ordinance early in March as the crossing of the rubicon by the parliamentarian majority, the point at which reform changed into rebellion or revolution. But the downward slide into armed conflict was a slow one. And the whole period from February to August 1642 can be thought of as a kind of cold war, with each side trying to put the other in the wrong and so to win support from the uncommitted. This war of declarations and counter-declarations revealed essentially that the parliamentarians' mistrust of the King now went so deep that they would be content with nothing less than control of the executive, if not the right to appoint ministers of state and privy councillors then an effective veto on whom the King might appoint. Charles was equally mistrustful of them and had no intention whatever of conceding this. Much of his propaganda, now largely in the hands of the ex-reformers or moderate parliamentarians, Viscount Falkland, Edward Hyde, and Sir John Colepepper, was effective and gave him the best of the debate. But his eventual response to Parliament's enforcement of the Militia Ordinance, when it appointed commissioners to take charge of each county, was yet another resort to a legal but archaic device. Royal 'Commissions of Array' were issued to selected individuals in the counties; in many cases there was an actual overlap, so that some of the same individuals were commissioners for both King and Parliament.

It is hard to know whether the Nineteen Propositions, which were sent to the King at the beginning of June, should be seen as a basis for serious negotiations or merely as a propaganda exercise. If implemented, they would have further reduced the royal prerogative, in some respects drastically so, in effect removing the royal veto and binding the monarch to abide by majority decisions in a Privy Council, itself to be chosen with a parliamentary veto on its membership, during the intervals between parliaments. The King's advisers (in this case Falkland and Colepepper) drafted a polemically effective reply. Much, however, has been made of one point in it, where it is alleged a fundamentally new principle was conceded. For it was now accepted that the King was himself one of the 'estates of parliament', and not—as previously portrayed—above the three estates of peers spiritual (i.e. the bishops), peers temporal (the nobles), and the commons (MPs). And, if the monarch was but

one estate, instead of presiding over them, was it not reasonable
that in cases of unresolved dispute he should give way to the
majority? So runs the argument, strengthened by Clarendon's
subsequent criticism of his colleagues for having made this
concession.[2] In fact contemporaries were more confused, or
anyway less consistent than this implies, and the two views
can both be found expressed long before June 1642. The
Propositions and the King's Answer should alike be seen
primarily as debating statements, designed for self-justification
but above all aimed at converting waverers.

Several historians have emphasized the extent of neutralism
in 1642. At least they have suggested the number and the wide
geographical and social spread of those who did not want a war
and, if one came, wanted to keep it out of their own localities
and, failing that, to evade involvement in it themselves.[3] If so
many people wanted an accommodation to be reached and if so
few wanted to fight, why did a civil war break out at all? The
answer seems to lie partly in the centralized nature of the English
State. There was no command point or power base which the
would-be neutrals and others in favour of compromise could
grasp and exploit, comparable to the Crown on the one hand or
Parliament on the other. Conceivably, if the House of Lords
had been less divided, depleted in numbers and demoralized,
then the peers with the judges as their 'assistants', or technical
advisers, might have acted as such a focus or rallying point. The
judges too were divided and some had already been the victims of parliamentary attack. The Privy Council was hopelessly
split, although the King had managed to obtain quite large
attendances for a short time in the winter of 1641–2. In the
absence of any possible inter-county organization, to co-
ordinate the various local and regional peace movements, these
were bound to appear merely localist, concerned to keep the war
out of their respective districts. The level of attendance in both
Houses of Parliament continued to shrink in the course of 1642,
as more peers and MPs withdrew, either to join the King or
simply to go home and keep out of trouble. When fighting began
in the autumn, the parliamentarians continued to set great store
by noble support, indeed to depend on aristocratic leadership of
their forces. Yet the House of Lords as an institution was
already what the Commons was derisorily to be called after

1648—a 'rump', or fag-end of its former self. Thus can be seen a dramatic change in the political role of the peerage between 1640 and 1642. Historians of the most varied persuasions are agreed in emphasizing the importance of noble opposition to royal policies, indeed to the whole regime, in precipitating the crisis which led to the calling of the Long Parliament and to the King's extreme weakness during almost all of its long first session. Yet by the autumn of 1641 the Commons was either acting alone, as with the passage, presentation, and publication of the Grand Remonstrance, or dragging an unwilling Upper House in its wake, as with the measures for further church reform and control of the militia. None the less, individual peers continued to play a crucial role, such as the Earl of Warwick in getting control of the navy for Parliament. Was it after all then an aristocratic rebellion?

Let us take one celebrated example in some detail, in order to explore this further. Robert Devereux had been restored to the peerage as third Earl of Essex by King James not many years after his father's execution for treason in attempting an unsuccessful coup against Queen Elizabeth. But soon after that, as a very young man, he had suffered a fearful humiliation, in which the King had connived and Laud had also been involved, when his marriage to Frances née Howard had been annulled on the grounds of his sexual impotence, so that she could instead marry the King's current favourite Robert Kerr, Viscount Rochester and later Earl of Somerset. Considering that the Countess of Essex, then of Somerset, was subsequently convicted of conspiracy to murder and was certainly also a perjurer, one may think that he was well quit of her; but the slur on his virility must have been traumatic. Thwarted in love, he sought consolation in war, serving as a gentleman volunteer and then as a commander in various of the Continental campaigns conducted by the German Protestants and the Dutch against Spain, Austria, and the Catholic Counter-Reformation. He reluctantly accepted the post of second-in-command, the Commander-in-Chief being both junior in social rank and of less military experience than he was, on the expedition sent by Charles I against Cadiz in the Spanish War of 1625, but he inevitably took some share of blame for its costly failure; and he was passed over for command in the 1627 expedition against

the French to relieve the besieged protestants of La Rochelle. He
held no office or position at Court from then until 1639.
Meanwhile a second marriage also appears to have foundered,
again not without suspicion of inadequacy on the Earl's part.
Perhaps more to the point politically were the troubles of the
Anglo-Irish family, the de Burghs, into which Essex's widowed
mother had married. His stepfather and stepbrother, successive Earls of Clanrickarde, were the victims of Wentworth's
plantation policy in county Galway and of his general high-
handedness. Essex accepted a place as second-in-command in
the Scottish expedition of 1639; then, when Strafford came
back and took charge in 1640, he was dropped without any
explanation.

So it is hardly surprising that Essex was firmly associated with
the anti-Court leaders in 1640–1 and was especially implacable
in his determination to see Strafford executed. He had already
been appointed to the Privy Council at the beginning of 1641
and later that summer, despite the strength of the King's feeling
against those responsible for Strafford's death, was made Lord
Chamberlain, in place of another long-standing associate of
the opposition, the Earl of Pembroke. He was also appointed
Captain-General of all the armed forces in the Midlands and
south of England (such as they were) during the King's absence
on his trip to Scotland, all of which may seem like a sustained
attempt to win him over to support of the royal cause—much
more so in fact than with Bedford, of whose case more is often
made. Essex himself told Parliament that he considered his
commission as Commander-in-Chief south of Trent had automatically lapsed with the King's return from the north, and there
is just a hint that Essex's position was more equivocal at the end
of 1641 than it had been earlier. None the less he continued to
act with the parliamentarian minority in the Lords, which only
became a majority with the disappearance of the bishops and the
royalist peers, and he accepted nomination as Lord-Lieutenant
of four counties in the Militia Ordinance and shortly after this
was relieved of his office as Lord Chamberlain. In June he took
the decisive, perhaps irrevocable step of accepting the post of
Lord General and supreme commander of all Parliament's land
forces; between then and September he was engaged in raising
and training an army. His name and prestige were certainly of

value to the parliamentary cause; his father had been the champion of the Puritan war party under Elizabeth I. But to leap from these facts and probabilities to the assertion that Essex planned or brought about the Civil War, that he revenged his father's fate by mounting a successful rebellion, is a travesty of historical reasoning. Essex was a proud, honest, stubborn man of rather limited intelligence with much about which to be disgruntled. But he was increasingly the instrument, if not the dupe of more radical and determined men with subtler minds than his: in the Commons, Pym, Hampden, Vane, and St John; in the Lords, Saye and Sele, Warwick and Brooke.

Mention of Pym brings us back to the Russell family. William, fifth Earl of Bedford, followed his father by taking a prominent part in the radical leadership during 1641–2, and was made second-in-command under Essex, as Lieutenant-General of Horse. But a year later he was to change sides twice in the space of less than twelve months. Quite apart from this, there is no suggestion in any contemporary source that he filled his father's vacant place in the parliamentarian leadership, or that Pym regarded himself as the new Earl's client or servant.

The case of the Earl of Bristol is different but equally instructive. John Digby had been James I's ambassador in Spain during the long-drawn-out negotiations for a Stuart–Habsburg marriage alliance in the 1610s and early 1620s. He fell from favour when Prince Charles and the royal favourite, the Duke of Buckingham, came to Madrid to further the Prince's suit in 1623. Although he had been raised to the peerage only the year before, Bristol was made the scapegoat both for the failure of the negotiations and then—most unfairly—when British foreign policy was dramatically reversed to become anti-Spanish in 1624–5, for the marriage ever having been promoted and pursued at all. He had demanded an open trial to clear his name in 1626, but this was dropped when Buckingham's own impeachment was ended by the dissolution of Charles I's second Parliament. In the Petition of Right debates of 1628 Bristol took a neutral stance, and he remained out of favour, or at least distanced from the Court, throughout the following decade. He came into his own at the Great Council of September 1640, when he virtually assumed the leadership of the non-Court peers, and he continued to pursue an active political career for the

following two years. Bristol was an able, ambitious, but
somewhat self-important man, who seems to have believed that
he could act as a mediator or bridge-builder because he was free
from any taint of involvement in the Personal Rule and its
immediate antecedents. He was restored to the Privy Council,
after a seventeen-year gap in his membership, when Bedford and
Essex entered it at the beginning of 1641. Yet his refusal to vote
for Strafford's attainder and his association, via his more
brilliant but erratic son George Digby, with the 'Army Plots',
and at the same time his evident lack of enthusiasm for the more
radical demands of the opposition, soon led to the collapse of
his work as a mediator. By the end of 1641 Bristol had himself
become the target of impeachment proceedings, moved by none
other than Oliver Cromwell. From 1642 until his exile in 1646 he
continued to be an influential royalist councillor and the object
of intermittent parliamentarian attacks. But, after the summer
of 1641, there was never any possibility of his leading any kind
of 'middle party' or Country–Court coalition. Whether the
King's elevation of his son to the Lords in June 1641 was
decisive in breaking Bristol's main link with the House of
Commons is disputable, for arguably the younger Digby was
always more of a liability than an asset.

Finally what of the two most undeniably radical of the peers?
William Fiennes, Viscount Saye and Sele, and Robert Greville,
Lord Brooke, were both perhaps more extremist in religion than
in politics. Saye and Sele, whose younger son, Nathaniel, was
a close associate of Pym, St John, and others in the Commons, would probably have liked to see an 'Erastian', that is
lay-controlled semi-presbyterian, semi-congregationalist state
church, whereas Brooke, cousin and heir to a minor politician,
poet and Court favourite of Elizabeth's and James's reigns,
advocated toleration for the sects and said nothing about a state
church at all. As for their politics after 1642, Brooke died of
wounds received in battle the next year; Saye remained a
parliamentarian but opposed the regicide and remained out of
public life until the Restoration. Neither was a major figure
among the nobility as a whole, although Saye had long been an
active member of the House of Lords (much more so than
Bedford or Essex); both had given a bold lead back in the
spring of 1639 by refusing to take an oath acknowledging the

King's right to military assistance against the Scots. But, compared with the great territorial magnates, their wealth was modest and their electoral influence slight. A glance at the league table of aristocratic landed incomes will underline this point.[4]

Causes and explanations

So much has been written of late years to explain away the extent of active support for both sides that it may well be asked how a war could have taken place at all. It may indeed be true that 'great events do not necessarily have great causes'.[5] And the Civil War may have begun partly through a series of accidents and misunderstandings. But this does not mean that people took sides, or avoided doing so, in a completely random, haphazard way. Eventually some did so because they were conscripted (as were foot-soldiers on both sides at different stages of the war); some out of loyalty or deference to their customary social superiors; some to ensure the survival of their fortunes and estates (even to the extent of close relatives fighting on different sides and sometimes one keeping out altogether); some out of individual cussedness or quirkiness or because they were against someone else who had already taken the opposite side. None the less, if we try to look at the country as a whole and at all social groups and classes, the divisions can be related to the religious issues of the previous eighty or more years and to the constitutional difficulties of the 1610s and 1620s. Any generalizations about overall social divisions can be contradicted from the cases of particular individuals, families, and localities. But this is not a sufficient reason for failing to offer any. Proportionately more of the upper crust of the landed classes— peers, baronets, knights, the wealthier esquires and gentlemen—were royalist, though the eastern counties may have been an exception to this at the gentry level. Probably the same was true of the traditional civic élites in the larger towns and cities. Proportionately more of the middling and lesser gentry, especially in the south-eastern half of the country, of the learned professions except the Church, and of the merchants, master craftsmen, skilled artisans, yeomen freeholders and substantial tenant farmers were parliamentarian. Below these levels of the social hierarchy, allegiance was more often decided by various of the other influences which have already been mentioned. According to the dominant interpretation among historians today, the war was 'made', that is brought about, by very small, resolute minorities on both sides. But once begun it was sustained, with varying degrees of enthusiasm, by a much wider range of people—positive neutralism and side-changing as well as sheer escapism being most strongly marked at the top; indifference, apathy, and involunatry side-changing at the bottom levels of society.

Some years ago it was found that among MPs in the Long Parliament, the royalists were on average nearly eleven years younger than the parliamentarians. This led to speculation about time having been on the King's side, through a possible anti-Puritan reaction among the young men growing up in the 1630s or boredom with the constitutional squabbles of the 1620s. It seems more likely to reflect a slight but perceptible social distinction between the two sides inside the Commons: more of the future royalists were relatives of peers and members of longer-established, well-connected landowning families, more too had Court or government connections. Hence they were more likely to obtain seats earlier in life than their future parliamentarian colleagues, who more often had to work their ways up in law, trade, royal service, estate management, or to establish themselves as respected figures in local and then in county government before they were so likely to find seats. Wentworth was first elected at 21; Pym at 36. A smaller, but perhaps still statistically significant age difference was also found between the future supporters of the two sides among royal officials, and is probably to be explained along the same lines. Attempts to correlate the taking of sides with differences between first and younger sons in families of the same rank or wealth have so far proved inconclusive. And we must of course remember that MPs and office-holders were small categories, representative of no one but themselves.

The most fashionable recent explanation of seventeenth-century politics has been in terms of local loyalties. Men are held to have felt more attachment to their county than to Crown, Parliament, State, or Country. The fact that the word 'country' was often used where we should say 'county' has been adduced in support of this. Thus the opposition to the Personal Rule of

Charles I and support for the reforms of 1641 are alike to be seen in terms of a revolt by the provinces against the centre; and the swing back to the King in 1641–2 signifies a feeling at the provincial level that Parliament was now going too far and was in turn beginning to encroach on county autonomy. As we shall see, this explanation can also be deployed convincingly to explain the backlash against the Long Parliament's regime which is evident by the later 1640s, likewise in resistance to some aspects of republican rule in the 1650s. The Restoration of 1660 is, in this sense, to be seen as the triumph of the local community, the victory of the provinces over the nation. While this approach has led to a salutary reassessment of political history as a whole, it involves considerable difficulties about the evaluation of evidence and its interpretation. Not least is the question whether the county was in fact so much of an entity as to be the focus of loyalty for more than a certain section of its gentry inhabitants; one might argue that the parish or manor was the most meaningful local unit for the bulk of the population. Moreover, if all English counties were equal in status, in that each sent two knights of the shire to represent them in Parliament and that each had a separate structure of local justice and administration, some (e.g. Yorkshire, but also Devon, Lancashire, Lincolnshire, and Norfolk) were more equal than others (e.g. Rutland, also Cumberland, and others). We may, however, grant the importance of the county community, the strength of local loyalites, the dislike of excessive interference and centralization in the lives and minds of many gentry and others. And this may indeed help to explain the support for reform through parliamentary action in 1640–1, and some of the recovery of support for the King in the following year or so. But, in itself, it goes very little way towards explaining why some counties and towns, or some districts within counties, were more or less royalist or parliamentarian than others in 1642 and after. Nor does it explain adequately why individual members of different social groups and classes divided as they did. What we have to account for is a huge number of personal and group decisions. Excessive emphasis on localism would lead to the conclusion that everyone was neutral except for the opposing leaders and their immediate followers; whereas even neutralism or simply a desire to keep out of the fight, although widespread, was not evenly distributed over the whole country nor universal. Some local communities toppled, if unwillingly, one way or the other; others had to be pushed.[6]

Did the religious and social differences between the two sides also correspond to a moral and cultural difference? This seems much truer of the subjective view which each side's supporters had of their opponents—witness the labels Cavalier and Roundhead—than of objective realities. Some royalists did behave like the Cavaliers of parliamentarian propaganda; some parliamentarians like the Roundheads of royalist propaganda. It may be of slight significance that the epithet 'roundhead' seems to have aroused more anger among those to whom it was applied than that of 'cavalier' did the other way round. Still, as with all propaganda if it is to have any effect at all, there was just a sufficient element of truth or anyway half-truth to make such grotesque caricatures seem credible. Prince Rupert had fought in the war on the Continent and was more inclined to sack captured towns and villages; there was, it seems likely, more plundering, drunkenness, gambling, swearing, whoring, and even rape on the part of the King's forces. There was an intolerant, 'kill-joy', aspect to the puritan outlook; if not hypocrisy, then self-righteousness, also suspicion of beauty and enjoyment, iconoclasm, and Old-Testament-style bloodthirstiness against papists and the Irish were not simply an invention of the King's journalists and pamphleteers. The main importance of these stereotypes was probably to sustain morale on each side by generating fear and hostility towards the other.

To say that the war had a social or 'class' aspect to it, is not the same as saying that it had profound long- or medium-term economic or social causes. In a negative sense of course it did. The kind of society that England was determined the kind of civil war that was possible; that could not be otherwise. The whole previous geography and history of the country helped to determine this, but did not actually cause the war which broke out as and when it did. Among such influences may be briefly listed: that Britain is an island; that England had no land frontier with a potentially hostile foreign state after 1603; that the country had been effectively unified for many centuries; that when the kings created parliaments in the thirteenth century the knights of the shire, or representatives of the *nobiles minores*,

sat with the citizens and burgesses in the Lower House and not
with the *nobiles majores* and the prelates in the Upper House;
that kings, chief ministers, favourites, even archbishops had on
previous occasions been brought to book for their failings or
misdeeds and in some cases had come to violent ends; that the
last nation-wide civil war had been a dynastic conflict between
rival branches of the royal house; that the revolts against the
Tudors in the previous century had been essentially regional and
at least as much religious as social in their motivation; that the
last (and utterly unsuccessful) baronial or nobles' revolts had
been by the Catholic Northern Earls in 1569 and then by the
second Earl of Essex in 1601. Above all, despite the extremes of
wealth and poverty in seventeenth-century England, there were
proportionately more people in the middle levels of society,
enjoying in good times at least a modest competence; and, by the
standards of pre-industrial societies, early modern England was
relatively affluent and commercialized. This was largely because
agriculture itself, the principal occupation of the majority and
the greatest single source of wealth, had long been geared to a
market economy, and in the case of the wool trade and the
woollen cloth industry partly to an export market. The country
was not as urbanized as parts of Italy or Flanders had been some
centuries earlier, nor as much as Holland and Zealand then
were, but the capital had grown dramatically in the previous
century or so, and now ranked among the major cities of
the Christian world. With its twin centres of London and
Westminster and its suburbs on both sides of the river, the
population of 'greater London' was over ten times that of the
next largest towns in the country—Bristol and Norwich. With
parliamentary backing, the Crown had seized the lands of the
religious orders a century earlier under Henry VIII and Edward
VI, but almost all had been sold and a few given away. Although
the Crown remained easily the largest single landowner in the
country, land was no longer its main direct source of revenue.
And, in real terms, the Crown's financial position had worsened
markedly between the reigns of Henry VIII and James I; over
this time-span inflation, though gentle by twentieth-century
standards, had affected all social groups and classes; the poor
had perhaps been getting poorer, though evidence about wages
is inferior to that on prices and in any case many people had

more than one source of income, were self-employed or did casual work as well as being wage-earners. Not only the rich, and in many cases not necessarily the very richest, had been getting richer; here we come back once more to those in the middle levels of society, 'the middling sort' as contemporaries called them. And it was among these groups too that radical Protestantism, latterly Puritanism, had made proportionately more impact than at the top and the bottom of society. Puritanism, if less a movement or body of ideas than a temper and outlook, was by no means the preserve of a single social class; none the less it was stronger in some social groups and in some parts of the country than in others. None of this caused, in the sense of directly bringing to pass, the Civil War which began, so gradually and raggedly, in the late summer and early autumn of 1642. All of it determined the kind of war which was and was not possible.

3
War

It is difficult to say exactly when and where the Civil War broke out, but in any case this is not very important. During the spring and summer of 1642 the King was twice denied entry to Hull, the main munitions magazine in the north; but since no assault was attempted, there were no casualties. Charles was much more successful at recruiting soldiers in the west than in the north, and the elevation of his standard at Nottingham in August, if equivalent to a formal declaration of war, was little more than symbolic. From the start, he seems to have been better supplied with cavalry than infantry or artillery, and may have had a surfeit of officers in relation to other ranks, although young men of middling and even gentry and noble families served as volunteers in cavalry units, on both sides, especially in the socially prestigious lifeguards of the rival commanders-in-chief. At any rate, by late September–early October the King had an army in the field. Under his own nominal supreme command, his senior generals presented some striking contrasts. His first choice as Captain or Lord-General, Robert Bertie, Earl of Lindsey, the Lord Great Chamberlain and a privy councillor since 1630, then aged about 59, had some previous military experience, but was far from being a professional soldier; in any case since he died of wounds in the first major battle, his successor is more noteworthy. Lord Ruthven, soon to be created Earl of Forth, was a Scottish professional soldier in his late sixties, who apparently suffered from quite severe deafness. Under them the infantry were commanded by Sir Jacob Ashley or Astley, also experienced in war, also over sixty, but considerably more active than Ruthven. By contrast, Prince Rupert, the King's nephew, who commanded the cavalry, although already a veteran, was only in his early twenties. His royal birth mitigated but did not prevent the jealousy and resentment caused by his early promotion, his prominence in the King's counsels, and his lack of tact.

Fighting had already broken out on a small scale in parts of

Lancashire and Yorkshire, in the south-west and elsewhere, when the two main armies took to the field. The core of Essex's infantry consisted of the London trained bands and was commanded by a professional soldier of lesser gentry origin, Philip Skippon. Many of the regiments and troops of horse had been raised by individual members of the parliamentarian nobility and gentry: for example, John Hampden led a regiment, Oliver Cromwell (MP for the borough of Cambridge) initially a troop of cavalry. These forces were raised principally in the south-eastern half of the country, but from the start volunteers probably travelled long distances to join up and were then drafted into various units, so that few regiments, or even companies and troops, were composed exclusively of men from particular localities. That was more the case with the local and regional forces on both sides, although the separate army which Parliament created in the eastern counties during 1643 may in this respect have been more like the main army under Essex. Parliament's cavalry was commanded by the Earl of Bedford, who seems to have had no previous military experience. As a whole the leadership of Parliament's army was at least as socially exclusive as that of the King's; but, if anything, even fewer of its senior officers had ever before seen a shot fired in anger. At the lower levels, of drill sergeants, master gunners, and military engineers, this was less true. Unfortunately there is no single comprehensive list of all those who had served in the Continental wars over the previous twenty years or so. In any case, the composition and leadership of the armies on both sides were to change greatly as the war went on.

The first campaign in the autumn of 1642 was nearly a total disaster for Parliament. Essex allowed the King's army to get between him and his base in London. The battle which followed at Edgehill in Warwickshire was hard fought: tactically a draw but strategically in Parliament's favour, since the King's forces then failed to prevent Essex from withdrawing to London. Rupert and the royalist horse had had the best of the cavalry action in the battle, but Skippon's regiments came best out of the foot-soldiers' battle, and the parliamentary reserves were used to better advantage. Altogether it was a presage of things to come. Rupert and the King's advance guard then approached the western outskirts of London, capturing Brentford in Middlesex. Large numbers of Londoners, urged on by preachers and pamphleteers, rallied to dig defences and lend moral support to their soldiers. Rupert was halted at Turnham Green, now part of west London, then a suburban village; the King was never to be nearer to victory. It is possible but unlikely that, if Charles had rushed up more infantry and all his available guns, Rupert could have blasted his way in through the defences and have ended the war there and then. More likely the natural advantage of the defence would have operated in built-up areas and London would not have fallen. Parliament could still have been defeated in 1643 or even in 1644, but the capital itself was never again to be threatened in this way.

From the winter of 1642–3 Charles I made his headquarters in Oxford, which indeed became a kind of rival capital city. Control over many different areas of the country and over different cities and towns was to vary with the fortunes of war. Broadly speaking, Parliament held London and most of the home counties, East Anglia, and the East Midlands, parts of Yorkshire and of Lancashire, and pockets elsewhere in the north, the south-west, and the far west of Wales. Most of the southern counties and much of the north were to be recovered by the King's forces during 1643. The royalist areas lay mainly in the west (the West Midlands, Cornwall, and Wales) and the north (parts of Yorkshire and Lancashire and almost all of the four northernmost counties). Among the main and secondary theatres of war and the districts which changed hands once or more times, were the middle Thames basin, large areas of the south from Hampshire across to Devon and Somerset, and in the central parts of England the counties of Gloucestershire, Warwickshire, Staffordshire, some of Leicestershire and even Lincolnshire, Nottinghamshire and Derbyshire, parts again of Cheshire and Shropshire, even of north-east Wales, and large areas, indeed almost the whole, of Lancashire and Yorkshire. The King's main army was normally based in Oxford, with delegated commanders-in-chief for separate armies in the north and south-west and local forces elsewhere. Likewise Parliament's main army under Essex was London-based, a separate command being created in 1643 for Sir William Waller MP in the southern counties, with two independent regional commands, for Lord Ferdinando Fairfax and his son Sir

Thomas in Yorkshire and the Eastern Association's army soon to be based on Cambridge and to be commanded by the Earl of Manchester; the most significant local forces were under Edward Massey, an ex-royalist, in Gloucester, and Sir William Brereton Bt. MP in Cheshire.

Brereton is an example of someone whose political role as a parliamentarian MP was secondary to his regional military career. He was the mainstay of Parliament's cause in his native county and served as commander-in-chief there from 1642 to 1645 and again, after being exempted from the Self-Denying Ordinance, in 1645–6. While less uniformly successful as a field commander than some others on both sides, Brereton none the less sustained the parliamentary cause in Cheshire and the surrounding region by a combination of political and military leadership; without him it would scarcely have had a single upper-class champion in that part of the country. Although initially an ally of the Independents, he took no part in the events of 1647–9 and was certainly no regicide or republican. Brereton may be contrasted with John Pyne MP and Sir Anthony Weldon, the political leaders and managers of Parliament's cause in Somerset and Kent respectively, who played no part in military affairs, and with Edward Massey, whose role in Gloucestershire and the southern marches of Wales was almost exclusively military not political. The nearest parallels are perhaps the position of the Fairfaxes in Yorkshire from 1642 to 1645 and during the same years that of Oliver Cromwell in the counties of Cambridge and Huntingdon.

It is often said that Parliament had superior resources. But it may be misleading if we therefore imply that a parliamentary victory was bound to come. The fact that very few regions were solidly for King or Parliament partly explains why so much of the fighting was local, and why there were so many small military units either in the field or in garrisons. This also helps to explain why the military history of the Civil War is hard to tell. If there had simply been two field armies seeking each other out where the situation seemed favourable, avoiding battle where it appeared otherwise, a single narrative of events would be possible. Even then the historian would have to try to deal with political and other non-military developments on both sides and in the country generally.

Rival strategies

From 1642 to 1644 it is hard to know whether the Long
Parliament and its senior commanders can be said to have had
any strategy at all. Their general aim was to avoid decisive defeat
and, if possible, to establish such a military predominance that
the King would be compelled to negotiate and eventually accept
peace on their terms. Maybe even this much of a common
denominator is a logical inference by the historian and not a
historical fact. Such a strategy might well have involved going
on the offensive in particular theatres of war and winning
victories. But the total defeat of the royal army, including the
killing or capture of the King, does not seem to have been in
Essex's mind, nor by 1644 in Manchester's, nor probably—
though this is less clear—in Waller's. Ironically in view of his
later political evolution, the latter was the commander most
favoured by the radicals, the 'win-the-war' faction in Parliament.

Whether the royalists had a single agreed strategy is almost
equally debatable. No doubt, if anyone had asked Charles I, he
would have said that his aim was to crush the rebellion, although
this might require quite generous surrender terms to be offered
to the rank and file of his enemies, indeed to all but the hard
core of irreconcilable rebel leaders. In order to achieve this aim,
his commander in the north, the Earl of Newcastle, was to
defeat the Fairfaxes and then advance southward, containing if
not destroying the enemy in Lincolnshire and East Anglia. More
or less concurrently with this, the 'western army' under Lord
Hopton and the Grenvilles of Cornwall was to consolidate its
grip on the south-west and then move eastward to enter Sussex
or even Surrey; meanwhile the King's own army was to take
advantage of any tactical opportunities, especially if the
parliamentary forces were diverted to cope with the other two
prongs of the royalist advance. At the decisive moment the three
armies would encircle London and advance on the capital from
the south, west, and north. If that was not the plan, it is very
hard to see what was. In the north the King's forces on balance
had the best of it until the winter of 1643–4, but they never
destroyed the Fairfaxes' army completely or captured Hull or
gained more than a precarious and temporary footing in
Lincolnshire and the Midlands. In the south, too, the royalist

forces won more victories and gained more territory but they never firmly controlled the whole of Dorset and Hampshire and made only temporary incursions into Surrey and Sussex. On the central front neither side suffered a decisive defeat. Bristol fell to Rupert, but Essex succeeded in relieving Gloucester. The largest set-piece battle in 1643, at Newbury, was a draw in Parliament's favour; yet the royalists often had the local initiative and tactical advantage, especially in their use of cavalry. Hampden was fatally wounded in a pointless skirmish which through faulty intelligence he believed necessary to the security of Essex's main army. The defenders of castles and fortified towns were already seen to have the advantage over their besiegers, given adequate supplies and good morale; both sides felt obliged to deploy what seems like quite excessive effort and resources in besieging those held by the other. This was perhaps less true of inland towns, but the King's forces held Newark in otherwise solidly parliamentarian territory continuously from 1643 to 1646, and Parliament's forces held Taunton in mainly royalist-controlled territory from 1643 to 1645.

One of the minor mysteries of the war is how the two sides got enough horses, both for their cavalry and for transport needs. Considering the length of time a horse takes to breed, from conception to maturity, and considering the probable number which were killed or seriously injured, this is only credible on the assumption that breeding mares were kept out of danger more than other horses. There can be no doubt that the farming community and inland traders suffered severely from the forcible purchase or even seizure of their animals.

The sinews of war

The two sides used broadly similar methods to finance their respective war efforts. The royal government in Oxford followed Parliament's example in sequestering, or confiscating, the estates of their enemies, and then letting all but the most incorrigible buy them back by paying a penal fine or composition. They also introduced a regular weekly, later monthly, tax of so much on each county or city, to be levied by an assessment broadly similar to that used earlier for ship money. Compared with the parliamentary weekly pay, after-

wards known as the monthly assessment, the royalist equivalent
seems to have been inconsistently applied and generally
ineffective. The royal government likewise followed Parliament's example in introducing an excise or sales tax on many
commodities, including semi-necessities as well as luxuries. The
very idea of an excise had been denounced in the Grand
Remonstrance; apparently it had been mooted in Council, not
even in Parliament, during the late 1620s. Likewise, although
the abuses of royal wardship over tenants-in-chief had also been
condemned, Parliament kept the Court of Wards in being, with
Lord Saye and Sele as its Master until the end of war in 1646;
the King set up a rival Court of Wards in Oxford. So, in theory
the estates of those holding land by knight service who died
without male heirs of age could have come under the control of
either of these bodies—or both! Generally speaking the
royalists' methods of exacting contributions, of getting the
supplies, accommodation, horses, even the men that they
needed, were more casual and high-handed. Parliament's were
more regular; the tax burden which they imposed was much
heavier because it was more efficient. Popular resentment and
resistance to the burden of maintaining the rival armies
culminated in the 1645 risings of the Clubmen, who have been
much studied in recent years. The evidence is limited, but it
seems almost certain that the Clubmen did more damage to the
royalist than to the parliamentarian cause, if only because of the
timing and location of the main outbreaks. But by then the
fortunes of war had in any case shifted decisively in Parliament's
favour.

In terms of planning and command structure the two sides
show both likenesses and differences. As his own generalissimo,
Charles I had a position which neither Essex nor his successor
could hope to rival. Yet he normally depended on field
commanders, staff officers, and advice from a frequently
divided Council of War. On one of the rare occasions when
Charles was on his own and followed his own instincts, he
administered a sharp defeat to Waller at Cropredy Bridge, north
of Oxford. In substance, as opposed to form, the position of the
King and his generals was perhaps normally not so different
from Parliament's relations with its various commanders. This
was at first exercised through a committee of safety (1642–3),

containing both peers and MPs, and then by the Committee of Both Kingdoms (1644–6). The latter body was so named because of the Scottish element in its membership, which followed the treaty of alliance, the Solemn League and Covenant of September 1643, in which the Scots undertook to come to the aid of the English Parliament and the English to adopt the Scottish church system in so far as this was compatible with scripture. In 1644 the Committee made some very damaging interventions in its orders to commanders in the field, trying to control them far more closely than the slowness of communications made it sensible to do; by 1645 the generals were on the whole given a freer hand with successful results. In the royalist camp, personal jealousies, notably those aroused by Rupert, political rivalry between Digby and Hyde, professional tensions between soldiers and civilians, were perhaps more damaging than strictly institutional weaknesses. The King's decision to summon all members of both Houses of parliament to meet in Oxford, while not a total failure measured by the number of those who attended, was no real help to the royalist war effort. On the parliamentary side and particularly within Parliament itself, factional or what we might call party conflicts, and profound disagreement between win-the-war radicals and 'peace-party' moderates, were more harmful than any equivalent among the royalists.

If we compare the two rival wartime governments, politically the King was the more secure, in the sense of being more completely master in his own house. Oxford was far smaller than London, and the town was utterly dominated by the presence of the royal army. However intense the personal rivalries and sectional jealousies among the leading royalists, no one seriously contemplated overthrowing Charles I himself: the contests were for access to and influence over him. Parliament, by contrast, was itself divided between Lords and Commons and within each House; it had a guard of its own, but there was no large army stationed in Westminster to overawe or ward off possible threats of violence, and its members were constantly open to pressures—financial, religious, and even physical—from different elements in the capital. There were at least three plots of varying seriousness, aimed at forcing Parliament to make peace with the King, or even at seizing power and then surrendering London to him, in the space of about two years from March 1643. Perhaps the most severe internal crisis arose in August 1643 when there was a sharp division between the two Houses, a majority in the Lords favouring something very near to outright capitulation. The Commons' rejection of this was at once followed by a massive and menacing demonstration by thousands of female Londoners, two of whom died in consequence of the riot which developed. A week later seven peers seceded from Parliament, some of them going straight to join the King at Oxford. In one way Parliament's very success in weathering these and other storms, or perhaps we should rather say the failure of any such scheme to succeed, again meant that time was on their side; every year, if not every month, that passed made victory harder for the King to attain. Only after the triumph of Parliament's forces in the field did their internal divisions prove to be insurmountable.

Fresh divisions

Between 1644 and 1646 there was a decisive shift in the alignment of the Scots, and one which had great importance to the future. They had entered the conflict very much as allies of the centre and left in Parliament, led by Pym and after his death (in early December 1643) by Vane and St John. A combination of religious and political influences, above all the priority which they gave to a Presbyterian church settlement, brought them into alliance with the conservative or moderate parliamentarians, the heirs and successors of the earlier peace party, of whom Denzil Holles and Sir Philip Stapleton became the most prominent leaders in the Commons. By 1646–7, when the war had been won, this party began to gain ground among middle-of-the-road or uncommitted members, to draw them away from their previous support of the radicals or war party. Much closely reasoned analysis, based on scrupulous, exact, and probing research, has been devoted to the study of 'party' and other groupings inside the Long Parliament and among its adherents, from 1642–3 through to 1648.[1] Recently the concept of a three-party model, to explain how things worked during 'the reign of King Pym', has been challenged in favour of a two-party one. An even more ambitious attempt has been made to rewrite the whole story in terms of a dialectic between 'consensus' and 'adversary politics', with an overall shift from the former to the latter as a result of Holles's predominance in 1646–7.[2]

The word party, like the word class, is probably one that the historian of the seventeenth century can not do without. The difference is that 'party' was used by contemporaries, but often to mean a following or movement rather than a definable organization. Perhaps we should think of individuals and groups of people who normally acted together but amongst whom realignments could take place on particular issues—military priorities and the settlement of religion being the two most obvious. Thus the religious labels Independent (what we should call Congregationalist) and Presbyterian were often also used as political labels, to describe radicals and moderates respectively, those who had earlier often been known, again very loosely, as the War and Peace Parties. Yet there were certainly religious Presbyterians in the Independent or War Party, and there were some—rather fewer—Congregationalists and even Baptists who were not political radicals. Nor must we forget in all this the parliamentarian peers; miserable a rump as the House of Lords had become, its concurrence was always important and sometimes decisive. So the historian has to try to keep in mind royalist politics and government, centred in Oxford, parliamentarian politics and government at Westminster and their key relations with the City of London and the Scots, as well as the developing events in England and Wales, Ireland, Scotland, and on the seas around the British Isles.

The outcome of the war was not a foregone conclusion, far from it. Measured in terms of morale, military leadership, horses, weapons, and successes in the field, the King's forces made a good showing, and had the best of a more or less even contest from the autumn of 1642 until the spring of 1644. It is of course tempting to say that the entry of the Scots, together with its own superior resources of wealth and population, led inevitably to Parliament's victory over the King, but it certainly did not look like that to contemporaries. And such an assumption seems dubious even now, looking back at the military events of 1644.

The fortunes of war

The northern campaign of that summer illustrates very well

some of the strengths and weaknesses of the contending forces. The slow but relentless advance of the Scots, the second Covenanter army, and their eventual meeting with the Yorkshire army of Lord Ferdinando and Sir Thomas Fairfax posed a sharp dilemma for the King's northern Commander-in-Chief, the Earl, now Marquis, of Newcastle. He had either to abandon York or to defend it. Clearly the King expected him to do the latter, and this led to his being besieged within the city along with a large proportion of the King's northern army. Although York was described as 'the second city of the Kingdom', its symbolic value to Charles I was clearly out of all proportion to its real strategic importance. A significant minor victory by the younger Fairfax at Selby in the spring had already seriously reduced the strength of the royalist infantry not long before the siege began, while the northern cavalry certainly did no good to their cause mewed up inside the perimeter of York (eventually reduced to the medieval city walls). Possession of York seems almost to have become an end in itself for both sides, though for the parliamentarians there was the added possibility of fighting a major battle with a massive advantage of numbers. Thus during June the army of the Eastern Association under Manchester with Cromwell in command of its cavalry moved north through Lincolnshire to join the besieging forces.

The King's response was to give Rupert an independent command in the north, with an overriding mission to prevent the loss of York. His rapid advance up the western side of the country, culminating in the occupation of all northern Cheshire, southern and central Lancashire, was something of a triumphal tour, marred by the sack of Stockport, Bolton, and Liverpool. He joined forces with the local Lancashire Cavaliers and added a large proportion of them to his own army. He then moved east across the Pennines and descended into the vale of York from the north-west, taking the allied armies quite by surprise. Strategically it was a superb operation, almost a textbook military exercise. The besiegers fell back to the east and south of York and the siege was raised. As to what happened next, whether the Prince genuinely miscalculated the odds against him, or whether he read his uncle's characteristically ambiguous letter as directing him to bring the enemy armies to battle as well as to relieve York, has never been clear. At any rate he provoked

an unnecessary battle, starting late in the evening when many of
the royalists who had been pent up inside the city for weeks were
still only limping out and most reluctant to fight. Newcastle
himself seems to have been against an immediate engagement.
The numerical odds were about three to two in the allies' favour,
against the Prince. Even so, the battle was a close-run thing. The
royalist left wing, consisting of the southern horse, under the
dissolute but redoubtable George Goring, broke through the
Yorkshire horse, who had attacked prematurely and suffered
heavy losses. At this stage two of the allied generals, the Scottish
Commander-in-Chief, Alexander Leslie, Earl of Leven, and the
elder Fairfax, followed by a considerable number of their men,
actually fled the field, thinking that the day was lost. But as with
Rupert at Edgehill, so it was with Goring at Marston Moor. The
tactically victorious royalist horse proved quite unable to reform
and rejoin the main battle until it was far too late. Meanwhile
Cromwell had broken the royalists facing him on the other side
of the field and then made a masterly encircling move, coming
right round to where Goring had been (and should by then have
been again); this, plus the doggedness of the Scottish foot in the
centre under the younger David Leslie, enabled numbers to tell
and totally reversed the outcome. It was probably the blood-
iest and hardest fought of all the major battles in the war. Although most of the royalist cavalry escaped to fight again, their
infantry losses were very heavy; parliamentarian casualties too
were severe, though light by comparison. Humiliated and
disillusioned, the Marquis of Newcastle left his command and
went abroad as a private exile. The surrender of York was
negotiated shortly after, more of the royalist soldiers who had
escaped from the field of Marston Moor being captured there.
Minor royalist forces remained in the field, especially in parts of
the north-west, and several isolated fortresses continued to have
a nuisance value; but the King never again had a major army
able to bid for control in the north. It seemed that only the
successes of the Scottish royalists, under the ex-Covenanter
James Graham, Marquis of Montrose, leading a mainly
Highland but also partly Irish army, could prevent the Scottish
Covenanter army from continuing to play a decisive role in the
war in England.

At the same time, and surprisingly in view of their superior

resources, things were going badly for the parliamentarians in
the south. Either misinterpreting his brief from the Committee
of Both Kingdoms, or misled by bad advice and by his own
obstinacy, the Earl of Essex, having successfully relieved the
beleaguered garrisons of Lyme and then Plymouth, plunged on
further south-west into hostile country in Cornwall. Freed by his
own recent victory over Waller at Cropredy, the King gave
chase; as in the Edgehill campaign of 1642 but this time with far
worse results, the Lord-General allowed the King to get between
himself and his home base. Eventually the main parliamentarian
field army was penned into the tiny Fowey peninsula in south
Cornwall. Despite Parliament's control of the sea, the army
could neither be kept supplied nor evacuated. Finally the
parliamentarian cavalry succeeded in breaking through the
royalist cordon to escape, though in a severely shattered state,
but the foot regiments all had to surrender. For reasons that are
not entirely clear, they were allowed to go free although without
their arms and other equipment; only Skippon's leadership kept
them together at all as they dragged their way back across the
length of southern England. Essex and his staff escaped by boat.
It was an ignominious and above all unnecessary, but not
actually a catastrophic defeat. After being re-equipped (less
difficult for them than for their enemies), Essex's army joined
that of the Eastern Association which had now come south, far
out of its own territory. But the next major encounter outside
Newbury again proved the dangers of divided councils, and
showed in the case of some, including Manchester, a disastrous
lack of the will to win. Even Cromwell came out of this battle
with a slightly tarnished reputation, although he was sensible not
to waste his men's lives in a futile struggle. The King meanwhile,
having partially retrieved his military fortunes in the southern
theatre of war, and with Montrose increasingly active in the
Highlands of Scotland, now planned to exploit the Irish
situation decisively to his advantage in England.

It is tempting to say that Irish involvement was as damaging
to the King's cause as Scottish participation was—in the short
run at least—helpful to the Parliament's. Whatever else may be
said about it, the situation in Ireland was complicated; there
were more like four or five contending parties than a mere two
sides. The revolt which began in October 1641 had initially been

led by Gaelic Catholic Irish from Ulster, some of them the sons of families dispossessed by the English and Scottish settlement there of the 1610s to '20s; several had served in Catholic armies on the Continent, usually those of Spain. In the course of the following winter they were joined by more Irish from the other three provinces and, more surprisingly, by many Anglo-Irish gentry from the Pale. Virtually all those who supported the rebellion were Catholic, but by no means all Catholics, either Old Irish or Old English, supported it and many remained loyal to the King's cause. In 1642–3 the rebels formed an alternative government, the Confederation of Kilkenny; in 1645 a papal nuncio arrived in the shape of an Italian cardinal. The Confederates were themselves divided on the question of allegiance to the English Crown, probably on whether to tolerate or wipe out Protestants, if they were victorious, and certainly on what sort of peace terms would be acceptable to them. The most active and consistent royalist leaders were the Earl of Inchiquin, of mainly Old Irish ancestry, and James Butler, first Marquis of Ormonde, leader of the Old English in Munster and himself a convert from Catholicism.[3] The parliamentarians, who can more or less be equated with the New English but included some Old English too, held Dublin and for much of the time little else. They had a semblance of constitutional authority from Charles's concession in 1641 making the moderate parliamentarian Earl of Leicester Lord-Lieutenant; although he personally never set foot in Ireland, his son Lord Lisle was there as general in 1642–3 and again as Lord-Lieutenant in 1647; by that time his father had long been superseded by Ormonde as the King's appointee. But the real driving force of the parliamentary, Protestant, cause was sustained by men of humbler social origins, such as the three brothers Jones, sons of a Church of Ireland bishop: one, himself a future bishop, extorted confessions, some under torture, from rebels captured in 1641–2 and so helped to build up the legend of the massacres and atrocities having been on a gigantic scale, which was to be so long-lasting and potent a source of English feeling against the Irish; another, Michael, was the most determined and the most successful of Parliament's military commanders and he helped to turn the tide of the war before Cromwell's arrival in Ireland at the end of the 1640s; the third was another future Cromwellian who had helped save Dublin in

1641. Finally there was the Scottish population in Ulster, much strengthened by the presence of a separate Covenanter army there from 1644 to 1648. This force co-operated somewhat uneasily with the English Protestant armies loyal to the Parliament.

On Charles's instructions his representatives negotiated two 'cessations' with the Confederates, in 1643 and again in 1645. It was during these intervals of temporary peace that the King either redeployed his own forces in England or on the second occasion had some thousands of Irish soldiers brought over to join his army in England. Although individual Irish soldiers and officers fought loyally and bravely for him, this apparent accession of strength was never enough to make a decisive military difference, unless very temporarily and locally in Cheshire and north Wales, while politically it was acutely counter-productive. The fact that Irish Catholics were fighting on the King's side in the English Civil War immensely strengthened the Puritan–Parliamentarian propaganda which portrayed the King, if not as himself the instrument then at least as the willing dupe of the far-flung, infinitely alarming popish plot to subvert the religion and liberties of England. We must also remember the existence of the Adventurers, who had advanced financial support, or provided men, arms, and ships, for the reconquest of Ireland on the security of the rebels' lands which were yet to be won, a measure to which Charles I had given his assent as late as June 1642. None of this excuses but it does help to explain what was to happen in Ireland from 1649 on.

Thanks partly to the Earl of Warwick's vigorous leadership as Admiral from 1642 to 1645, Parliament enjoyed naval superiority throughout the war. How much this had to do with the political and religious convictions of the seamen, as opposed to the officers, is unclear; at any rate the ship-money fleet was largely used against its creator. But this did not, could not, mean total command of the seas everywhere all the time. The parliamentarian navy could not prevent the Queen bringing substantial military supplies from the Continent to the Yorkshire coast in 1643, nor other shipments getting through (including the Irish soldiers already mentioned), especially to royalist-held ports in the west and south-west on and off through the years 1644 to 1646. None the less, negatively speaking Parliament's general command of the sea was of great importance. If the King had gained naval superiority, his strategy could have been more flexible; London might have been frozen into submission by a total interruption of the sea-borne Newcastle coal trade; and his prospects of victory at various stages during the war would have been much brighter.[4]

Other wartime developments

If the entry of the Scots helped to win the war for Parliament and that of the Irish to lose it for the King, and if seapower helped prevent Parliament being defeated, we must also relate all this to the non-military developments on both sides during the course of the war. Changes on the King's side can be dealt with more briefly if only because subsequent military defeat meant that many potentially important developments never took effect. There were fundamental latent divisions between absolutists and constitutionalists, as between Catholics and Protestants. More immediately and on the surface, there was chronic friction and mistrust between soldiers and civilians. The fact that one of the leading civilian constitutionalists and Protestants, Edward Hyde, later Earl of Clarendon, was also the greatest historian of these events makes it difficult for us to obtain a balanced picture. Indeed the other near-contemporary histories by royalist participants (those of Sir Philip Warwick, Sir Edward Walker, and Sir William Dugdale), while all written independently of each other and of Clarendon, reflect the same broad viewpoint, although arguably Dugdale became more of an absolutist in his latter days. We have no sustained history or even personal apologia from Rupert (as opposed to his letters and dispatches) or Goring or Digby, too little from Hopton or the Grenvilles, or even from Newcastle, apart from his wife's hagiographic life. But important advances in our understanding of the royalist armies and war effort generally have been made in recent years. As the war went on more self-made men rose in the King's service, and correspondingly attitudes hardened. The Catholics were readier than the Anglicans to advise doing a deal with the Presbyterians; here too, as in matters political and strategic, the King characteristically oscillated, although ultimately he refused to abandon the Church of England. By the mid- or later 1640s Falkland was dead; Hyde and the Queen

were both in exile; Digby and Rupert discredited. In a sense
Charles was at last his own man; but for better or worse it was
by then too late.

On Parliament's side there was a series of shifts, both
ideological and institutional, between 1643 and 1645, which
generally tended in a more radical direction. Politically the kind
of coalition over which Pym had presided did not long survive
his death and may already have been crumbling before that. The
only other man with the possible combination of qualities to
have succeeded him, John Hampden, had already died of
wounds the previous summer. In the Commons, St John and the
younger Vane were probably the ablest of the radical leaders;
and, visiting the armies encamped round York before Marston
Moor, Vane is said to have sounded out the various generals on
the idea of deposing the King. As we have seen, the key question
in parliamentary politics was to what extent and for how long
the radical leadership could keep a sufficient hold over the
so-called middle party, or rather (as they have been portrayed
here) over the uncommitted men in the middle. Scottish pressure
for a fully Presbyterian church settlement and the increasing
number of English parliamentarians who came to favour this,
largely through fear and dislike of the more extreme Puritan and
other religious sects, were perhaps the decisive factors in the
realignment.

It had been agreed way back in 1641–2 that an Assembly of
Divines should be called to settle the future of the Church. And
this body duly came together in 1643; but already it was a very
different body from what it might have been earlier. A few
Anglicans or Episcopalians were invited but none took part in
the proceedings; moreover, in their main dissenting statement,
arguing for a decentralized system of church discipline and
government, the Congregationalists could only muster five
supporters out of well over a hundred members while the equally
or more numerous Baptists were unrepresented. So the great
majority in the Assembly, pushed on by the Scots and stimulated
by clericalist preachers and writers in London, set about turning
the English Church into a fully Calvinist and presbyterian one,
more or less on the model of Geneva, Holland, and Scotland.
And it was only the lay, or 'Erastian' element in the two Houses
which cut across denominational boundaries and acted as any

kind of brake on this programme. Even so, a series of proposals from the Assembly was enacted, some with modifications others not, as parliamentary ordinances, to set up Presbyterian church government first in London, then in the country at large, and to replace the Elizabethan Prayer Book with one called the Directory of Worship.

In practice the full presbyterian structure may never have come into existence in many parts of the country. But despite this and the fact that the Scots denounced the whole thing as 'a lame Erastian presbytery', the settlement aroused intense opposition, not only from Episcopalians but also from radical Puritans. They key question came to be provision for what Cromwell called 'tender consciences', by which he meant mainly Congregationalists and Baptists, though in principle he would have extended it to cover all Protestants who had renounced prelacy and were not blasphemers. Of the other sects or movements, the most active and vocal were rapidly coming to be the future Levellers, at this time usually known as the party or following of Colonel John Lilburne after their most colourful and best-known leader. These divisions went back at least to 1641. Indeed perhaps they had always been inherent in Puritanism and were only masked by a common hostility to Laud and the Arminians and the consequent determination in 1640–1 to make any return to that system for ever impossible. The sudden appearance of sectarian preachers, who were often not ordained clergymen at all, and who did not restrict the worship which they conducted to consecrated church buildings, alarmed all who wanted a reformed state church. The 'Root and Branch' abolition of episcopacy again was a kind of common denominator but only a negative one, which alienated moderate, reforming Episcopalians and pushed them into political royalism without re-unifying the Puritan cause. It was widely assumed by the enemies of the sects that 'popularity' or democracy in the Church would lead to the same in the State, and vice versa; and that both alike threatened the whole social order.

Not only radical Puritans and sectaries began to publish their views with virtual impunity for the first time in 1641. The censorship had collapsed with the abolition of Star Chamber and the overthrow of the bishops' authority; admittedly, the would-be monopoly of the London Stationers' Company remained. Effectively only the laws of libel and those relating to heresy and treason restricted what could be published. Although the Long Parliament tried to reintroduce a system of censorship in 1643 and this became a renewed point of conflict, it did little to diminish the volume of publications. The output of printed works in the 1640s was larger than that of the entire previous period since Caxton had begun printing in England in the 1470s, and probably greater than it was to be again until into the eighteenth century. Our fullest evidence for this is due to George Thomason, a Presbyterian London bookseller, who started collecting a copy of every item that was published at the end of 1640 and astonishingly kept this up until 1661. Naturally he was not completely successful, missing quite a lot put out by the royalist presses in Oxford during the war and by other provincial publishers; he excluded some categories such as expensive reprints of the classics and earlier authors, and he missed a few occasional flysheets, anonymous broadsides, and clandestine pamphlets. Even so, his collection, now in the British Library, contains over 20,000 items (many of the short ones are of course bound up together in composite volumes).[5] The individual pieces vary from single sheets (petitions, declarations, etc.) to stout volumes. From the political and military historian's point of view, among the most significant are the eight- or sixteen-page weekly 'newsbooks', equivalent to modern newspapers, and the huge mass of short, polemical pamphlets (anything from a few pages to a hundred or so).

It should not be supposed that all these were ultra-radical. The most successful single newsbook of 1643–5 was *Mercurius Aulicus*, published for the King from Oxford; and the best established parliamentarian newsbooks were moderate rather than radical until at least 1644 or 1645. At the level of less ephemeral religious and political tracts, too, the royalists gave as good as they got, until they were overwhelmed by military defeat in 1645–6. Even after that some of the classic apologies enjoyed great popularity: for example, the King's real or spurious book of autobiographical devotions, the *Eikon Basilike*, published in repeated editions from the morrow of his death on; or Dr Henry Hammond's defences of Anglican theology. Also from a royalist pen were Izaak Walton's *Lives* and his *Compleat*

Angler. But when all is said, the main effect of this great outpouring of the printed word was to influence and shape opinion in a radical direction. This was partly a matter of economics, the fact that so many editors and authors were appealing to a wider audience than the previous political nation and the minority who had received a formal higher education; they were addressing not only peers, MPs, and other gentry and affluent city fathers, but the middling citizens of London and other smaller towns and their rural counterparts—yeomen and substantial tenant farmers. Whether more women were reading or having things read to them is impossible to prove but seems probable; certainly more men were in the army who would previously have been outside the cultural world of all except popular chapbooks. Some of the editors of weekly newsbooks became politically influential, even if they had often begun as the clients of leading parliamentary figures. Above all, viewpoints favourable to democracy in Church and State could at last be freely expressed despite the abortive attempts by Parliament and the Assembly of Divines to bring the press under control once more. The few prosecutions or examinations of authors and editors before committees were—as we shall see in particular with Lilburne and his associates—highly counterproductive. The flood of pamphlets and other publications continued even if it fluctuated somewhat from year to year, in tone as well as in volume.

The Sects and toleration

Yet from the viewpoint of orthodoxy and tradition, mainstream Puritan as much as Anglican, moderate parliamentarian as well as royalist, much of this output seemed ever more seditious and subversive. By 1645–6 even some of those who had suffered at the hands of Archbishop Laud and the prerogative courts, and who had at first demanded the right of the godly to preach and publish freely, came to see toleration as the fundamental evil which opened the way to all the others—to heterodoxy, heresy, blasphemy, unbelief, even indirectly back to prelacy and popery. This is the theme of Thomas Edwards's extraordinary three-part catalogue of errors, *Gangraena* (1646), a rich if unreliable source book for identifying the names and opinions of some small and otherwise obscure radical sects and their leaders. This

renascent intolerance, and especially the activities of the
Assembly, pushed Milton into one of the classic defences of free
speech and free publication in the *Areopagitica*; likewise it
helped to push John Goodwin, a leading radical Independent
clergyman, away from predestinarian orthodoxy and eventually
away from belief in a state church of any kind. The future
Leveller leaders, Richard Overton and William Walwyn, were
led into supporting their friend John Lilburne when he became
the victim of this persecution, even though they seem themselves
to have disagreed with aspects of his theology. Hence the critical
importance of Cromwell's stand for the 'liberty of tender
consciences', however far he may have meant that to go. This
had first come to a head after the treaty with the Scots, when the
Solemn League and Covenant was imposed as a sort of loyalty
oath on all civil and military officers. As we have seen, the main
English negotiator of the treaty, the younger Sir Henry Vane,
was no Presbyterian, and the oath does not seem to have
troubled him; but then Vane, in Clarendon's hostile but
admiring and perhaps apt phrase, was 'a man above
ordinances', that is to say one whose personal convictions
enabled him to bend means to ends. The men for whom
Cromwell spoke were mostly more prosaic and straightforward:
Baptists for example or extreme Congregationalists who could
not bring themselves to accept the entire text of the Covenant.
Some people in the seventeenth century were coming to see that
tests and oaths were snares and pitfalls for the ultra-scrupulous,
no real barrier to the cynic or casuist: perhaps like lie detectors
today.

   Very few people were prepared to tolerate all and any
opinions, beliefs, and unbeliefs: certainly Milton was not, nor
Cromwell. The real measure of whether those on the Puritan
side believed in toleration for its own sake or only as a means
to their own victory is to be found in their attitude towards the
expression of episcopalian and even more of Catholic views and
the practice of such worship, and also towards blasphemers
and atheists. The issue of defining blasphemy and then of
suppressing it became increasingly urgent, reaching its climax
with the later emergence of the Ranters and then of the Quakers;
but it was a matter of heated not to say violent controversy
before either of these groups had appeared or at least were

known by these names. The toleration of blasphemy, like that of the popish Antichrist, seemed to many contemporaries, not only those whom we might think of as bigoted, calculated to bring down the wrath of God upon the whole country. Belief in God's foreknowledge and purpose, the core of what is more often called predestination, never—or very seldom—induced fatalism and passive acceptance of events. Whatever the logical difficulties, its adherents acted on the assumption that human beings could affect their own destiny both by correct religious observances (mainly prayer but also fasting) and by right actions; they could not, however, affect their respective destinations in the next world. The anti-tolerationist argument was sometimes different from this when applied to Catholics. For some Protestants, particularly for those Puritans who took the doctrine of the millennium literally, the papal Antichrist had to be destroyed as a prologue to the rule of the saints, the conversion of the Jews, and eventually the Second Coming of Christ. So to suggest that its adherents should be allowed freedom of expression and worship was tantamount to giving the devil a residence permit in your midst. For others, however, the argument had a more modern ring to it: the Roman Church was a vast international organization, itself absolutely committed to the destruction of all heresies and rivals, including the Protestant churches, and the forcible reconversion of their members; its victory would mean the end of freedom of expression, worship, and publication for non-Catholics. This remains a classic dilemma for liberals and believers in a free society: is full freedom of expression owed to those who would, if they had the chance, deny it to us and to everyone else not toeing their line?

We must not suppose that the entire religious debate was concerned with such fundamental issues. Many of the controversial sermons and pamphlets might be said to have kept within the bounds of a broad Protestant consensus, and to have been concerned with what might seem today much narrower, sometimes almost technical points of disagreement: infant versus adult baptism, the role of elders in a true church, the minister's right to control access to communion, the qualifications and payment of clergy, and many others. Even then their tone was often intemperate if not violent. On the political side no one openly attacked the King himself as opposed to his wife and his advisers until his secret papers were captured in the summer of 1645. None the less, the majority in both Houses of Parliament and most of the mainstream Puritan clergy still wanted a negotiated settlement with him, although on terms which Charles would never have accepted. But quite apart from theological and ecclesiastical issues, the general tone of stridency, if not bitterness, probably contributed to the development of more extreme policies and made conciliation less likely.

Winning the war

As in most wars and perhaps especially civil wars, the very fact of having to wage war and eventually to win it led people in directions which few if any had foreseen. The parliamentarians claimed to be fighting for King and Parliament, to save Charles I from his evil councillors—as a kind of legal fiction—but we have to remember that by the mid-1640s Parliament itself comprised no more than some three-fifths of the MPs and perhaps a quarter of the lay peers. The royalist MPs, having either withdrawn or been expelled, were later declared to be disqualified from membership and it was decided to fill their seats; this led to a large number of by-elections from 1645 on, to which contemporaries gave the name 'recruiting' the House. Although historians have found little discernible difference between the recruiters and the original members in terms of their social origins, proportionately more of them do seem to have been radicals in politics and religion. The entry into the Commons of Cromwell's son-in-law Henry Ireton, Edmund Ludlow, Thomas Scot, Thomas Harrison, and Thomas Rainsborough more than counterbalanced that of such moderate stalwarts as John Swynfen and John Birch or the Presbyterian polemicists, William Prynne and Clement Walker.[6]

The measures taken by Parliament to improve the effectiveness of its war effort likewise led in unexpected directions. In earlier times there had been parliamentary committees on bills and more general topics, and there had been royal commissions, sometimes on national problems such as the cloth trade, more often on a county by county basis for taxation and other purposes such as land drainage or even the protection of swans.

The JPs, often described as the backbone of English local government in this period, were technically commissioners of the peace of each county; the assize judges received commissions of oyer and terminer and gaol delivery, to deal with more serious crimes. Although the Long Parliament had its own great seal made, and appointed lords commissioners to have charge of this in 1643, the groups of people whom they appointed for different branches of business in the various counties and regions were almost invariably commissioners, named in parliamentary ordinances rather than appointed under the great seal; occasionally they were simply named by order of one or both of the Houses. Parliament's own committees of course continued in being, the most important often being joint ones of the Lords and Commons; indeed their number multiplied, some ossified and faded away, others overlapped and competed with each other. Parliament was slow to create any kind of central executive body, to replace the royal Privy Council. The nearest to this was the Committee of Safety in 1642–3 and then the Committee of Both Kingdoms (with peers, MPs, and Scottish representatives) from 1644 to 1647 and later, when the Scots dropped out and the alliance had lapsed, the Derby House Committee, named after its meeting place, from 1647 to the winter of 1648–9. None of these should be thought of as an equivalent of a modern cabinet; they served principally as links between the Houses and the army commanders, and in no way controlled or managed parliamentary business. For many routine purposes others were of more consequence: committees which might be composed exclusively of peers and MPs or of these plus others, or else be non-parliamentary. The duties of the different regional, county, and local committees included responsibility for military forces, the penal taxation of some royalists and the administration of the confiscated property of others, the eviction of Episcopalian clergy and their replacement by more thoroughgoing Puritans. In some counties a single undifferentiated committee had charge of military, financial, and religious matters; in others there were separate bodies; some counties had a more elaborate structure of subcommittees, subordinate to a central parent body. From 1645 there was a separate network of subcommittees of accounts, answerable direct to the Committee for Taking the Accounts of the

Kingdom in London. Contrary to what its name might suggest, this body was concerned exclusively with those who had handled money on Parliament's behalf: army and civilian paymasters, collectors, etc. From 1647 on there was a central Indemnity Committee, to receive complaints from all who, having acted in Parliament's service during and since the war, were now being sued in the ordinary courts of law.

Ordinary people were most aware of the county committees and of those in the capital responsible for penal taxation— sequestration and compounding. It was their activities, together with the direct tax on property—the monthly assessment—and the excise that impinged on the course of life from day to day. These various levies meant that the country was supporting a far heavier fiscal burden than ever before; as a percentage of national income or gross national product (if we had the information to measure these with any accuracy) it was possibly not to be exceeded until the world wars of this century. Government borrowing was still on a short-term basis; so loans made to the Parliament, on what was called 'the public faith', had to be secured on particular branches of the incoming revenue, as had been true under the monarchy, or else on capital assets such as Irish or bishops' lands. What became increasingly unbearable was the combination of the burdens resulting from years of civil war, the seemingly arbitrary methods by which these were imposed, the kind of men involved in the system, and its continuance after the King had been defeated and any large-scale fighting had come to an end. The peace without a settlement which followed the war indeed saw tax reductions; the excise was taken off meat and some other basic commodities, and the assessment was lowered, but only with the result that the army's pay fell into arrears. There were local mutinies and in some areas a return to 'free quarter'. Most of the royalists had by then compounded, that is paid a penal fine graded according to the extent of their delinquency as well as their net landed wealth; the 'advance', as it was called, payment of a fifth of real and a twentieth of moveable wealth by all who had failed to come forward voluntarily with money, silver plate or horses and men back in 1642, which generally speaking meant many neutrals as well as royalists, had also by this time been wound up. Instead the final abolition of episcopacy, which had been effectively suspended since 1642, led to the sale of bishops' lands in 1646, although the great bulk of these went direct to the government's creditors, rather than providing a new source of ready capital. As with the monarchy's use of monastic and chantry lands a century before, the property confiscated was used as a windfall addition to income or else to pay off existing debts, not to form a new capital endowment for the provision of additional income. It may have been assumed by many people that a formal settlement with the King would bring to an end all the taxation which depended on the authority of parliamentary ordinances; it is not clear whether this was ever the official view in Parliament or the army. Finance came into the various negotiations with the King, but only in relations between the army and Parliament did it become briefly the central and most contentious issue.

New Model and Self-Denial

The Civil War was not decided by taxes and committees alone, effective and unpopular as they were. During the autumn of 1644 there was profound and widespread dissatisfaction with the parliamentarian war machine and its leaders. Probably this had been building up for some time, but it now came to a head. In spite of their evident superiority in manpower and resources and the great victory won at Marston Moor, Parliament's forces had signally failed to defeat the King; and there was more than a suspicion that they or some of their leaders were not really trying to do so. After the disgrace of Essex's defeat in Cornwall, the three armies (his, Waller's and Manchester's) had again brought the King to bay near Newbury and again had had the worst of it; at least with inferior numbers the King had achieved a draw. Cromwell blamed his own Commander-in-Chief, the Earl of Manchester (the Lord Mandeville of 1641–2) who had now shifted over to the peace party in the Lords; others blamed Essex, and Essex blamed Waller, whose independent command in the south of England had—despite some minor victories— bedevilled affairs for too long. All this helps to explain how two, in theory distinct, movements came to fruition together: a scheme to 'new model' the Parliament's forces, that is to create a single field army under a unified command, and the more

controversial principle of 'self-denial', to make membership of
either House of Parliament incompatible with the holding of
any military command. The latter became a test of radical
enthusiasm, rather in the way that support for the Committee of
Both Kingdoms having effective powers had been the year
before. If the proposed self-denying ordinance went through, it
was bound to remove all peers from army and navy commands,
including Essex, Manchester, and Warwick; and all MPs,
including Waller, Cromwell, Brereton, and Hesilrige. The
recruiter elections had not yet begun, so the position of new
members did not arise. The Lords threw out the first version;
some concessions and alterations were made. The ordinance was
extended to cover all civil offices of profit unless the holders had
been in them by a certain date (1641 or earlier); on the military
side, garrison commanders were no longer included.

Essex retired without waiting for the ordinance to take effect,
and Warwick ceased to be Lord Admiral. Already the younger
Fairfax, Sir Thomas, had been selected to be Captain-General
of the newly modelled army, with Skippon, Essex's veteran
infantry commander, as his Major-General of Foot; the post of
Lieutenant-General of the Horse was significantly left vacant.
Meanwhile Cromwell and Waller spent part of the spring
conducting a useful minor campaign in the southern counties,
which did something to redeem the failure of the second battle
of Newbury. Then both gave up their commands and, as MPs,
returned to Westminster. There is no evidence of the contrary
happening, of anyone resigning his seat in order to retain an
office of profit or a field command. As a result of ambiguous
drafting, it seems to have been assumed when the recruiter MPs
were elected that the ordinance did not apply to them. The elder
Fairfax was a peer of Scotland and so did not have a seat in the
English House of Lords, and Sir Thomas was not an MP (in fact
he was to succeed his father in 1648 and was to be elected to the
Commons in 1649 but never sat). He was about as upper class
a commander-in-chief as could have been chosen, granted the
constraints of the Self-Denying Ordinance. Many regiments
continued to be commanded by members of the landowning
classes, and from the upper crust of it at that—wealthy and well-
connected knights and esquires; and even below the rank of
colonel many of the field officers were neither radical nor

plebeian. A number were still allies of the moderates or peace party in Parliament, but the great majority was Puritan in some broad sense cutting across denominations, although in theory all had to take the Covenant. In short, new modelling did not change the social composition or the ideological colouring of the officer corps overnight; whether it made much difference to the rank and file is obscure. It may be that proportionately more of the volunteers who served right through the war were men of strong religious commitment, but even to say this much is to risk straining the evidence. As we shall see, by 1647, after two years, the New Model is a very different story—and one for which the evidence is more plentiful, if open to conflicting interpretations.

The officers and men of the horse regiments clearly wanted Cromwell to be allowed to join them to take command. But his popularity may have been more as a successful field commander, a proved trainer of men, with a reputation for taking care of them and their horses, than as the champion of the sectaries and their tender consciences or as a leader of the win-the-war party in Parliament. His own attitude towards the Self-Denying Ordinance has puzzled historians as it did his contemporaries. The fact of his having moved its original adoption back in December 1644 and of having consistently supported its passage and then later being exempted from its provisions from June 1645 onwards (by a succession of special ordinances relating to him and later to two or three others) has always provided one of the strongest arguments for those who see him as a scheming hypocrite, who used religion and self-denial as a cloak for his ambitions to become the ruler of the whole country. Since Thomas Carlyle's publication of Cromwell's letters and speeches 140 years ago, it has been difficult to see him in that light, and modern studies have not made it more plausible. Obscure and inconsistent his mind may indeed appear to have been, but insincere he was not. His strong belief in divine providence explains much of his conduct, including his position during these months. If someone's interpretation of providence always seems to serve his own interests as well as that of the cause which he supports, the need to be hypocritical or insincere is providentially removed.

Decision in the field

In the early summer of 1645 the New Model was an untried force. Most of the officers and men had served before, in the armies of Essex or of Waller or under Manchester in the Eastern Association but not in their new units and under their present commanders. After a successful feint manœuvre, the King and Rupert attacked and quickly captured Leicester. The town was then sacked (the scale and severity of the atrocities is hard to gauge); news of this was used to stiffen parliamentary determination to have revenge and to destroy the ungodly. It may also have made the royalists over-confident. The King had, most unwisely, allowed Goring to go off to the south-west, in order to try to retrieve royalist fortunes there and link up with the Cornish; he and Rupert were then caught in the Midlands with greatly inferior numbers to those at the disposal of Fairfax, who was dramatically joined on the very eve of the decisive battle by Cromwell to take up command of the cavalry. The parliamentarians certainly ought to have won the battle of Naseby, again with a numerical advantage of at least three to two in their favour, and Charles should never have risked giving battle. Even so, the royalists looked at first like being the victors. Once more Rupert's charge broke through the enemy's cavalry opposite to him, but yet again he lost control of his men who rode off the field after the parliamentary baggage and supplies. Again Cromwell rolled up the royalists' other wing, but kept his men under tight control, so that superior numbers told against the royalist foot in the centre. The proportion of prisoners to those killed was higher than at Marston Moor, and the King was left almost without trained foot-soldiers outside Devon and Cornwall. Charles turned abruptly west and embarked on a recruiting drive similar to that of 1642 in Wales and the border counties. Rather than chasing him over the Welsh hills, the New Model was redeployed to pursue Goring down into the south-west; unlike Essex's foray of the year before, this time it reflected a sound strategic instinct. Goring and his army were caught at Langport in Somerset and then in Bridgwater, and his army was virtually wiped out.

Another royalist defeat had severe political repercussions. Just as Lord Saye and Sele's younger son, Nathaniel Fiennes, had been disgraced and his political career blighted by his surrender of Bristol to Rupert in 1643, so now Rupert was discredited and alienated from the King by his surrender of the same city to Fairfax. In both cases pointless slaughter and destruction was thus prevented; but the taint of cowardice or treachery remained. And, although they were later to be formally reconciled, Charles never really trusted his nephew again.

The royalists were now in disarray. The Queen had already left the country after the birth of her youngest child. The Prince of Wales and his councillors, including Hyde and other leading royalists, were to join her the following year.

In Scotland, too, the fortunes of war changed decisively in a short space of time. Montrose's final whirlwind campaign in the summer of 1645, if not a nine days' wonder, was little longer than a nine weeks' one. Considering the paucity of his resources and the rapid turnover of men in his army—the Highlanders being particularly reluctant to serve for long far away from home—his achievement was remarkable. The best part of the Covenanter army was away in England; but this can only partly explain the rapid string of victories which he won, several against heavy numerical odds. This culminated in his entering the Lowlands and decisively defeating the 'home army', leaving Edinburgh and Glasgow at his mercy. What Montrose would have made of his opportunity, politically speaking, whether he would have conciliated enough Lowlanders and split the Kirk's following then, as it was to be in 1648 and after, is mere speculation. The younger Leslie led a part of the army back from England by a series of forced marches; Montrose's intelligence was poor and his army was caught at a hopeless disadvantage and destroyed less than four weeks after his last victory. Although he escaped and carried on a guerrilla campaign in the Highlands until the following year, when he evaded capture and went into exile, Montrose was no longer a serious threat to the Covenanter regime. But his activities had had an inhibiting effect on the Scottish army in England, which wasted its time in a somewhat futile siege of Hereford lasting several weeks; this did not even pin down the King, and the city was later captured by a far smaller force of English parliamentarians, who used cunning as well as force.

The King scraped another army together after the disastrous

defeats of 1645, quite a feat in the circumstances. The royalists
continued to hold Oxford, parts of Wales, a fast-shrinking area
of the extreme south-west and isolated strongpoints elsewhere.
But the military outcome of the war could no longer be in any
real doubt. As Sir Jacob Astley reputedly said when he was
captured at Stow-on-the-Wold with the last royalist foot
regiments still at large rather than in garrisons: 'You have now
done your work, boys, and may go to play, unless you will
fall out amongst yourselves.' Only conflict within the
parliamentarian camp or between English and Scots could lead
to a royalist recovery and prevent the total defeat of Charles I.
A political settlement with him was to prove impossible. Yet for
most of his enemies, though no longer for all, such a settlement
was still unthinkable without the King's participation.

4

Revolution

It is difficult to see how the King's military fortunes could have been retrieved after Naseby, but it took a long time to end the war. Charles I's cross-country flight to join the Scottish army at Newark in the spring of 1646 and the consequent surrender of Oxford soon after marked its practical conclusion in England. A few pockets of royalist resistance still lingered on, but presented no more than a symbolic token, or a nuisance value in military terms. Politically, however, time was now on the King's side; and he knew it—one might say that he knew it too well and so overplayed his hand. Just as during the war many parliamentarians had not wanted to win a complete victory over the King, but to gain enough superiority to persuade him to come to terms, so now many of them were much keener to restore Charles I to his position as monarch and head of state than to insist on the exact conditions to be imposed upon him. In the course of 1646 the Court of Wards and Liveries was abolished, together with the feudal rights and tenures which justified its existence, and the parliamentarian office-holders in it (exempt by date of appointment from the Self-Denying Ordinance) duly compensated; the royalist Court of Wards, like the rest of the King's wartime government and administrative system, had disintegrated and disappeared with the fall of Oxford if not before. Only a few councillors and officials were with the Queen and Prince in exile. More important to the peace negotiations were Parliament's abolition of episcopacy and sale of bishops' lands, and its parallel introduction of a modified Presbyterian system of church government and worship. The latter was to prove a real obstacle to settlement, both with the King and with their own allies and supporters. It was not presbyterian enough, or at least it was insufficiently theocratic, to satisfy the Scots and their fellow-travellers among the Puritan clergy of London; yet it was too much of an intolerant, exclusive state church for the Independents, Baptists, and other sects. For the King it was in principle unacceptable, but in practice a possible bargaining counter if he would agree to accept this settlement for a fixed number of years with a private right of Anglican worship reserved for himself and his household. By its legislation on such fundamental religious matters as church government and liturgy, the Long Parliament was also denying, indeed subverting, the royal supremacy. Charles I was, like his predecessors since Elizabeth I and his successors to the present day, 'supreme governor' of the English Church. In the context of Church–State relations, at least as most people had seen them before the 1640s, this was not the least revolutionary aspect of Parliament's actions. And it had effectively taken place some years before the abolition of the monarchy. The other main difficulties in the way of a treaty between Parliament and the King included the position of the active royalist leaders: would Charles have to condemn all of them to perpetual banishment as the price of his own restoration? Another familiar theme from the past was control over the armed forces, or—since everyone assumed, or pretended to do so, that no standing army would be retained—command of the militia; the appropriate restrictions on the King's choice of ministers of state and councillors were another unresolved issue from 1641, in spite of all that had happened since then.

There had been two sets of negotiations during the course of the war: one at Oxford in the winter of 1642–3, and the other at Uxbridge early in 1645. In many ways the King would have come off better from either of these draft treaties than from the Nineteen Propositions, Parliament's last comprehensive demands before the war had begun. Even so, he would have had to make concessions over the Church and control of the armed forces and would have had to be ready to part with many of his closest supporters. Still undefeated in battle, this he was in no way prepared to do. The parliamentary majority's new, post-war scheme, put to him at Newcastle-upon-Tyne where the Scots had established themselves after his surrender to them, was understandably more severe, in view of the royalists' military defeat since the time of the Oxford or the Uxbridge proposals. None the less, if he had been prepared to concede on episcopacy and the militia, Charles would still have been left with very spacious prerogatives. Whether such a constitutional settlement would have worked, in the sense of lasting for any length of

time, seems a pointless question to ask. The King repeatedly
stalled and played for time through the rest of 1646 and much
of the year after. In a sense he began the whole process over
again, in discussing a revised version of the Newcastle Propositions, in the later months of 1648, until all negotiations with
him were summarily brought to an end by the Army's final
intervention. But in 1646-7 Charles succeeded in dragging out
the negotiations until the situation was dramatically altered by
the emergence of a new and quite different crisis.

Army and Parliament

Within Parliament, and particularly the House of Commons,
what might be called the broad centre-left coalition of 1644-5
had by this time disintegrated. Perhaps the very fact of military
victory and the consequent end of large-scale fighting was bound
to have helped the political moderates or conservatives, the heirs
of the peace party from 1642-4. But, as already suggested, the
crucial fact was the number of relatively uncommitted members
who had drifted over, to give Denzil Holles (one of the Five
Members) and his associates a comfortable majority on most of
the big issues. Having imposed their church settlement, and
having presented their terms to the King, Holles and his party
then managed to raise enough money to pay off the Scots and
get their army out of the north of England, as recompense for
which the King was handed over to the English early in 1647.
Holles and his allies then seem to have hoped to pay off the
Army in England except for such units as were designated to
undertake the reconquest of Ireland. (For on the Irish issue the
so-called peace party was no more peaceable or ready for
compromise than anybody else, including the one-time war
party.) In this scheme Fairfax was to be left as the only general
officer in England; by implication Cromwell's military days
were over. The regiments selected for service in Ireland were
given no choice; nor was anything like adequate provision made
for the pay arrears of the Army as a whole. By early 1647 these
had reached shocking levels, especially in several of the horse
regiments. The Army's initial objections to these plans for their
own future were on what might be called professional and
technical grounds, affecting their vested interests as members of
an army: indemnification against legal proceedings for actions

during and after the war; the settlement or at least the substantial reduction of pay arrears; a voluntary choice between demobilization and service in Ireland; the right of those who were to go to Ireland to have commanders of their own choice in whom they had confidence. All this, especially the last point, might be thought of as a kind of military syndicalism, exactly the reason why trade unions are not allowed in the armed forces today; but it was far from a revolution.

In the early spring of 1647 the initiative in resistance to Parliament's programme seems to have come from among the rank and file. There are hints in the evidence that they were already being egged on by the London radicals, one of whose leaders, John Lilburne, was himself an ex-Lieutenant Colonel of dragoons, having left the Army because he would not take the Covenant. Although he spent much of 1646–7 in prison because of the dispute with the House of Lords, this never seems to have prevented Lilburne from publishing nor from maintaining political contacts with his associates outside. But the army officers' interests were at stake too. The position of those who were also MPs was particularly delicate, not to say equivocal: these included Skippon, Ireton, Harrison, Rainsborough, and Fleetwood and, of course, Cromwell if he was at this time a member of the Army and not excluded because his exemption from the Self-Denying Ordinance had lapsed. According to royalist propaganda and the views of some subsequent royalist historians, the whole of the Army's resistance to Parliament was being secretly orchestrated by Cromwell, with Ireton's help, to advance his own personal ambitions; some of his one-time parliamentary and republican allies were later to accept this same version of events. Certainly his and Lilburne's relations with each other were ambivalent and far from consistently hostile; that does not mean that they jointly master-minded all that happened.

A decisive step towards the politicization of the Army came in late April. The soldiers began to elect two delegates from each regiment, to speak on their behalf. These were called variously 'agents', 'adjutators' or 'agitators', the last of these terms not yet having its modern pejorative sense. Three of them were examined at the bar of the House of Commons; it is not quite clear on what grounds, perhaps as irregular petitioners. In the course of May the officers of several if not all regiments followed suit and themselves elected two officer–Agitators apiece, to act with the elected soldiers. Even more important than this, Cromwell and several senior officers in the Commons decided to throw in their lot with the Army, however exposed this left them in Parliament. Many other officers of more conservative political and religious persuasions, some of whom were also recruiter MPs, resigned their commissions and left the Army, and others were promoted in their place. At this stage the officer corps became markedly less upper class and correspondingly more radical. Too little and too late, Holles and his party began to offer concessions: an indemnity ordinance, votes of money to reduce pay arrears, a halt to the forcible drafting of units to Ireland and to mass demobilization.

The Army's demands had now ceased to be limited to military grievances as officers and soldiers. By June the Army had its own political forum, the General Council, which consisted of the general officers and commanders of regiments and the delegates of the regimental officers and the soldiers. Moreover, it had a programme which owed something at least to Lilburne and his party, whose 'Large Petition' embodying the programme of the civilian radicals in London had not only been rejected by the Commons but insultingly ordered to be burned by the common hangman as a seditious if not treasonable document. Both the Large Petition and the various declarations and engagements issued by the General Council emphasized the Parliament's failures to honour its own obligations and to secure what many of its supporters thought they had been fighting for. Included were a wide measure of religious freedom, an end to monopolies, legal privileges and inequalities, reform of the law and of Parliament itself, and a settlement with the King and the Lords such as to secure the rest of these gains. The Army's hostility came to focus increasingly sharply on Holles and his immediate associates, as the source of their ills, in fact as enemies of their cause and of the public interest, more so now than the defeated King and his party. So the Army had become, for the first time, a political instrument and force in its own right.

Events moved rapidly with real danger of a new civil war breaking out between the two wings of the parliamentarian cause. Early in June a detachment of the Army equivalent in strength to several companies or troops but commanded only by a cornet (the lowest commissioned rank in the cavalry) seized the King, offered him no violence but moved him further into the heartland of the radical cause in East Anglia where the main part of the Army was then based. At the same time the train of artillery and the magazine were secured in Oxford. It is a mystery whether these steps were taken on the initiative of the Agitators alone or with the secret connivance of Cromwell; even if he had no foreknowledge of these events, the Lieutenant General certainly evidenced no disapproval of them. Parliament meanwhile, urged on by the militant Presbyterians in London both lay and clerical, began to reorganize the city militia and to recruit a rival army consisting partly of demobilized ex-officers and ex-royalist rank and file. In Sir William Waller and Colonel Edward Massey, the successful defender of Gloucester in 1643, now an MP, they had potential commanders of proven ability, and there were recruits in plenty if pay and other conditions of service could be made attractive enough. The crisis came technically on the question of the London militia and the composition of the committee to control it, but in reality it had become a struggle for power. The Army demanded the impeachment of Holles and ten of his closest allies, or at least announced its intention of impeaching them if the Commons did not conduct a self-purge (as it had done with monopolists and others in 1640 and with large numbers of royalists in 1642–3). Perhaps because of its reduced importance by this time, they made no corresponding demands about members of the Lords. Parliament backed down over the London militia, and the projected counter-coup with the aid of an anti-army seemed to have collapsed. In mid-July the General Council of the Army grudgingly accepted Cromwell's advice not to occupy London as was demanded by some of the Agitators and even by some of the most radical of the officers.

The next stage of the crisis was precipitated by a right-wing backlash in the City. Crowds of apprentices and others, inspired by the Presbyterian preachers and pamphleteers, surged down to Westminster, forced their way into the Parliament buildings and compelled the two Houses to start implementing the very measures from which they had so recently drawn back. This was a massive affront to the privilege of Parliament and, as it turned out, a disastrous precedent. A substantial minority of the sitting members in both Houses, including both their then Speakers, the time-serving Lenthall and the Presbyterian Manchester, withdrew in disgust and fled to the Army outside London for protection.

The Army's enemies had played into its hands. An advance on the capital and its occupation could now be plausibly represented as the restoration of the freedom and privilege of parliament, as well as a means of settling with Holles and company. The Army entered London eleven days after the forcing of the Houses by the Presbyterian 'mob'. Many respectable conservative Londoners seemed to have feared loot, rape, and massacre at the hands of the soldiers, perhaps combined with a popular sectarian uprising inside the City. Nothing of the sort happened; perfect discipline was preserved, and there was no bloodshed or plundering. According to Fairfax's admirers, even bad language was punished in this most unusual of armies. But the impeachment of the eleven was immediately recommenced and they fled rather than attempt to meet the charges against them. The Army had, however, made a serious political miscalculation. Even without Holles and his ten associates, and in spite of the obvious dislike felt by someone such as Manchester for the forcing of the Parliament, the Presbyterians or moderates still had a clear working majority in both Houses on many issues. The proceedings of the eleven days were declared null and void, but the radicals or Independents could only reckon on control of the Houses when the King's behaviour or other external circumstances proved too much for the uncommitted members. To see how this might have come to pass, we must now return to the King's role and the various negotiations with him.

Army and King

During the brief pause before the forcing of the Parliament and the Army's final decision to occupy London, the General Council had appointed a subcommittee to draft its own plan for the settlement of the kingdom. The 'Heads of Proposals', as the scheme became known, were drafted by Cromwell's son-in-law Commissary-General Henry Ireton MP, assisted by a young

Yorkshire officer of unusual talent both military and political, Lieutenant-Colonel John Lambert. We do not have full enough records of all the General Council's meetings to be sure whether or not the Heads were supposed to be referred back for approval before being submitted to the King, or if those negotiating with Charles were intended to have any freedom to amend them according to how he might respond. As often in human affairs, there may have been a genuine element of misunderstanding. But it was certainly a serious tactical error on the part of Cromwell and Ireton, and one which was to cost them dear, to appear to be negotiating with the King on their own initiative without a clear mandate to do so from the General Council. The King and members of his entourage implied that he found the Heads of Proposals potentially more palatable than the Newcastle Propositions, but he never in fact committed himself to any formal response on paper. Broadly speaking, the Heads were less severe on leading royalists and other active Cavaliers, less insistent on any specific type of church settlement so long as it was not papist or prelatical, but tougher on reducing the King's executive powers, and insistent on an element of moderate electoral reform (on which the Propositions had been deafeningly silent). Ireton and Lambert—assuming their authorship—seem to have contemplated something like a uniform taxpayer franchise together with drastic redistribution of seats away from decayed boroughs towards centres of wealth and population; they may have envisaged the number of seats allocated to each county being in proportion to its share of the monthly assessment, the current direct tax on property and other income, which was being used to maintain the Army. Many lesser reforms were classified as desirable but not as essential parts of the terms which the King must accept. The wording of one key clause, which gave another hostage to fortune, apparently meant that the Crown would recover all its powers and prerogatives not explicitly modified or removed in the proposals, including the royal veto on future bills dealing with matters not in the original treaty. The general tone was more pragmatic, in some ways more generous, than that of anything submitted to the King since the middle of 1641.

It is therefore tempting to say with hindsight that Charles should have accepted the Heads of Proposals. He would still

have enjoyed at least as much power as his grandson William III
was to do after the second revolution of 1688–9. But Charles I
had not the slightest intention of becoming a parliamentary
monarch, even one who could still within limits rule as well as
reign. On the contrary, his purpose was to recover by manoeuvre
and negotiation what he had lost in the ordeal by battle. In any
case, when Parliament returned to the problem of negotiations
with the King in August–September, peers and MPs did not
consider the Army's rival scheme but went back to their own
propositions of the previous year, though these now confusingly
became known as the Hampton Proposals or Propositions, from
the fact that the King was now residing at Hampton Court under
an easy-going form of house arrest. Charles, however, was
losing interest in both sets of proposals as his main aim shifted
towards a new alliance to bring the Scots back into England as
his allies, a scheme in which Hamilton was the key figure and
Montrose was tacitly abandoned.

The Leveller challenge

Meanwhile a fresh division was opening up within the Army.
The 'grandees', as the generals and their supporting officers
were called by their opponents, became increasingly suspect to
the alliance of Army and London radicals, Agitators and those
who, from November on, would come to be called Levellers.
Lilburne remained in the Tower for another three months after
the occupation of London which gave an added edge to radical
bitterness; but the real disillusionment was with the failure to
press reforms on either King or Parliament. The grandees were
seen as corrupted by royal favour and the promise of future
rewards from a restored monarch. New Agitators were elected
by some regiments, the Leveller concept of mandated delegation
being applied to them as strictly as was intended that it should
be to MPs. The radical programme was embodied in a pamphlet
of mid-October, *The Case of the Army Truly Stated*, and then
summarized in the *Agreement of the People*, issued at the end
of that month. The extent of popular support for this programme remains acutely controversial and largely a matter of
informed guesswork. Probably it never had the backing of more
than a minority in the Army, perhaps a large one among the
cavalry troopers and a smaller one in the foot regiments, and

of some thousands of people in and around London. Presumably as a concession to radical pressure, a special meeting of the General Council or maybe a committee of the whole was called to discuss the *Case* and the *Agreement*.

This resulted in the famous 'Putney debates', so-called because they were held there, whether or not actually in the church. The Agitators were allowed to have with them two spokesmen of the civilian radicals from London; not Lilburne or Overton but two less well-known men, the sharp-minded legally trained John Wildman and a London tradesman called Petty. The only senior officer to speak on the radical side in the debates, Colonel Thomas Rainsborough, son of a naval commander under James and Charles I before the wars, had already clashed with Cromwell in the Army Council and in the Commons; he was also at odds with the House of Lords over being posted to the fleet to replace a Presbyterian vice-admiral, correctly suspected of crypto-royalism. The extent and fervour of Rainsborough's democratic sympathies were hitherto unsus-pected. With Fairfax absent through illness and Cromwell there-fore in the chair, the anti-radical case was largely sustained by Ireton, who often seems to have been arguing single-handed against several opponents, including Edward Sexby, the most articulate of the Agitators. Setting aside for the moment many important qualifications which have to be made and overlooking other points of detail, the general argument of the two pamph-lets and the radical speakers in the debates represented a giant stride forward towards democracy. That is both a central truth and an over-simplification. The debates ranged over several distinct but often overlapping issues: who had been true and untrue to the 'engagements of the army', mainly the agreed declarations of June; on what conditions could one be absolved from obligation to keep an engagement or 'covenant' if it tended to one's own destruction or was wrong in principle; the meaning of the *Agreement*'s first substantial clause about the future parliamentary franchise; the general political future, including relations with the King; the specific issue of army discipline and the question whether the *Agreement* should be submitted to the Army as a whole at a mass rendezvous.

It has been argued recently that we should not think of two sides in the debates, that all—grandees, the other officers present, the Agitators, the two civilians—wanted consensus not confrontation. But the text of the discussions (taken down in shorthand by the Army secretary William Clarke and transcribed by him some fifteen years later, after the Restoration) makes it abundantly clear that Ireton on the one hand, Rainsborough, Sexby, and Wildman on the other only wanted consensus on their own terms. The role of the other officers present, some of whom probably never spoke at all but were readier to go further than Ireton in meeting the radicals part way, is of particular importance; even Cromwell showed himself more pragmatic, less of a theorist than his son-in-law on the franchise. Thus the debates were at least partly an exercise in persuasion; and, to judge from Clarke's briefer notes taken after the three days which he recorded in full, the Council accepted a substantial measure of reform on the suffrage and other issues. On the matter of discipline and a rendezvous, by contrast, the generals had their own way. There was to be a series of separate smaller meetings where order could be more easily preserved and a mass movement to subscribe the *Agreement* nipped in the bud. Whatever we may think about consensus or confrontation, almost all those concerned set great store by the unity of the Army.

In the immediate aftermath of the Putney debates and the continuing dispute about the rendezvous, the King became persuaded that his life was in peril at Hampton Court. At least he either was convinced or pretended to be—the evidence is ambiguous—that a party of Agitators, inspired by those whom he and others now called Levellers, was planning to murder him. This is not logically impossible; we shall find Sexby involved in assassination plots against Cromwell eight or ten years later. But there is no evidence to support it, except what Charles said that he had been told and a letter from Cromwell to the officer-in-charge there, and it seems wholly uncharacteristic of Lilburne and the rest, who if anything were too gentle and humane to be successful revolutionaries. The contrary view, as with the earlier seizure of the King too clever by half, is that Cromwell planted the misinformation on Charles I, via the local commander, intending the King to discredit himself by escaping, but then providing that he should fall into the Army's hands again by going to the Isle of Wight where the commanding officer was conveniently another relative and admirer of Cromwell. Unless there was a double agent among the King's own close attendants and confidants, acting throughout in Cromwell's interest, it is simply not credible to suppose he could have known that Charles would head for the Isle of Wight rather than all the possible alternatives. Every argument of common sense would have urged the King to try to get across the Channel, out of his enemies' grip altogether, so that he could then attempt a comeback as his son was to do later, either via Ireland or Scotland. Only if Charles had been misinformed, deliberately or in good faith, that the governor of this island was a royalist sympathizer does the choice become credible. This is not impossible: plots and double agents did exist; dispatches were intercepted, read, and then allowed to go on their way. But when evidence is lacking and the historian has to weigh probabilities, it is normally sensible to prefer the simpler explanation of the alternatives available. No doubt Cromwell was already deeply suspicious of the King's sincerity in negotiations, but the decision to cross the Solent and not the English Channel was yet another blunder on Charles's part, and one which helped to cost him his life just over a year later.

Discipline was soon restored in the Army and, more surprisingly, so was its unity. At one of the three rendezvous for groups of regiments of about brigade strength, one regiment, having mutinied and parted from all but one of its officers, turned up contrary to orders; these soldiers and some of those in one other regiment then took part in what can best be called a mutinous demonstration, with copies of the *Agreement* stuck in their hats. This was on Corkbush Field at Ware near Hertford; Lilburne, by now at last released from the Tower, was lurking on the edge of the field but took no part in the proceedings. Still more remarkable, Rainsborough also seems to have been present and to have done nothing to prevent Fairfax and Cromwell[1] from regaining control of the situation. Three ringleaders from the mutinous regiment were court-martialled and sentenced to death; one, chosen by lot, was summarily executed. It was all very anti-climactic, and by most standards not a harsh way of restoring military discipline; three or four officers, one being an otherwise little known MP, were arrested and kept in prison for varying lengths of time.

It has also been suggested that there was a divergence of interest between the Levellers and the Army. Leveller emphasis on decentralization and their neglect of the executive and adminstrative aspects of government conflicted with the practical necessity for a strong central authority to enforce the indemnity ordinances and to collect the assessment and other taxes. When the power of the State was so used, by agreement between the Army command and parliament, as it was during the winter of 1647–8, then large numbers of troops could be paid off without all the trouble that the attempts to do this had caused during the previous spring and summer, when Parliament and Army were at odds and the Levellers had exploited this division in order to convert the Army to their cause. This appears persuasive, but there is no clear evidence that contemporaries actually perceived such a contradiction to exist at the time.[2] It is more convincing simply to point out that Leveller–Agitator influence was only dominant for a relatively short spell between May and July, and that it was already waning again by August–September, well before the events at Putney and Ware.

The King and the Scots

More than anything else the King's continued activities helped to bring the Army together again, and likewise gave the initiative back to the radicals or Independents in Parliament. Charles was now in the process of clinching his secret alliance with the Scots. A fuller, more comprehensive set of demands, known from the way they were formulated as the Four Bills, amalgamating parts of the Propositions and the Heads, was now carried in both Houses, submitted to the King and—for once—not simply laid aside but rejected. This led Cromwell and his allies in the Commons to move a vote of 'No Addresses', to break off negotiations with the King, regarding him as incorrigible but leaving open the question of what to do instead. This was carried in the Commons but not at first in the Lords, who again gave way after pressure and threats of action by the Army. Clearly, as a result of the King's trickery being made plain for all to see, an alliance of a sort between radicals and moderates had again re-formed; or, to put it another way, enough of the uncommitted members had swung back to the line taken by the Independents rather than the Presbyterians. For the first time since the rumoured sounding out of the generals by Vane back in 1644, the King's deposition was apparently discussed, though not in Parliament or in any formal way. The escape of the young Duke of York (the future King James II) to join his elder brother overseas made such a scheme less plausible and may explain why it was dropped, though James in any case was old enough to have refused to co-operate.

The royalists' plan for 1648 was an ambitious one, and required careful co-ordination and very successful timing. They aimed to reverse the outcome of the Civil War by simultaneous risings or revolts in several areas, to coincide with a Scottish invasion by land from the north and an amphibious assault led by the now eighteen-year-old Prince of Wales by sea from across the Channel. This was to be dependent upon the defection of the fleet to the royal cause. It was further hoped that many ex-neutrals and even ex-parliamentarians, especially perhaps the London Presbyterians smarting after their defeat in 1647, would rise too. This was a bold and ingenious scheme and not without strategic and political insight, but if part went wrong all was likely to do so. The so-called Second Civil War only lasted for a few months, but the outcome was by no means a foregone conclusion.

How did it come about that the Scots, who had defied Charles I back in 1639–40 and had entered the war against him in 1643–4, were now prepared to invade England on his behalf? When we speak or write of Scotland or the Scots in the seventeenth century, it is easy to forget from an English point of view that our northern neighbour was no more a single homogeneous entity, in religious, political, or social terms, than was England itself. The National Covenant of 1638 had been very widely subscribed. Notionally indeed most of the adult male population, except for the Gordon-led Catholic pocket in Aberdeenshire and clans in parts of the Highlands and Islands, adhered to it, with only a tiny minority of anti-Calvinist Episcopalians otherwise standing out. Probably this unity was always somewhat superficial or, as with opposition to Laud in England, the unity was negative only. Of the King's ministers in Scotland and his Scottish friends in England, the only one to have retained any substantial following in his own country was Hamilton, despite his reputation for deviousness. He and the

King's other agents now succeeded in splitting the Covenanter leadership.

It might be safer to say that they helped to precipitate a division already taking shape, between pragmatists and fundamentalists, or moderates and zealots. Among the former, John Campbell, Earl of Loudoun, the Lord Chancellor, and the two Leslies, Alexander, Earl of Leven and his son David, held sincerely to the cause but coexisted uneasily with such as Archibald Campbell, Marquis of Argyll and Archibald Johnston, laird of Warriston. Nor were the Presbyterian clergy all on the zealot side. The alarm at the toleration accorded to the non-Presbyterian Puritan sects in England together with dislike for the radicalism manifested in the Army's growing prominence, was bringing out the inherent royalism of the Covenanters, or at least their basic monarchism, which was now felt more and more also to be the cause of the Kirk itself. Even so, the opportunist alliance of 1647–8, known as the Engagement, made with Charles I and leading to Hamilton's invasion, was too much for many to swallow. Only in the extreme south-west did the clergy as a whole not merely oppose but actively campaign against it, and this division was to be a lasting one among the Scottish Presbyterians. Others simply dissociated themselves. Of the two leading lay fundamentalists, Argyll was the more influential because of his great clan following as head of the Campbells, but also the more devious; Johnston, the surviving parts of whose autobiography provide one of the more extraordinary personal testaments of the period and a political source of some value, typifies the man of extreme and strict principle partly corrupted by the pursuit of wealth and power, and the end he aimed at was ultimately ruined by the means used to attain it. Still, compared with most of the Engagers, they were certainly men of principle. The opponents of the alliance, later known as Remonstrants or Protesters from the retrospective statements of their case, were only a serious force in the south-west.

The Engager or Hamiltonian army was ill organized and ill led; it got as far as mid-Lancashire. Very few English royalists joined it, though, even if more had done so, the outcome would hardly have been different. Delayed by Lambert and Harrison, commanding numerically far inferior forces, the Scots were decisively defeated when Cromwell reached Preston. The anti-

Engager leaders and their more moderate allies then invited the English to help them break the power of the Engagers. So in one of the stranger episodes of the whole era, an English flying column under Cromwell and Lambert crossed southern Scotland virtually unopposed to enter Edinburgh early in October 1648. When the English force returned south to continue mopping up operations against the royalists in Yorkshire, the zealots were left nominally in control of the capital and the government of Scotland. As events shortly revealed, to oppose the Engagement with Charles I was by no means the same as to approve of regicide or to favour the establishment of a republic.

Cromwell's sweep north, to win the easiest major victory of his career at Preston, was only possible because the outcome of the Second Civil War had already been decided in the rest of England and Wales. At first things had seemed to go well for the royalist design. A large part of the Navy did mutiny, allegedly resenting Rainsborough's political extremism, though this seems to have been a justification more than the cause of the sea-men's action. Forgetting self-denial, Parliament quickly re-appointed Warwick as Admiral; and under his adept leadership the majority of the ships' crews reverted to their previous parliamentarian allegiance; the rest, a sizeable proportion of the whole fleet, drew off and put themselves under the command of the Prince of Wales, later being transferred to that of Rupert who was now trying his hand at sea. There was a spontaneous neutralist-cum-royalist rising in Kent, against a particularly unpopular county committee as well as against Parliament's rule in general. A serious revolt broke out in South Wales, led by a combination of ex-parliamentarian officers and royalists. The main rising planned for the home counties was to be led by the young Duke of Buckingham, son of James and Charles I's favourite who had been murdered before the Personal Rule back in 1628, and by the Earl of Holland, one-time favourite of Queen Henrietta Maria, a side-changer in the first Civil War and—ironically—Warwick's brother. They were an incompetent and implausible pair; their plans went thoroughly awry and the forces which they got together very quickly fell apart, most disappearing again. No rising took place in London; and Fairfax, having crushed the Kent royalists, chased the survivors of their army round the north of the capital and into Colchester on the Essex coast. A long-drawn-out and increasingly ill-tempered siege followed. When the town fell, Fairfax alleged-ly broke the laws of war by having some of the royalist commanders summarily shot after being court-martialled; this may partly explain why a group of royalists broke out of Pontefract Castle where they were being besieged and killed Rainsborough, who was lodging at an inn in Doncaster while directing the siege operations; two of them were in turn tried and executed at the York assizes after their capture the next year.

The general conduct of the war was taking on a grimmer aspect with vengeance increasingly in the ascendant. On the other side of the country, Cromwell finished off the neo-royalists of south Wales, who had already been defeated by the local parliamentarian commander with two New Model regiments. This was before his march north against Hamilton. Over most of the country, whatever people's sympathies with the now imprisoned King and however much their disgruntle-ment at the continued burden of taxes and committees, there was never any question of a mass uprising on the King's behalf.

Purge and regicide

The Second Civil War was fatal to Charles I, in that the Army came to hold him personally responsible for the renewed bloodshed. Some, like Harrison, probably already felt that he should be brought to justice; others, like Ireton, were now converted to this view. The same was true of a small minority in the Commons. But, while the Army was away fighting the Second Civil War, the majority in both Houses was still bent on a settlement which would restore the King. The vote of No Addresses was therefore repealed, as were the impeach-ment proceedings against Holles and his surviving colleagues, and shortly after this a committee was appointed to resume negotiations with Charles I, on the basis of the parliament-ary majority's continued preference, the revised Newcastle Propositions. It is hard to escape the feeling that the Pres-byterians or parliamentary moderates were living in a dream world during the late summer and autumn of 1648. Some of the radicals such as Vane agreed to serve as commissioners to treat with the King at Newport in the Isle of Wight, presumably believing that it was their duty either to sabotage any un-acceptable agreement or to insist on provisions which would make it acceptable to their allies in the Army. If so, this was indeed a vain hope! The General Council of the Army, including the Agitators, had not reappeared after 1647. It was now the Council of Officers, mainly inspired by Ireton while Cromwell was still absent in the north, which spoke on the Army's behalf. Two successive declarations called for an end to negotiations with the King, demanding instead proceedings against him and a purge of the Parliament as well. Presumably feeling that they needed allies, or at least to secure themselves against attack from the popular radicals, the grandees with their civilian and clerical Independent allies had already reopened discussions with the Levellers, each party hoping to win the other's backing for its policies if not its principles.

By the end of November 1648 the Army's exasperation with their parliamentary masters was reaching an explosive pitch. Whereas in 1647 it had been the Levellers who had been demanding a single chamber parliament without a monarch, during the winter of 1648–9 they became increasingly alarmed that, if the King were proceeded against before a general political settlement including safeguards for individual rights, then such reforms as they wanted might never come about at all. From their point of view this was a correct analysis; it was their negotiations with the Independents which in restrospect appear anomalous or misconceived. To understand what went wrong or, to put it another way, why a grandee-Agitator or Independent-Leveller common front was impossible, we need to look back over the previous year and a half to the summer of 1647.

The fate of the Heads of Proposals shows that settlement often depends more on the political context than on the actual content of such packages. Taken out of context, we may readily agree that Ireton's and Lambert's scheme offered the best hope of any put forward for settling the country's government on a sound basis. But in the event it was unacceptable—to the King, to the majority in both Houses of Parliament, and to the popular radicals in London and the Army; indeed one could go further and suggest that the Army leaders' negotiations with Charles I weakened their own position and exacerbated tensions.

It was the King who solved their predicament for them, by the blatant evidence of his duplicity as well as obstinacy from November 1647 onwards; opinion in the Army now turned irrevocably against him, whereas even during and after the Second Civil War the majority of sitting peers and MPs still gave the highest priority to a settlement with Charles in spite of all that had happened. Only this can explain their reversal of No Addresses, readmission of the Presbyterian leaders, and resurrection of the Newcastle Propositions in the Newport negotiations. It is in no way surprising that the Army's patience finally snapped, although the action it then took may seem mistaken.

What alternatives were open to the Council of Officers? They could have repeated the temporarily and partially effective measures taken in the summer of 1647: compel Parliament to purge itself, although it must have been clear that they would have to insist on the removal of considerably more than a mere eleven members, with the threat once more to occupy London and Westminster to back up their demands. But what then? The King had already effectively refused to consider their own offer to him for a settlement, and on the contrary had shown himself to be intolerably untrustworthy and an impossible person with whom to have dealings. Might a further purged parliament remove Charles I and then dissolve itself, thereby making way for a new legislature, elected on a different basis, which would in turn implement the other reforms for which the Army had been striving, many of which had been listed in the Heads of Proposals? The alternative was to borrow the ultra-royalist argument that the body still sitting at the end of 1648 no longer constituted the Parliament intended in the May 1641 Act, and that it could therefore be removed without breach of that statute. Might it not be better to replace the Long Parliament by a fresh and differently chosen 'supreme authority' before getting rid of Charles I and embarking on other reforms? Whether the officers would have decided otherwise if Cromwell had been present we cannot tell.

To speak of 'the Army' or even of 'the Council of Officers' is to suggest a unity and a harmony of outlook which existed only seldom and on a limited range of issues. The officers included moderates such as Fairfax who wanted the minimum possible intervention needed to get them out of their present impasse. Then there were the pragmatic reformers like Ireton, who were coming round increasingly to accept the idea of a republic but otherwise wanted improvements rather than fundamental changes in government, law, religion, and society. There were even a very few Leveller sympathizers who wanted a more democratic or 'popular' type of settlement, accompanied by more sweeping reforms, though since Rainsborough's assassination they had no spokesman of any standing among the field officers. More important were the millenarians, of whom Colonel Thomas Harrison MP was emerging as the most articulate: they lived in a psychological atmosphere of constant expectation and excitement, where drastic action against the parliament might well be a justifiable prologue to action against the King, who was increasingly identified as a 'man of blood', indeed as a limb or agent of Antichrist. What other reforms would follow the institution of a republic modelled on Old-Testament lines was probably less clear to them; or rather this might have found them in turn divided between piecemeal reformers and those who truly believed in a 'brave new world'. It may also help us to understand what happened if we think of Cromwell himself as a man of two minds: his instincts drew him to the conservative reformers like Ireton, his religious convictions to the apocalyptic revolutionaries like Harrison. The contradiction was never to be resolved.

The action on which the Army officers and their civilian allies decided may well be seen as the worst of every world. At the end of a stormy all-night sitting the Commons had finally voted by 129 to 83 that the King's final reply in the Newport negotiations provided a satisfactory basis for proceeding with a treaty. The Army had by then already entered London, again unopposed. The famous episode known to history as Pride's Purge, after the Colonel immediately in charge, shows how easy it is to take direct military action against an elected assembly, and more fatally how it can become a habit. With the help of Edmund Ludlow and one or two other MPs to identify them, the members were picked off as they came to enter the House on the day after the morning of their fatal vote. About 45 were held under arrest (though most of these were released in a matter of days or a few weeks) and between 95 and 120 more were prevented from entering and later told that they would only be allowed to resume their seats if they publicly disavowed the vote of 5 December. The Purge removed at a stroke something like three-fifths of the members then eligible to sit, including recruiters, and left at first only fifty or sixty prepared to do so, whom Cromwell joined the next day on his arrival from Yorkshire.

It was this truncated House of Commons, first elected eight years earlier, to which the aptly derisive nickname of the 'Rump' was soon to be applied. Prolonged informal and secret discussions, of which no record survives, took place between various of the remaining MPs and some of the officers. Eventually it was decided that the King should be brought to trial on capital charges of committing treason and levying war against his people, before a specially constituted 'high court of justice'. The first ordinance to establish such a body and proceed with the trial was defeated in the Lords where a few more peers than usual turned out to vote. The Commons then carried a series of resolutions declaring in effect that they represented the will of the people, and that they alone could and should make laws. If this had been done by a full and properly elected House of Commons, it would still have been a revolutionary act, but the claim might at least have had a certain moral and political force; as it was, their assertion can only be called a preposterous travesty. But the Lords no longer commanded any following (Essex had died back in 1646; Warwick was away at sea; they had no real leader), and made no further attempt to oppose these unilateral proceedings. An act (as the Commons' legislation was now once more styled) instituting the High Court of Justice to try the King was then carried. The commissioners named in it were to be both judges and jurors. Of the 150 or so listed, at least 60 never sat at all. For different reasons, Hesilrige and Lilburne were both conveniently absent in the north of England, and Vane refused to take any part, though he remained an active member of the government (which was to cost him his life after the Restoration); so did Fairfax, whose wife reputedly denounced the whole proceedings. In the end fifty-nine men signed the warrant for the King's execution, and another ten, having been present and assenting when sentence was given, may also be counted as regicides. The first three signatures were those of John Bradshaw, an obscure but respectable Cheshire lawyer who acted as President of the court, next Lord Grey of Groby, the heir to an earldom, and Oliver Cromwell. Much has been written about the illegality of the trial and how little it accorded with the popular will. But the great impact which the regicide made on contemporaries both at home and abroad was precisely because it did take the form of a public trial and execution. A summary court martial, followed by the shooting of the King, where and whenever it might have happened, would indeed have been no more unjust but would have had far less effect. In Thomas Carlyle's words: 'I reckon it perhaps the most daring action any Body of Men to be met with in History ever, with clear consciousness, deliberately set themselves to do.'

These two actions—the Purge and the regicide—largely shaped the pattern of politics during the following ten or eleven years. The limited and partial, conservative rather than radical or 'popular' nature of the revolution no more predetermined the Restoration of 1660 than Charles I's Personal Rule had predetermined the outbreak of the Civil War in 1642. But in a comparable way it was a necessary cause, without which what followed would most certainly have been very different from what it was. It is unreasonable to blame people for making mistakes if they have no choice. The act against the Long Parliament's dissolution without its own consent proved a fatal inhibition for men whose political thinking had such a strongly legalistic cast. Just as the parliamentarians had maintained the legal fiction that they were fighting for King and Parliament throughout the period from 1642 to 1645 or 1646, so the Army could not bring itself to say openly that in the circumstances of 1647–8 the so-called Parliament was no longer the body of 1640–1, and that therefore that act was no longer binding. It is all too easy to say that the removal of a majority of the sitting members by imprisonment or exclusion was either too much or too little, that the Army should either have reactivated the impeachment proceedings against Holles and company, or else have summarily dissolved the whole parliament and called a new one on a different basis.

It is indeed possible that some of the more radical officers hoped, even intended, that the Purge should be merely a prologue to dissolution in the very near future. This partly turns on how to interpret the Army's negotiations with the Levellers at the end of 1648, and how seriously the proposals then being made were to be taken. The discussions were broken off by Lilburne and his colleagues because (so he tells us in a pamphlet written in changed circumstances the following summer) he had become convinced that Ireton, who was effectively in charge, was totally insincere. However, the Council of Officers went on meeting. The Levellers published a second, more detailed but also (notably on the franchise) more moderate version of the *Agreement*; the officers then did likewise on behalf of the Army, presenting theirs to the House of Commons with a covering petition in January on the eve of the King's trial. It seems an elaborate exercise if the whole thing was just a device to gull the Levellers or even—as is perhaps more likely—their potential fellow-travellers in the Army especially among the rank and file. That at any rate is the view of most historians. We might do better to assume that Ireton and others were sincere in the absence of evidence to the contrary. Perhaps it was more a matter of priorities; they would have liked voluntary dissolution followed by elections for a reformed parliament, but were not prepared to force it on the Rump so soon after the December Purge. The monarchy and the House of Lords were abolished by the purged House of Commons shortly after Charles's execution, and a second High Court of Justice in turn sentenced to death Hamilton (as a peer of England) and other royalist leaders from the Second Civil War, including Holland; but little more happened.

It is tempting to argue that the regicide too could and should have been avoided. If only the Army had been less imbued with the ethic of revenge born of too much reading in the Old Testament, they might have deposed Charles I and then securely imprisoned him beyond the possibility of escape. The royal cause would thus have been denied the emotional leverage of martyrdom; the external threat from the Prince and the other royalist exiles would have been no greater than it proved to be after the King's execution. The monarchy could have been left in a state of suspension with a commission of regency or some similar device. As it was, many Presbyterian parliamentarians both clergy and laity, who might grudgingly have come to terms with Pride's Purge and the Rump, utterly rejected regicide and republic. In short, the events of December 1648 to February 1649 narrowed the basis of support for the regime without any corresponding access of strength except among that minority comprising the Army and the radical Puritan sects, whose support could have been ensured by something less than this. All that being said, it may seem remarkable that the English republic lasted as long and—in many respects—operated as effectively as it did.

Just as it had required all the circumstances and developments of the 1630s to bring about the situation of 1640–1, so it took the whole of those of 1640–2 to make possible the Civil War of 1642 and after. Likewise it required all that happened during and after the Civil War, and especially its renewal in 1648, to bring about the events of 1648–9. Only by thinking of the historical process in this way can we possibly make credible what happened between the summoning of the Short Parliament and the King's appearance on the scaffold some nine years later. There had been alternative possibilities at many stages along the way. The King and his ministers might have persevered with the first of the two Parliaments called in 1640, so that it had not been 'short'. Civil war might have been avoided; the King might have won it. Where events could so plausibly have been different at so many junctures and in so many possible directions, it may seem pointless and even misleading to suggest any long-term underlying causes of what happened. But it is the argument of this book that, whereas contingent circumstances did indeed in a multitude of ways help to determine what did and did not happen, at the same time several of the necessary causes, without which events could not have been what they were, lay far back in time, some in the very roots of English history.

Some of these earlier influences and more recent coincidental or contingent circumstances are more obvious than others. The precise events of the 1640s were not caused by the seizure and sale of the church lands under the Tudors, by the Protestant Reformation and the subsequent rise of Puritanism, by the failure to reform royal government after the mid-sixteenth century, by the inadequacies of the first two Stuart kings, in the international as well as domestic context of their time, or by the early death of Charles I's elder brother Prince Henry, by the vigorous longevity of Bishops Laud and Neile, by the ambitions and abilities of Thomas Wentworth, by the strength of the reformed faith in the Scottish Church, by the reactions of the Old Irish and the Anglo-Irish to English policies in Ireland—and so forth: of course not. But without these elements in the situation and many others, the events of the 1640s would not, could not, have taken the form that they did. It is in this sense that we may properly speak of 'necessary causes'. To enumerate the sufficient causes of almost any significant and complex event in human history is perhaps so difficult as to be beyond our capacity. The historian is not God, and should not try to be.

5

The quality of life

A twenty-year span is probably too short a time to measure changes in many aspects of life. It is after all less than a generation, if we reckon that as the average age of parents at which their first children are born. Before we come to matters affecting the family and the material basis of society, what can be said about the 1640s and 1650s in relation to thought, culture, and the arts? We may start by asking what was distinctive about each aspect and what differences, if any, arose from the public events of the time.

Culture and the arts

One caricature can be dismissed straight away. The Puritans were certainly not anti-intellectual and not against the arts in any general undiscriminating way. At the same time, like adherents of other strongly articulated and directed bodies of ideas with a great conviction of their own righteousness, they were suspicious of certain tendencies and manifestations. For example, most Puritans were strongly in favour of higher education and moral and theological training, but not of free speculation and expression if these led in unacceptable directions. Some of those whom we think of as the greatest, even as the most representative of Puritans were in fact heterodox, not to say deviants and rebels against these very orthodoxies: Milton, Bunyan, perhaps Cromwell himself. Thus, in the great outpouring of creative political and social thought, little of what was most original and seems to us most remarkable can be called puritan in any meaningful sense. It is only necessary to think of Thomas Hobbes, the philosopher of absolutism, the Levellers, Gerrard Winstanley the Digger—a kind of pantheistic Christian communist—James Harrington—the agrarian classical republican—or the secular-minded defenders of the Commonwealth, to become aware that most of the truly original ideas were produced by people in varying ways out of step with prevailing orthodoxies—Anglican, Puritan, royalist, parliamentarian.

Such exciting new theories about the individual, the State, and society were in the fullest sense the product of their time, yet produced as it were against the grain.

Historians and autobiographers

Interest in contemporary history received a predictable stimulus from political and other public events. Writing probably in the later 1640s, Milton inserted his untitled excursus, usually called 'The Character of the Long Parliament', into his *History of Britain* at the point where the Romans have withdrawn leaving the natives to their own devices, just before they are overwhelmed by the Saxons and other invaders thanks to their own divisions and other follies; the clear message is that people are often not equal to the burden of freedom.[1] Milton felt that this applied particularly to the present rulers in Church and State—the Assembly of Divines and members of the Long Parliament. Others who wrote contemporary history or memoirs of their time in a distinctive way included Harrington, an economic determinist for whom the distribution of landed property normally dictated the kind of government that a country would have, and explained the whole course of English history since 1485. But there were lesser-known histories, some written even before 1660, which reflect a response to events in an even more direct and sometimes cruder fashion. Thomas May's *History of the Parliament begun in November 1640* (first edition 1647), although a semi-official, 'sponsored' work, is remarkable in criticizing the parliamentarians for having made too much of the religious danger, the great popish conspiracy and its Arminian instruments, and correspondingly too little of the royal design for absolutism, and suggests that they lost support in consequence. The side-changing medical doctor George Bate's *Elenchi motuum nuperorum in Anglia* (Latin 1649, English translation 1652), if indeed he was its author, can claim to be the first published pro-royalist history, and certainly analyses causes as well as recounting events. Sir Richard Baker's *Chronicle of the Kings of England*, which was continued to 1660 by Milton's nephew Edward Phillips, suddenly becomes a valuable near-contemporary source for the last years before the Restoration, the second author having access to new information. Various books criticizing James and Charles I published in the 1650s, some by royalists, evoked conflicting replies. There was basic disagreement as to whether the monarchs had had any faults or made any mistakes; alternatively everything that went wrong was ascribed to the wickedness and malevolence of their enemies. Thomas Fuller's classic *Church History of Britain*, which daringly came down to 1648 although only published in 1655, was stingingly attacked, from the High-Church or Laudian side, for being too moderate and yielding, although Fuller had himself been a royalist army chaplain and had later suffered at the hands of the Puritans. His opponent, Peter Heylyn, had been a protégé of Laud's and a royal chaplain under Charles I, and was to write several works in the high Anglican interest, although he went blind and barely survived the return of episcopacy, from which he gained no reward. The fashion for political biography owed much to classical influences, particularly the English translation of Plutarch's *Lives*. The only life of Cromwell with any pretence of objectivity came out within two years of his death; the next was not to be until well into the next century.

Edward Hyde, a privy councillor and Chancellor of the Exchequer since early in 1643, started to write his *History of the Rebellion* when he was on the island of Jersey in 1646. For reasons that he gives in the text, he begins his story effectively in 1625 with the accession of Charles I; by the time that he left to join the Queen and the Prince in France during the spring of 1648 he had got to 1644 with fragments written on 1645 and 1646. He did not resume work on his history until his second exile as an elder statesman, an earl and ex-Lord Chancellor, in the late 1660s. He had been in the process of being impeached and it was the threat of attainder and the King's inability to promise him protection which sent Clarendon abroad once more and led to the completion of the book. Hence the rest of the *History*, covering 1645 to 1660, and the openly self-justificatory *Life* by Himself written more or less parallel with it, were composed at a much greater distance in time from the events with which they deal. As against this, the exiled Earl's sons were allowed to send large numbers of documents across for his use. The main motivation of the first version of the *History*, covering 1625–44, is to show how such disasters had come upon the country since 1640, although Hyde had only gone over to the

King late in 1641. By 1668–74 his motives were more complicated: to account for the débâcle of the royalist cause, the
destruction of monarchy and Church and their near-miraculous
restoration. In the *Life* (which was continued in much greater
detail from the Restoration to his exile, for which years it was
more nearly contemporary) he sought to explain how he had
taken so prominent a part in the exiled King's councils and had
helped so much to make Charles II's return possible, but had
then been driven from office and from his country seven years
later. No other work of contemporary history has so complicated a history itself in its chronology and the reasons why it was
written;[2] no other can compare with it in detail, sweep and
sheer intellectual force, let alone richness of prose style.

  The only leading parliamentarians who attempted to write
contemporary history (at any rate which has survived), for
different reasons produced vastly inferior works. The memoirs
written by Denzil Holles and by Sir William Waller are slight
and self-justificatory. Holles's in particular are little more than
a sustained diatribe against 'the violent party', or Independents,
and a correspondingly partisan defence of 'the moderate party',
that is of himself and his allies; and he tells us nothing about his
relations with Hampden and Pym during the early years of the
Long Parliament. Bulstrode Whitelocke, a conservative-minded
lawyer and political trimmer, was largely concerned to exculpate
himself from responsibility for the political and other events of
1647–53; but much of his *Memorials of the English affairs* . . .
(first published after his death in 1682) is no more than a
compilation, padded out from newsbooks, pamphlets, and other
available contemporary materials.[3] Edmund Ludlow's *Memoirs*
set out to be more of an account of his own part in events, not
a general or comprehensive history. It has two main limitations:
one arises from Ludlow not having been a very sophisticated
political observer; the second from the fact of his text having
been seriously tampered with by its probable editor before it was
first published in 1698–9.[4] Ludlow's motives were to explain
both the victory and the downfall of what came to be called 'the
Good Old Cause', that is of a Puritan, parliamentary republic;
from the late 1640s onwards the published *Memoirs* read
much like a prosecutor's case against Cromwell, who is
portrayed as an ambitious hypocrite, bent upon attaining

supreme power. Curiously, Henry Ireton is treated very favourably; although Ludlow sympathized with the Levellers and even defended them in the House of Commons, he disagreed with their view of Ireton as Cromwell's *éminence grise*—'that chief of Machiavellians' in Lilburne's striking phrase.

Science

There is almost total disagreement among scholars as to whether Puritanism helped or hindered the advance of sciences, or had no effect either way. It is tempting to suggest that individual scientists can be found in each camp and in neither, and subscribing to almost every political and religious tenet; in short that the public events of 1640–60 were tangential to the progress in mathematics, physics, mechanics, astronomy, optics, chemistry, anatomy, and physiology, which taken together have without exaggeration been called the Scientific Revolution. This movement was not limited to a single country or to one twenty-year period. And the closer that we look at mathematics and pure science, the less direct connection there seems to be with current affairs. But in the applied sciences, and what we nowadays call technology, things look different. Here the needs of governments, the influence of pressure groups or economic incentives, and the general temper of the time may well have acted as a stimulus or catalyst. Navigation, ballistics, surveying and mapping, land drainage, the most efficient use of available sources of energy (water, wind, wood, charcoal, and coal), the collection of accurate information and statistics are only some of the areas where war and revolution might have had a positive effect. But it is quite another matter to demonstrate that the Puritan or republican ethos was more favourable than the Anglican or royalist to progress in such areas. And it seems most unlikely to be provable either way. Let us consider medicine and the life sciences: William Harvey, discoverer of the circulation of the blood, was a royalist; Thomas Sydenham, one of the foremost diagnostic clinicians of his time, a very committed and active parliamentarian and republican. It seems pointless to go on name-swapping in this way. Perhaps more significant, the radical Nicholas Culpeper, as well as being an astrologer, was strongly in favour of apothecaries (ancestors of today's pharmaceutical chemists) being allowed to prescribe drugs direct and not only as prescribed by physicians. The College of Physicians was among the monopolies attacked by the Levellers and other radicals; as in other cases, the attack was not pressed home. The College had not enjoyed a complete monopoly, at least in the provinces, before 1640, but retained its privileges more or less intact through the Interregnum.

Literature

There is disagreement about literature, imaginative and creative writing, too, although the arguments are somewhat different. Some writers were more directly caught up in public events than others: the so-called Cavalier poets, for example, were dispersed by the break-up of the royal Court, some meeting death in battle, others suffering penury and deprivation. Even Robert Herrick, hardly an ideological militant, was sequestered from his Devonshire vicarage. Once more, we cannot possibly tell how the writing of poetry would have proceeded without the war and its aftermath. Some of what might be called the 'public' verse of John Milton, Andrew Marvell, Edmund Waller, George Wither, the young John Dryden on the parliamentarian side would, by definition, not have been written had events turned out differently. But the relationship between the poet and the events of his time is not always a simple one. Andrew Marvell's pastoral poems—'The Garden', 'Upon Nun Appleton House', etc.—may be represented as a private escape or withdrawal from an unattractive public world, but plainly this is not true of his 'Horatian Ode'. Nor does this apply to all of Milton's sonnets; as to whether his great epics would have remained unwritten without the decline and fall of the Good Old Cause, we can only surmise that, if written at all, they would have been different. The foremost living historian of the seventeenth century has pointed out that there were more eminent poets in the State's service in the 1650s than ever before or since.[5] But this still does not quite answer the question of what was the relationship between Puritanism and literature, poetry and politics.

In the case of English prose, a more positive answer is possible. Just as there was far more overtly political writing after the collapse of the censorship, and a greater interest in and market for contemporary history, so too there was more satire, allegory, and polemical writing generally. Moreover, much of it was now directed at a readership without the background of classical learning normally taken for granted earlier, a new audience whose staple diet was likely to be the Bible and perhaps Foxe's *Book of Martyrs*. The use of irony by William Walwyn, of sarcasm and invective by Richard Overton, a little later of metaphor and figures of speech from everyday life by John Bunyan are illustrations of this. But royalist newswriters and polemicists, too, were aiming at a readership wider than an academic or courtly élite, at being read in ordinary homes as well as colleges and great country houses. We should not equate Puritan and parliamentarian with simplicity and Saxonisms; Milton's prose may not be so elaborate as the sermons of Donne or the works of Robert Burton and Sir Thomas Browne, but it is by no means simple and in some ways is nearer to their style than to that of the truly popular pamphleteers and newsbook writers. Some of the Puritan preachers claimed that they cultivated 'the plain style', by contrast with the elaborate style of the Arminians and others enjoying Court favour who aimed only to reach select, upper-class, and educated audiences. As literary historians have shown, this is at best a half-truth; perhaps the interesting thing is that they should have wanted to make such a claim, but it applies mainly to the period before 1640. Since the censorship was reimposed in 1649 and, in different circumstances, even more tightly in 1660, we cannot tell how English prose, either secular or sacred, would have developed untrammelled out of the 1640s. It seems difficult to speak of a popular press existing again until the eighteenth century. The chapbooks continued, but their best historian has not related their development decisively to the events of 1640–60.[6]

Theatre and music

The quarrel between the Puritans and the stage, or perhaps we should say between some Puritans and some dramatists, is well known. Plays continued to be written after the theatres were closed in 1642, but, except for the modest revival of opera at Cromwell's protectoral court in 1657, there were no public productions again until 1660. Again the discontinuity in the English theatre is susceptible of more than one interpretation. It can be argued that Elizabethan–Jacobean drama was already in full decline, that a forced interval was salutary and made a fresh start easier. It can be maintained with equal force that the playwrights of the 1630s were more original than the former view would allow, and that they should be seen as the precursors of the so-called Restoration dramatists; the forced interruption is to be seen on this view as unfortunate and for some concerned, as with the Cavalier poets, personally tragic. Some authors, actors, and producers lived to fight another day—on the boards so to speak; others did not. And the court masque disappeared virtually for good—something of an irony when the author of *Comus* was a distinguished public figure.

With music the case looks even clearer at first sight. The absence of the royal Court after the fall of Oxford in 1646 and the abolition of the previous liturgy and its musical accompaniment, especially in cathedrals and college chapels, by definition ended this type of church music, both for composers and performers. Although Puritans were against choirs and organs (and to some extent also church bells), they were not against music as such, once it was dissociated from a form of worship which they regarded at best as stiff, formal, and hierarchical, at worst as infringing the Second Commandment. Many individual Puritans, from Cromwell downwards, were devoted to music, but it was now to be found in a secular, often a domestic, setting.

The visual and applied arts

The influence of theology impinged on the visual arts, too, but for the most part only in respect of church ornamentation—sculpture and painted glass. It is now generally agreed that less damage was done to carvings, statuary, and windows in the 1640s and 1650s than had been done in the age of the Protestant Reformation a century earlier; blame is often attached to Oliver Cromwell in local folklore which if anything should belong to Henry VIII's great reforming minister, the 'hammer of the monks', Thomas Cromwell. None the less, Puritans were iconoclasts, and we do their memory an ill service by pretending otherwise. The Long Parliament had its own image-breaking committee for the London churches, under the well-to-do, educated, Herefordshire gentleman and ex-office-holder, Sir

Robert Harley, who, however, rebuilt his own village church in the 1650s to make good its near destruction by royalists during the war. According to tradition, Fairfax protected York Minster from the parliamentarian and Scottish soldiery after Marston Moor and the Bodleian Library when the New Model entered Oxford; he may have been politically naive, but he was certainly a Puritan and a parliamentarian as well as a formidable commander in the field. Two cathedrals, Carlisle and Lichfield, suffered serious damage and were left in a more or less ravaged state, and the lunatic fringe of zealots more than once suggested the demolition of all cathedrals as a money-raising device. But there was nothing like the ruin which befell the monasteries and other religious buildings after the dissolution of the religious orders in the sixteenth century.

Architecture as a whole presents a rather different case. Inigo Jones, the greatest designer of his age, had been closely associated with the absolutism of the Stuart Court, was almost certainly a practising Catholic, and was captured in arms after one of the fiercest sieges of the war. Yet other architects influenced by him continued to design new houses or additions and alterations to existing ones. In such house building as took place after the end of the war, there was no major reversion to the pre-Jonesian style, which has been called 'artisan mannerism'.[7] Few very large houses were built or rebuilt, although Wilton, which belonged to the parliamentarian Earl of Pembroke, who sat as an MP after the abolition of the House of Lords, was a conspicuous exception. Possibly tastes had changed, but more likely fewer huge fortunes were being made by Court favourites and ministers of state. The houses designed for Oliver St John, then Chief Justice, and Cromwell's Secretary of State, John Thurloe, were modest indeed measured by Hatfield or Audley End, or even by Wentworth's now demolished mansion at Jigginstown outside Dublin. Perhaps the test would have come if the Cromwellians had survived to produce a second generation of rulers in the 1670s and after. Once more we have to be careful to compare like with like, but there is more than a hint of a shift in wealth and influence away from the very top towards the middling levels of society: not a 'bourgeois republic' in the modern sense of the word, but on the whole a non-aristocratic one.

Charles I had been a great collector and connoisseur. The many paintings which he had acquired, including several masterpieces of sixteenth-century Italian art, were dispersed in 1649, along with the rest of the royal possessions. Most of them were sold, some finding their way to the Continent, others remaining in this country; a few were reserved for official display, and of these some later found their way into Cromwell's residences when he became Protector. The break-up of this magnificent collection was due less to rabid anti-aestheticism than to the Commonwealth's financial exigencies. Nor was the concept of a national art museum or gallery yet born.

In painting and sculpture there was undoubtedly change, but at least in the former this should not be read as decline. Van Dyck, who had in fact painted some 'opposition' peers and their families as well as those connected with the Court, died before the outbreak of war; the portraitist of the Oxford Cavaliers, William Dobson, fell on hard times and died in obscure poverty. Peter Lely, however, who is often thought of as the Restoration court painter *par excellence*, offered his services to the Rump Parliament, suggesting a series of historical murals to commemorate their great victories by sea and land! He received the famous commission from Cromwell with the command that he should be portrayed 'warts and all'. In one branch of painting— the portrait miniature—the 1650s saw supreme achievement. Samuel Cooper, the greatest of all English miniaturists, produced a series of incomparable likenesses of the republican–Cromwellian ruling circle and members of their families. This did not prevent him from becoming 'court limner' to Charles II, in which capacity he is inimitably described at work in Pepys's diary.

The early seventeenth century had not been a great age for English sculpture. Apart from ornamentation on and inside buildings, plaster work, and wood-carving, there had been relatively little figure sculpture except on funeral monuments in churches. In such work two or three artists of considerable quality stand out from the rest whose achievement, while of much interest to the social historian, is of slight aesthetic merit. As with house building, so with funeral monuments. There was by no means a cessation after 1640, but fewer examples can be found of really large and elaborate tombs and wall monuments.

Again what the successors to the rulers of the country in the 1650s would have done subsequently by way of commemorating their fathers and other predecessors, we can only guess. Considering the government's financial straits at the time, a great deal was spent on Oliver Cromwell's funeral, but no monument had been set in hand when his son's regime collapsed eight months later. A reminder of the social conservatism of the Long Parliament is to be found in its ordinance of 1643, echoing a proclamation of Queen Elizabeth, that the destruction of images in churches was to stop short of desecrating tombs and monuments.

In what may loosely be called the applied arts, we have to reckon not only with the impact of Puritanism and war, but more importantly the relative eclipse of noble patronage in addition to that of the royal Court. A large number of the wealthiest families, in the case of peers an absolute majority, were royalist and suffered some degree of financial difficulty in consequence. They were not the only people who commissioned fine silver, glassware, porcelain, tapestries, furniture, expensive clothing, and jewellery, not to mention garden layouts; but as patrons they had been trend-setters out of all proportion to their numbers, possibly even to their proportionate share of national wealth. Likewise with the pleasures of the table. The rulers of the republic were not, for the most part, against good food and drink, but the absurdly extravagant Court feasts of pre-war days did not reappear, although perhaps in any case these had been more prevalent under James than his son. So, if we include gardening, cookery, and dress, there may have been a slight tendency towards solid simplicity, away from the ornate and elaborate; away from conspicuous and wasteful expenditure as an end in itself. Would the wig have come into fashion when it did without the restoration of the monarchy? The answer may well be yes, but not as rapidly or carried to such elaborate extremes.

ECONOMY AND SOCIETY

What of the material basis of life and the relations between different social groups and classes? In considering the economy and social structure, we need to distinguish, so far as our evidence permits, between the causes or origins, the nature and immediate effects, and later consequences of reform, rebellion, war, and revolution. Enough has been said already as to the suggested distinction between necessary and sufficient causes. Discontents with monopolies, controls, and other government interference in agriculture, industry, trade, and transport should most certainly be included among the many elements in the situation before 1640 without which the events that followed would not have been as they were. This may be related to the fact that support for the Puritan–parliamentarian cause was strongest in the middle levels of society; while that for the Crown and the bishops was biased towards the top, whatever may have been true of those at the bottom. Some monopolies and controls were indeed swept away as early as the reforms of 1641, others simply lapsed with the cessation of royal commissions, e.g. to investigate wrongful enclosures and excessive conversion from arable to pasture which allegedly led to the depopulation of the countryside. Others, such as the privileges of the great London-based overseas trading companies, remained, even if some, like the East India Company, were broadened in the 1650s. Attempts to correlate the most radical Londoners with the 'interlopers', independent merchants outside the chartered companies, have only been partly convincing. But the Long Parliament and its successor regimes at least lacked Charles I's apparent passion for incorporation, even if there were no sudden dramatic victory of the capitalist spirit or the policy of *laissez-faire*.

It is tempting to conclude that the State interfered less internally and more, or more purposefully, externally in the economy. And this appears the more convincing if we include the use of naval power to support the navigation laws. But we must remember that the peaceful years of the 1630s had seen an expansion of English sea-borne commerce, not least in the entrepôt and carrying trades between other parts of Europe. The ship-money fleet had ostensibly been meant for trade and fishery protection. So it could be argued that Charles I and his advisers deserve some of the credit for developments which were resumed under the Republic, and became more prominent from about 1650 onwards. Some historians would go further and maintain that the Civil War was no more than a temporary interruption or setback, a brief distortion of commercial and other developments in respect of which a semi-absolute monarchy in the 1640s, 1650s, and after would have made little if any difference compared to a republic and then a restored, semi-parliamentary monarchy. Common sense suggests that there would have continued to be more controls and interference, more monopolies and Court rackets, and not necessarily more altruistic and benevolent paternalism on behalf of the poor and needy. Recent studies have shown that the system of poor relief was administered more on the initiative of local magistrates and did not collapse with the end of activity by the royal Privy Council. On the other hand, taxation would presumably not have been as heavy as it was, if Charles I had kept his head in both senses of the phrase. But then could any major state in seventeenth-century Europe have kept out of war indefinitely?

Effects of civil war

How much difference did the events of 1640–60 make to people's lives? The casualties, damage, and other losses arising directly from the fighting, together with the generally disruptive effects of war on agriculture, industry, trade, transport, recreation, social intercourse, even marriage and family life—all seem obvious on the debit side. As against this, war and revolution often have a socially loosening effect; careers are opened to talents, and this was true within limits in mid-seventeenth-century England. Numbers of gifted young men were able to break clear of a constricting environment and upbringing, and to achieve far more than would have been possible for most of them in more normal times. As for the female half of the population, some widows and others left in charge while husbands, sons, or brothers were away at the wars took more responsibility and enjoyed greater powers of independent decision than would have been the case in peacetime. Some women, too, played a larger and more positive part in the radical religious sects than was possible for them to do in the established Church or its main rivals—either Roman Catholic or mainstream Puritan. The number of people whose deaths were a direct result of the civil wars can only be guessed at; for England and Wales alone perhaps a few tens of thousands, certainly less than in the worst epidemics of the time. Population losses in Ireland must have been much more serious; in addition, both in Ireland and in Scotland there were losses due to the transportation of prisoners of war to the West Indian colonies, from which few returned. Physical damage, to buildings, roads, bridges, and crops, was limited to the zones of actual fighting; in England and Wales there was no 'scorched earth' policy by the combatants. Despite the destructive effects of some sieges and the sacking of a few towns and villages after capture, the overall loss of buildings was probably less than that due to accidental fires. The permanent or temporary absence of menfolk and horses and the much heavier tax burden were probably the most widely felt and painful consequences. How many people on the contrary profited from war is another question: some contractors and suppliers clearly did so, but the public faith often proved a poor investment, and even the winning side—let alone the losing one—was notoriously bad at settling its debts. The psychological effects of war are even harder to judge. How many people got a sense of uplift and enthusiasm, and whether this compensated for loss, suffering, deprivation, and shock, can be little more than a subjective opinion which is likely to vary with the outlook and sympathies of the historian.

   It should be possible to say a little more about the economic consequences of the war and other changes. The casualties, damage, and disruption to which we have already referred were followed by partial demobilization in various stages between 1646 and 1652, accompanied by a slight reduction in levels of taxation. For the majority of people in the country the three consecutive bad harvests of 1647–9 may well have been more traumatic than any man-made misfortunes. There is some evidence that the long-term price rise had already slowed down and that it levelled off, except for short-term fluctuations due to good and bad harvests, by the 1650s, whereas money wages rose more than they had done earlier. So in the 1650s real wages may have been rising for the first time since the end of the fifteenth century. This can plausibly be linked to the temporary cessation of population growth and a possible labour shortage in consequence. Gaps in the keeping of accurate parish records make the 1640s and 1650s the worst-documented decades for population history since the mid-sixteenth century. In the most recent and best history of English population the authors have found a statistically valid way of interpolating across this gap, for their calculations of longer-term movements in the levels of births, marriages, and deaths; but the fact of short-term deficiencies in the evidence remains.[8]

As we have seen, a large proportion of the confiscated lands was not really sold but used to settle outstanding debts owed by the Long Parliament. Others were sold, and in addition there were technically voluntary sales by royalists who could not otherwise pay their debts and composition fines. All Church and royal lands and private lands sequestered and then sold by the State were restored without compensation in 1660, although by then the new owners of episcopal lands had been enjoying them for thirteen years or more. Even without this dramatic reversal, however, it seems unlikely that a substantially new landowning class was in the process of establishing itself. A number of individuals—MPs, army officers, other officials, war contractors, and state creditors—made a lot of money and some acquired a lot of land, and did not lose it all again at the Restoration. But many of these individuals came from families already in the landowning class, and it makes better sense to think in terms of a changed ruling élite rather than of a new class. In Ireland the effects of confiscation and sales were altogether different, and there much less of a reversal took place in 1660 and after.

Again we are left guessing what the effects of these changes would have been if a republican regime had maintained itself for much longer. The recovery, even resurgence, by the aristocracy which many historians have remarked after 1660 would presumably either not have taken place at all or have done so in a very different way. Granted that the Republic did collapse and that the monarchy, bishops, and House of Lords were restored, are we to suppose that the nobility and great landowners were actually richer and more influential after 1660 than they would otherwise have been, without the upheavals of 1640–60? This seems a little far-fetched, but is not logically impossible. There is certainly evidence that the rank and file of the Cavalier gentry and perhaps also humbler royalists below them in the social scale recovered less well and, if they had to sell lands in order to pay debts, were less likely to get compensatory benefits under the restored monarchy than their wealthier, better-connected colleagues.

Is it possible to offer any general conclusions, even if these are statements of opinion rather than fact? Two may be suggested. There was no sudden shift in the economy, or radical alteration of the social structure; for all that, England after the 1640s and 1650s was a society more favourable to the development of business enterprise at home and mercantilist empire overseas than had been the case before 1640. And, in spite of short-term damage and dislocation, the atmosphere was more conducive to these trends than would have been the case if Charles I's Personal Rule had continued indefinitely, or if the royalists had won the Civil War.

REFORMS AND REFORMATION

When people talk about reform being needed, they often mean no more than getting rid of what they regard as abuses in order to get back to the way things once were and should be again. Sometimes they also mean making positive changes and innovations in order to arrive at a new, different, and supposedly better state of affairs than any that has existed before. In most historical situations we find some mixture of both elements, and the England of 1640–60 was in this respect no exception.

Principles and objectives

It is natural, indeed vitally necessary, to look first at religion and the Church because of their prominence in people's lives and in their minds. The initial impetus for change may have come principally from hatred of Laud and the Arminians and fear of Popery. But the divisions which began to emerge as early as 1641 show a concern with more than merely negative reformation, important as this was and continued to be. Some wanted a reformed and improved episcopacy, others a presbyterian structure, others again were for a more decentralized system with every parochial congregation enjoying near autonomy provided it avoided prelacy and Popery. Some wanted pastors or ministers supported out of the revenues of the bishops, the cathedral clergy, and perhaps the wealthier schools and colleges; others preferred the idea of some new kind of tax to maintain the clergy. Almost all reformers wanted the existing system of tithes, impropriations, advowsons, and glebes to be either swept away altogether or at least drastically curtailed. But some of the radicals opposed any such system, being against a state church in any form and wanting their pastors and ministers either to be maintained by the voluntary offerings of their respective church members or to earn their own livings as ordinary members of the community, serving only as part-time clergymen. That distinction went very deep, to the roots of what place people believed religion should have in society. Again, almost everyone wanted an educated clergy who would preach regularly and in a suitably edifying fashion. As to what constituted a proper education and the right kind of preaching, there was wide disagreement. For the most conservative of the reformers, educational reform probably meant simply more of the same: classics and traditional Protestant theology, with a bit of Hebrew being added to Latin and Greek for those who could manage it. For others, however, their idea of a properly educated clergy was only one aspect of their wider conception of educational change and intellectual reform.

Much of this took the form of popular, watered-down Baconianism. Several of the writings of Francis Bacon, James I's Lord Chancellor, who had been created Baron Verulam and Viscount St Albans before his downfall on charges of judicial corruption, were republished in the 1640s and 1650s. His ambitious reclassification of the different branches of human knowledge, his scathing denunciation of the obstacles in the way of rational advance towards improved understanding—what he called 'the idols of the tribe, the cave, the market-place, and the theatre'—his emphasis on practical learning or applied knowledge (technology in our terminology) were taken by some of his latter-day disciples during the Interregnum to offer a dramatic means of human improvement. Although the extent of Bacon's own theological heterodoxy, like the significance of his mother's Puritan influence, remains highly controversial, some of the neo-Baconians appear to have supposed that by harnessing the forces of nature the fall of man could be undone. Or at least they believed that God's curse on Adam, that he and all his posterity must live by the sweat of their brows, could be modified if not overcome. In that sense, whatever the direct influence and importance of Bacon as a philosopher of science, he and his followers can fairly be seen as prophets of the modern world, of what has been aptly called 'Prometheus Unbound'. That Bacon himself believed human nature could be restored to its prelapsarian perfection seems unlikely; his famous *Essays* suggest no such thing.[9] Of all the reformers, actual and would-be, during the 1640s and 1650s, only Gerrard Winstanley believed that such a restoration was attainable, through a combination of technological advance and the abolition of private property, buying and selling, and wage labour. In that sense, too, Winstanley was a proponent of the modern world, anticipating Lenin's dictum that Communism equals Soviets plus electrification.

Practical measures

Most of the reforms intended and attempted in Church and State, in the professions and the economy, were far removed from such notions as these. If they had a scientific or social programme, it was more anticipatory of eighteenth-century thought: the Scottish enlightenment, Adam Smith and the classical economists, Bentham and utilitarianism. On this line of thought, represented best perhaps by Henry Robinson but also by other 'improvers' among the pamphleteers, the State should provide external protection, maintain law and order, disseminate information, undertake those services which private enterprise could not or would not, sweep away the archaic restrictions on rational improvements, prevent obstructive monopolies, etc., but otherwise leave people free to pursue their own avocations. Although he was a believer in absolutism, preferably monarchical, this could also be said to have been Hobbes's socio-economic programme. The pursuit of such objectives might entail quite radical, indeed drastic changes: the abolition of wardship, purveyance, and other fiscal relics from the feudal past, a lowering of the legal maximum rate of interest, a stable coinage with proper credit instruments, a rationalization of the laws affecting debtors and creditors, an end of outworn restraints on agricultural improvement such as anti-enclosure laws, a naval and mercantile policy designed to maximize the country's export and carrying trades, at the same time as far as possible shifting the tax burden on to luxury imports, above all a government that was strong, just, and honoured its debts. These were but some of the requirements for what Hobbes called 'felicity' and what we might call the pursuit of the good life.

How much of this came anywhere near to being achieved during the 1640s and 1650s is a very different matter. Changes in the fiscal system from feudal dues to excise have already been noted and were made permanent in 1660. The lowering of the rate of interest and the restriction of the sea-borne carriage of imports to English ships were also re-enacted. Of the Long Parliament's statutes which had received the royal assent, only one was rescinded after 1660, although other measures had automatically lapsed. The last anti-enclosure bill was to be moved in Cromwell's second Parliament, but was withdrawn, and no such measure ever reappeared. A few other reforms had been implemented as parliamentary ordinances or republican acts, and either lapsed or were positively reversed after the Restoration. One small but useful measure will serve as an example: the Commonwealth had enacted that all legal proceedings, both written and oral, should be in English, not in Latin or 'law French', and that all legal documents should be written in normal contemporary handwriting, not in the deliberately archaic scripts practised in the law courts and various branches of the administration. The first part had to await the reign of George II for re-enactment; the latter really only came about with the use of the typewriter and duplicating machine and the more widespread printing of government papers and official forms.

Changes had also been made in the administrative system, although here, too, not as many or as far-reaching ones as some of the radical reformers would have liked. The salaries paid to many grades of officials were increased; the fees on which they had previously depended were either prohibited or strictly limited; gratuities were in theory forbidden, though in practice this proved largely unenforceable. Some treasurers and pay-masters were still allowed to receive poundage (a percentage of turnover); others were put on salaries only. More appointments were made on the basis of qualifications, but these included moral and religious fitness and political loyalty; fewer were made on grounds of social connection or birth and favour. The tenure of officers under the State was designed to be made dependent on good conduct and not to be for life; above all, posts in the public service were not to be bought and sold. The 'Service of the State', a collective abstraction, rather than of the King (or Queen), may have encouraged something more like an impersonal bureaucratic outlook. Although Cromwell, as Lord Protector, had a sizeable household, it occupied nothing like the place in central government which had been taken by the royal household under the monarchy. Those cases of official corruption and other administrative abuses which were proceeded against suggest that a somewhat different standard was being applied from that operative before 1640.

It would be a mistake to suppose that anything like the civil service of the early nineteenth century, let alone of the twentieth, had already been instituted. In particular, the various types of penal taxation (compounding, sequestration, advance, decimation) and the para-legal role of administrative bodies like the Indemnity Committee and then Commission must have afforded all too much scope for favouritism, informing, and petty persecution. Public measures which discriminate against categories of people on the basis of their beliefs or their membership of some party, church, or movement provide a natural breeding ground for the bully, the toady, and the sneak. The same had been true with the laws against recusant Catholics under Elizabeth I and the early Stuarts, and was to be so again with those against Quakers and other dissenters after the Restoration. None the less, measured by the level of taxation and the total turnover of public funds, proportionately less money remained in the private hands of officials, middlemen, and others than had done before the Civil War, and was to do afterwards under the restored monarchy. Except where the direct interests of the State were involved, the legal system probably operated more efficiently and with greater objectivity, if not exactly humanity, than under royal auspices. So, despite the disillusionment of their radical supporters with the Long Parliament and then with the successive governments of the Republic, reform was not simply a pious aspiration. Godly reformation was altogether another matter; but, as we have seen, it meant many different things to different people, and in some respects could even conflict with secular reform.

In the past much argument was devoted to the relationship between religion and witchcraft, or rather witch-hunting. It has now been demonstrated that the initiative in most accusations of witchcraft arose from tensions within village communities, often between neighbours. Except for one very bad epidemic of accusations, trials, and executions at the end of the Civil War, in Essex during 1644–5, there is no special reason to connect such outbreaks with the period of Puritan domination. Moreover, there is evidence that English soldiers in Scotland were shocked by the readiness with which alleged witches were condemned and executed there. Parliamentarians, Puritans and other radicals, including some leading figures, were as ready to consult astrologers as their Cavalier and episcopalian counter-parts, perhaps marginally more so. Popular resort to white (or 'good') witches, faith-healers, and soothsayers long antedated the rise of Puritanism. The most comprehensive study of popular beliefs and superstitions in early modern England argues that there was a greater need for this kind of unofficial magic when the quasi-magical official practices of the Catholic Church were replaced by the austerer forms of Protestant teaching and worship. Their decline in the later seventeenth century is ascribed to the growth of a more rational outlook and a less imperfect understanding of the natural world and, in the case of witchcraft, a reduced readiness to blame misfortunes on the devil and his human agents. It is difficult to say more than that belief in the reality of witchcraft and the existence of witches was probably already beginning to decline by the 1650s, and that the rule of the Puritans neither hastened nor retarded this process.

The importance of information being available is something that we tend to take for granted in modern Western society. But before mass circulation of daily and weekly newspapers, to advertise beyond town or even beyond parish boundaries was often difficult, not to say impossible. This applied whether people were offering some service or commodity, or conversely were in search of something, including lost property or individuals who had disappeared. The absence of regular police forces and other public services that we take for granted accentuated this deficiency. Hence the importance of the campaign for an 'office of addresses'—the name which Samuel Hartlib, a Baltic refugee reformer with wide connections, gave to his scheme for a nation-wide information service. The reduction of the weekly newsbooks to only two officially approved publications from 1649, and their virtual disappearance in 1660, retarded the development of modern press advertising which certainly goes back to the 1640s, and heightened the need for something like Hartlib's proposal. The improvement of communications was a longer-term development, and it would seem far-fetched to credit the Interregnum with advances towards the later systems of stage-coaches and turnpike roads or the extension and enlargement of the canal network.

Hartlib was associated with many other schemes for reform, including agricultural improvement. Compared with some of his contemporaries among the radical theorists, he may not have had an original mind; his role was rather that of an intellectual broker or middleman, helping to transmit a popularized Baconianism, at the centre of a circle which included other, more creative intellects. William Petty, medical doctor, land surveyor, social statistician, and Robert Boyle, the father of English chemistry, were perhaps the circle's most brilliant members. The Czech educational reformer, J.-A. Comenius, of comparable originality, had returned to the Continent in disillusionment when civil war overtook peaceful reform in the early 1640s.

The professions

Reform of the learned professions was another key area where high hopes existed, disappointingly little was achieved, and still less survived the downfall of the Republic. In the Church, the main consequences of the victory and then defeat of the Puritan cause was the permanent split between episcopalian Anglicans and the dissenters or non-conformists (in turn divided into Presbyterian, Congregationalists, and General and Particular Baptists). Nothing more was done to provide for the better maintenance of the poorer of the parish clergy until in 1704 the Crown made over part of its revenue which had been annexed from the church in Henry VIII's time, in a scheme known as Queen Anne's Bounty. Statutory toleration even for Protestants outside the state church was not achieved until 1689, subsequently being extended to Unitarians and Quakers and gradually to Catholics also; religious equality, giving full civic rights to adherents of all religions and none, was not attained until the nineteenth century. It seems quite unhistorical to consider whether all this would have happened sooner or later if the Puritan Republic had survived; we can only be certain that it would have come about in a different way. Broadly speaking the Anglican clergy abandoned any attempt to play a distinct political and even social role, and became, to a much greater extent than they had been in the time of Laud, an adjunct of the ruling class of peers and squirearchical landowners.

Paradoxically, in doctrine and liturgy the Church of England became more 'Laudian' or Arminian than it had in fact been in Laud's own day. And, although there was to be another great popish plot scare a generation later in 1678–9, it did not extend to accusing the bishops and other Anglican clerics of being fellow-travellers or secret papists themselves. And by this time the descendants of the Puritans had either conformed within the Church, or else were firmly excluded from it as 'Dissenters'. Some historians would in any case argue that the irrevocable split within English Protestantism came much earlier, around the middle of Elizabeth I's reign, and therefore would see the settlement of the 1660s as no more than a confirmation of this. That seems an odd reading of religious developments from the 1600s to 1641, but to imply that 'Root and Branch' caused this fatal breach will seem equally arbitrary to others. In any case, this suggests a value judgement—namely that ecclesiastical unity, with everybody belonging to one church, is more desirable than a plurality of churches; from the point of view of true religious freedom, including non-Christians and unbelievers, this seems open to question.

In the law the aspirations of reformers were to a large extent frustrated even before the return of the monarchy. The hope of a salaried legal profession, with means-tested legal aid for all, which was demanded by some pamphleteers in the 1640s, was probably a lost cause by 1653, and of course has still not been attained in Britain today. But we must remember that the law reformers were not themselves a united body; far otherwise, they were deeply divided. The most radical wanted to abolish the legal profession altogether, along with the central law courts and assizes, and to rely for the enforcement of such criminal and civil justice as was needed on courts staffed by members of the local community, that is by part-time amateurs. In one sense, of course, that is precisely what JPs are, and this approach could be represented as simply the democratization of quarter and petty sessions, plus the resurrection of the extinct county and hundred courts of earlier times. If all legal actions were to do with either straightforward crimes on which there was a common view (homicide, rape, burglary, etc.) or simple disputes between neighbours about property rights and other local interests, some of which were still handled by manorial courts in the seventeenth century, then such a system of popular, amateur local justice would have had much to commend it. How it could have met the needs of a more complex society, with a national market, a strong urban sector, and an active commercial life, linked in turn to the outside world, passes the understanding. Others, even more alarmingly, wanted what they called 'the Law of Moses', that is the full paraphernalia of prohibitions and penalties prescribed in the Pentateuch. Fortunately for England, law reformers of this species were found only among the millenarian fundamentalists; and, with the defeat of Fifth Monarchism as a political force in 1653, this ceased to be a serious possibility.

Some of the complexities can be seen in the fact that two reformers as earnest and committed as Walwyn and Robinson could disagree about the jury system. As it then operated this tended to favour the propertied and respectable within the male half of the population. Aside from the Acts about language and writing, and for civil marriage and the registration also of births and deaths (1653), various attempts at reform of the law of debt, and the temporary Cromwellian reform of Chancery (discussed in the following chapters), little, if anything, was achieved and most of that was undone again. Internal orders by the judges for the minor reorganization of the two common-law courts, Common Pleas and King's (under the Republic called Upper) Bench, if unspectacular and little studied, may have done more to expedite cases than the campaigns which got more publicity and have received more attention from historians.

This paucity of achievements is the more surprising considering the degree of discontent with different aspects of the legal system. That is, unless we are to suppose it was a factitious discontent manufactured by the pamphleteers, but there seem to be too many speeches recorded from different parliaments and, more significantly, references in Cromwell's own letters and in near contemporary sources like Ludlow's *Memoirs* for this to be a tenable view. In general, spokesmen for the propertied interests—landowners and merchants chiefly—called for the laws affecting inheritance, settlements, and other property transactions or disputes to be speedier, less expensive, and more uniform, less dependent upon procedural quirks or obsolete precedents. Spokesmen for the broader mass of the people—radical Independents, like the army preacher Hugh Peter, the Levellers, some Baptists and millenarians—demanded reform of the criminal law, especially as regards witnesses, the rights of defendants, and the restriction of the death penalty to major offences (i.e. not for theft), and better treatment of debtors.

Some saw that such a programme would in turn require structural changes in the courts and in the legal profession. The permanent disappearance of the prerogative courts and the temporary closure of the church courts (at national and diocesan level) may have satisfied the constitutional and religious aspirations of Puritans and parliamentarians, but did nothing by way of meeting these other demands. Indeed, by increasing the pressure of business in the remaining courts, it may even have exacerbated the very evils, especially the delays, of which the reformers were complaining. The basic system of half-yearly assizes held in the county towns by the common-law judges and of quarter sessions by JPs continued to operate unchanged, except for temporary interruptions during the Civil War itself and in one or two other periods of acute crisis (most notably on the eve of the Restoration in 1659–60). It is also unclear whether these years were of any special importance in the longer-run evolution of the legal profession, towards the modern dichotomy between barristers and solicitors. The attorneys and law clerks at the base of the system seem to represent a kind of 'also-ran', with a potential for broadening and popularizing the profession which was never realized. Here again, this is all a negative argument. We can know what did not happen between 1640 and 1660 and what was done but then reversed; by definition we cannot know what would have happened if the political and other upheavals had not happened or had taken a different course.

In the third of the great, traditional learned professions—medicine—the impetus for reform must again be contrasted with the meagre amount that was achieved. The College of Physicians' charter was not revoked as a vexatious monopoly; apothecaries remained excluded and surgeons in an insecure and inferior position. Proportionately more medics seem to have served under the Republic, often in administrative posts unconnected with their profession, than can be explained on a random distribution; this may tell us something about their political and religious convictions, but it may also suggest the hopelessness of trying to reform their own profession. Despite Nicholas Culpeper's fulminations against the Physicians, maybe the potential for major reform simply did not exist. Most people still had a much better chance of survival if they kept out of the hands of doctors altogether, and this for all the advances in knowledge and understanding made by Harvey, Sydenham, and others and the technical innovations like the midwives' forceps patented by another radical doctor and pamphleteer of refugee origin, Peter Chamberlen. The development of anything remotely like the modern medical profession was to be a very slow process, covering much of the eighteenth and nineteenth centuries; and the best medical training was available on the Continent at Leiden or Padua and later in Scotland. England's record in this respect until the nineteenth century could not easily have been worse under a Puritan republic than it was to be in fact.

Divisions and achievements

All this may seem to be to concentrate too much on institutions and policies, too little on individuals and ideas. And, as already suggested, a slightly less negative conclusion is reached if we emphasize instead the content of education, the development of scientific knowledge and of some applied skills. But the debate about the origins of the Royal Society—Puritan, royalist or neither—seems either sterile or at best irrelevant. Of course the particular way in which certain groups of scientists and mathematicians came together in Oxford and London during the 1640s and 1650s would have been different if Charles I's regime had survived; equally obviously, it would not have been a royal society for the advancement of science that would have received a charter from Charles II in 1662 if he had not recovered his throne two years before. To jump from this to assumptions about which side in the Civil War or which regime of the Interregnum and Restoration was more or less favourable to the discoveries of Boyle, Hooke, Newton, and others is quite unacceptable. What can be said again is negative: some kinds of regime—a repressive, clericalist autocracy, or a literalist biblically-minded holy commonwealth—might well have been less favourable to the growth of scientific enquiry and advances in knowledge than any of the regimes which did hold power or contest for it between the 1640s and the 1660s.

Not that all good and sensible people were neutrals, eclectics, trimmers, or latitudinarians. There are some historical situations where individuals are forced to take sides, distasteful as they may find it to do so. In the context of mid-seventeenth-century England, scientists, teachers, scholars, and other intellectuals were by no means exempt from these pressures. Some, it is true, did 'opt out'. We do find a few 'internal refugees', to borrow a useful phrase dating from the French Revolution of the next century. One or two Anglican bishops earned a modest living as local school teachers or private tutors, one or two of Charles I's officials and courtiers took to practising medicine with or without formal qualifications; after the Restoration slightly more one-time republican office-holders entered or returned to the world of private business. By what means many members of the defeated party kept themselves from beggary or starvation— royalists from 1646 to 1660 and republicans after 1660, laymen as well as clerics—is something of a mystery; many clearly became dependent on the charity of others more fortunate than themselves, those who were either less committed in the first place or more successful at sailing with the prevailing wind.

Radicals and reformers by definition stand to suffer more disappointment in life than conservatives and cynics. Because attention has been focused in this chapter on the hopes and aspirations and the consequent disappointments and disillusionments of the radicals, mainly supporters of the

Puritan–parliamentarian cause, we should not forget the psychologically traumatic effects of successful rebellion and then regicide on royalists and Episcopalians. The state of mind of those Catholics who had supported Charles I must in general have been somewhat different, because they were already subject to discrimination if not persecution, unless they belonged to the very small minority who enjoyed exemption through connections at Court. Whose morale was raised to greater heights in the hour of victory—reformers in 1640–1, revolutionaries in 1648–9, or conservatives in 1660—is as impossible to measure as the converse of who suffered the sharpest disappointment. To argue that the achievements of the Interregnum were negative rather than positive is not to imply that the whole of English history would have been better if none of it had happened. Then, as now, some people took a stand on principle (for Church and King, or for the Good Old Cause) because of passionate conviction in its truth, righteousness, and justice. Others chose with reluctance, supporting the less unpalatable alternative. Such basic differences in human temperament were as apparent then as they are now. But the sum of human achievement is only partly the outcome of people's motives for acting as they do. Good intentions often go awry; conversely, good things can come out unplanned and unintended.

6
The contradictions of the Commonwealth

Charles I had amply proved himself to be an impossible person with whom to negotiate. No settlement to which he was a party could have been expected to last, even if it had ever been achieved in the first place. None the less his trial and execution can be seen in retrospect to have constituted a disastrous mistake. This was doubly so: both for the legal, not to say moral dubiousness of the proceedings, and as an amoral political action too. The regicide was to prove a fatal barrier to the reconciliation of so many, not only royalists, but also neutrals and even moderate parliamentarians, Presbyterians, and others, who might without it have been persuaded, if not to support a republic, at least to accept a regency or protectorate on behalf of the King's eventual hereditary successor. Not enough people of sufficient importance were won over or consolidated behind the new regime to counterbalance the alienation of so many others. If we accept the findings of the best recent studies of the parliamentary scene and the political groupings during the years 1647–53,[1] the astonishing fact is how few MPs and other political figures outside the Army welcomed or positively supported the Purge and the regicide, let alone actually believed in a republic as being a superior form of government to monarchy. The very name 'Commonwealth', which the new regime gave itself some three months after abolishing monarchy and House of Lords, was a kind of compromise with the English past, and seems to have been thought less doctrinaire than the word republic. As we shall see, the Levellers, who certainly did in principle believe in a single-chamber parliament without a monarch or an upper house, saw the new government as a potentially self-interested, irresponsible, and tyrannical oligarchy. For the inherent contradictions and weaknesses in the very nature of the Commonwealth, Oliver Cromwell as the single most powerful person in the country must bear a heavy responsibility. It is worth considering his position, and probable

outlook, as of 1648–9, in order both to assess his responsibility
for the situation and the better to understand what happened
during the four years that followed.

Oliver Cromwell

Cromwell had become a Colonel of Horse in 1643, and then
Lieutenant-General and second-in-command of the Eastern
Association army in 1644. After a short hiatus due to the
implementation of the Self-Denying Ordinance, of which he was
himself a co-author, he held the same position, in command of
the cavalry, in the New Model Army from June 1645. His
military career until the summer of 1644 had been noteworthy
but no more so than that of other successful and vigorous
regional commanders, especially Massey. He was credited,
probably justly, with a major share in the victory of Marston
Moor and, nearly a year after, in that of Naseby; his share of
responsibility for the defeat of Second Newbury was largely
overlooked. And more recently he was rightly given credit for
the overwhelming victory over Hamilton at Preston in August
1648. During the autumn of 1647 he had presided over the
Putney debates while Fairfax was on sick leave, and he took a
leading part in the defeat of the Levellers that followed. Yet his
relations with John Lilburne were by no means of uniform,
constant hostility. Cromwell had introduced the motion for
the future Leveller leader's release from prison at the very
beginning of the Long Parliament; and, to judge from his
intervention on behalf of others, he must have sympathized with
Lilburne's resignation from the Army because his conscience
forbade him to take the Covenant. He shared Lilburne's
disillusionment with the Earl of Manchester and his wider
opposition to an intolerant Presbyterian state church; he too
wanted liberty for tender consciences, provided that they were
not papist, prelatist, or blasphemous. He also shared Lilburne's
conviction that the law and the legal profession needed drastic
reform, as much as the Church and the clergy. Where then did
they part company? Or, to put it another way, why did not
Cromwell put himself at the head of what has come to be known
as the Leveller movement? In the view of his enemies, royalist,
republican, and to some extent even Leveller, he deliberately
encouraged the Agitators, connived at Joyce's seizure of the

King, and used the Levellers for as long as he could, in turn discarding and then destroying them, when they no longer served his purpose and even got in his way. At Putney he was both more vehement than his son-in-law Ireton, denouncing their opponents not as anarchists but as standing for what must end in anarchy, yet also more conciliatory, for example readier to envisage extending the franchise to leaseholders and copyholders if they were men of substance; indeed, he almost jumped at a compromise whereby all men might have the vote except household servants, apprentices, paupers, and delinquents (that is, royalists). At the same time he was essentially a traditionalist and a believer in a hierarchical society. His genuine wish to settle with the King on the basis of the Heads of Proposals proves his commitment to what we should call mixed or parliamentary monarchy. His reluctance, even as late as December 1648, to agree that the King's execution was the only way out of the political deadlock, in spite of his acceptance, indeed approval, of Pride's Purge, is further evidence of this conservatism.

The theory that each stage of Cromwell's political career marked a deliberate step towards absolute power cannot be proved or disproved. But, true or false, this explains very little. To say that his breach with the Levellers and later with parliamentary and millenarian republicans in turn was a struggle for power may be true but is no more than a restatement of the obvious. His support for mixed monarchy was characteristic of the Long Parliament as a whole, at least of all except a few extremists on either side. But in the very different context of the early 1650s, his notion of the most desirable government having 'something monarchic' in it, had very different implications: this and his growing dislike for what he called 'perpetual parliaments' were to bring him into collision with many of his old allies and supporters. By contrast with these constitutional principles and preferences, his breach with the Levellers was much more a matter of class interest. Cromwell was determined that the landowning nobility and gentry should remain the predominant social class, and he instinctively recognized that this required their keeping political control of parliament and local government. Certain categories within these social classes might have to be excluded: papists, courtiers, incorrigible royalists, and episcopalians. And after the events of 1648–9

(Pride's Purge, the regicide and the Republic) this might come to involve the exclusion from the political process of an actual majority of those very social groups whose interests and predominance he was so passionately committed to preserve, while they remained in irreconcilable opposition to the regime. Cromwell's own power base was in the Army and among members of the radical Puritan sects; yet his aims were never the same as theirs, or only temporarily and fortuitously so in what they were against. Although he took the chair for the first week on the newly created Council of State in February 1649, Cromwell was no committee-man, just as he was, though educated, no intellectual. Not that he was the narrow-minded or killjoy type of Puritan. This can be seen in his letter to the Governor of Edinburgh Castle, criticizing the Covenanters' opposition to religious toleration: 'Your pretended fear lest Error should step in, is like the man would keep all the wine out of the country lest men should be drunk. It will be found an unwise and unjust jealousy, to deprive a man of his natural liberty upon a supposition he may abuse it.' His conduct is sometimes hard to explain on rational grounds. But it may help if we think of Cromwell as having had a relatively simple, straightforward mind, but a complex, even contradictory temperament. No one else in the country combined his strengths, qualities, and limitations. Yet, if he was the most powerful single individual in England from 1647 on, he was not to become its ruler, as a 'single person', until the end of 1653.

An interim regime?

It is tempting to see the infant Republic of 1649 as beset with problems and dangers, and to write its history in terms of how these were tackled and, in most cases, successfully overcome. But first we should remember how few people expected the new government to last more than a short time. Apocalyptic Puritans saw it as merely a stage, for some a decisive, for others a hesitant or even regressive one, towards the rule of the Saints on earth and the destruction of Antichrist. More secular-minded republicans wanted and expected further constitutional reform, including that of parliament itself, along the lines of 1647 but now with a single chamber only. Royalists and many ex-parliamentarians could regard it as no more than a temporary usurpation. Levellers, Diggers, and Ranters, from their own widely differing viewpoints, saw the Republic as acceptable only on the assumption that it would speedily lead on, or give way to something better. This attitude was encouraged by the Rump Parliament's act of May 1649 proclaiming the people of England to be 'a free state' under the name of a Commonwealth. Already by then, it might fairly have been asked: who were the people, and what was freedom? The Rump had already assumed the sole right to legislate in the name of the people, but on what basis other than a sheer assertion of political power it could claim this was unclear. Indeed one distinguished twentieth-century historian has seen the Army as a truer embodiment of the national will than that of any parliament of the time.[2] Since there were neither plebiscites nor opinion polls in the seventeenth century, and since none of the elections held then were by our standards either free or democratic, this particular argument may best be laid to rest. We simply cannot tell whether the people of England had wanted their surviving representatives to proceed with the trial of the King, his execution, the abolition of monarchy and upper house, and the declaration of England as a Commonwealth.

The Levellers again

Lilburne and his associates saw the whole sequence of events as an organized hypocrisy, a mere camouflage for the institution of a repressive, tyrannical system. In two characteristically rambling yet in parts closely argued pamphlets, *Englands New Chains Discovered*, he and his fellow-authors highlighted the Rump's own utterly unrepresentative nature and the unconstitutionality of its proceedings. The two High Courts of Justice denied the basic principle of trial by jury, the commissioners being appointed by the legislature. The Council of State's executive powers, given it by the Rump, were likewise a usurpation. Even more arbitrary was the use of martial law in peacetime by the Council of War, especially when men were still being compelled to serve in the army against their wills. Part Two of this tirade proved to have the quality of a self-fulfilling prophecy, although it was probably fear of renewed Agitator-style activity in some of the regiments that precipitated the government's action. On the basis of a warrant from the Council of State transmitted to various army units in London, large bodies of soldiers were sent to the respective residences of the four leading civilian Levellers (Lilburne, Overton, Walwyn, and their treasurer, a dealer in cheese and butter called Thomas Prince). They were arrested in the early hours of the morning and later brought before the Council of State; needless to say they gave as good as they got in verbal exchanges, Lilburne and Overton being particularly in their element. According to Lilburne, listening through the keyhole, he heard Cromwell thump the table, declare and repeat again: 'I say you must break these men, or they will break you.' The four were then committed to the Tower, but continued to smuggle out what they had written, so that the pamphlet war went on.

A few weeks after these arrests a leading sympathizer in the ranks of the Army was court-martialled and shot for having tried to organize a mutiny in his regiment, stationed in London. And only a little later the larger part of two and a half regiments, based in the south of England, did mutiny, got rid of their officers (without killing any, so far as is known), and began a cross-country march, hoping that the men of more and more units would join them *en route*; where they were heading is unclear, perhaps for Bristol, where there were Leveller sympathizers.[3] This was indeed one of the crises of the revolution: the sharpest radical challenge since the fiasco on Cork-bush Field, but this time with Rainsborough dead, Lilburne once more in the Tower, Sexby and Wildman temporarily out of things, pursuing their respective careers. Hence there was a grave, as it turned out fatal, lack of leadership on the mutineers' side. On receiving news of the mutinies, Fairfax and Cromwell showed no hesitation. The equivalent of a picked brigade was mustered in Hyde Park, inspected by the Lord-General, addressed by the Lieutenant-General, and they then set off in pursuit. Within a few days it was all over, when the generals and their force caught up with the mutineers who had unwisely dossed down for the night in Burford. The rest of the story is familiar: how those of the mutineers who had not escaped under cover of dark were crowded into the church, made to listen to a reproachful speech by Cromwell delivered from the pulpit, and then to watch the ringleaders' execution outside, one of the four being pardoned at the last minute because he repented and later turned informer. Some of those who escaped, despite technically being deserters, made their ways back into civilian life; many of those captured were in fact re-embodied in other regiments or else paid off. Only one 'mutineer', actually a civilian ex-NCO, died fighting against his pursuers, in a separate encounter in Northants. What are we to infer from this sorry tale? It is impossible to see how a pro-Leveller mutiny or rising could have succeeded against the high command of the Army as well as against the civil government of the country. The foremost commanders of their day were not to be lightly challenged, let alone overthrown. By seventeenth-century standards, perhaps indeed by those of today, the punishment meted out was minimal. This was no Thermidor—or Kronstadt—but only a damp squib.

For all that, the civilian Levellers continued to have the best of the war of words. The third and last *Agreement of the People* and their self-justification called *A Manifestation*, issued from the Tower, record for posterity, and for such of their contemporaries as obtained copies, their vision of a better world; that is, of a decentralized, democratic state with wide popular participation, yet strong safeguards for the individual and strict checks to prevent even a majoritarian dictatorship. Eventually Overton, Prince, and Walwyn were released without being charged, conditional on their taking the Engagement, the Commonwealth's loyalty oath to the rule of Commons without King or Lords. Lilburne was tried for treason (not by a High Court of Justice) and acquitted by a London jury amid scenes of tumultuous enthusiasm—as he was to be again nearly four years later; meanwhile he temporarily withdrew into private business. There had already been another incipient Leveller-inspired mutiny by a regiment stationed in Oxford; and, as the greater part of the Army had by then crossed over to Ireland under Cromwell's command, a serious situation might still have developed. But as an organized movement and a potential threat to the government, the Levellers were finished.

Ranters and other radicals

The republican regime faced, or rather its members felt that they faced, other dangers on the even more extreme left. From the spring of 1649 the Diggers, small groups including women and children, were attempting to cultivate unused waste and common land in Surrey and elsewhere. A few other settlements or colonies sprang up in imitation of Winstanley's original one, but no mass movement developed, and the Surrey Diggers were bitterly harassed (and physically assaulted) by the local land-owners and clergy, and their henchmen including some free-holders.

The Ranters were a more amorphous movement: numerous, but also obscure and, except for a few itinerant Antinomian preachers and pamphleteers, hard to identify. 'Antinomian' was an abusive label, meaning against the law (moral as much as statute and common law), given to those who preached and wrote in favour of the doctrine of free grace coming from God to humanity and the possibility of general salvation. From the Calvinist, or indeed the Pauline–Augustinian point of view, this was the same heresy as that of the Arminians, but Antinomians were alleged to believe in addition that recipients of divine grace, the saved, could then do no wrong—and could therefore in practice commit any sin, wallow in any vice, without danger to their souls, being likewise exempt from man-made laws. The potential popular appeal of a kind of debased Arminian–Antinomianism is easy to understand; indeed strict predestinarian Calvinism is one of the least attractive dogmas ever formulated in any religion, namely that God created Man knowing from the start that the greater part of humanity would suffer the eternal torments of Hell after their lives on earth. The wonder is that it got so great a grip on so many people for so long; but it only did so at a terrible price in nervous breakdowns, suicides, and sheer misery. Whether there was really a risk of Ranterism developing into a mass movement against law, government, and morality, as a kind of 'opting-out', anti-work ethic, is an altogether different matter. It would be easy to assume that the Commonwealth authorities invented Ranterism as a kind of bogy to justify repressive legislation and that thoroughgoing Antinomians were isolated, eccentric figures. There is a little independent evidence from the (admittedly prejudiced and retrospective) testimony of two great evangelists, neither of them adherents of official Puritanism let alone of the Episcopalian Church: George Fox, the co-founder and then leader of the Quakers, and the highly individualistic Baptist, John Bunyan. Both of them portray Ranterism as widespread and themselves as reclaiming large numbers of people from its clutches. But if Ranters were really anti-work, how did they survive in days when social security benefits were unknown, or at least when the tests of indigency were far stricter? Sexual promiscuity, or to be more exact what was called 'community of women', was both the main target of anti-Ranter moralists and legislators and perhaps also for some roving men its main attraction. Interestingly, Winstanley was anti-Ranter precisely on those grounds; his kind of communism went with strict monogamy and the maintenance of family life under paternal authority.

This should also caution us against another assumption. Much has been written recently about the prominence of women in the radical Puritan sects and in support of the Levellers, indeed about the greater readiness of many people, men and women, to challenge the whole range of accepted beliefs and standards of conduct. It may seem anti-climactic, and is certainly not from lack of sympathy either with seventeenth-century popular aspirations or with the present-day historians of such movements, to suggest that the scale of any such challenge, male or female, can easily be exaggerated. There was a popular dimension to the English Revolution. At times, especially in 1640–2, mass involvement played a crucial part in the course of political events. There was a slight but real threat, and a much greater imagined one (rather as with the popish conspiracy at the other extreme), of a popular rising or attempted takeover in 1647 and 1649; but there was at no time an incipient or abortive radical revolution on the brink of success. If Rainsborough and Lilburne wanted to be revolutionary leaders and to challenge Fairfax, Cromwell, and Ireton for control of the Army, their only opportunity was in 1647; they did not take it, and the opportunity did not recur.

There has also been an opposite tendency lately, to play down the significance of the Levellers and other radicals. This is an understandable reaction; historians who are attracted by the ideals and personalities of particular individuals and groups of people in the past undoubtedly need to beware of exaggerating their contemporary importance. That said, the Army took a large part of its radical programme from the Levellers in 1647, even to the extent of parts being borrowed by their future opponents for the Heads of Proposals and later for the officers' *Agreement*. Furthermore, the Levellers were clearly regarded as a real menace in the autumn of 1647 and again in the first half of 1649. Cromwell and many of his contemporaries may, of course, have overrated the likelihood of a populist coup; and those further to the right, royalists and Presbyterians, we must remember, portrayed the Agitators, if not the civilian Levellers, as Cromwell's creatures. As we have seen, this is both to exaggerate his control over events and to make him more of a calculating long-term planner than his temperament and his convictions made it possible for him to be.

Royalists and Presbyterians

At the same time the Commonwealth faced a real threat to its existence from monarchists of various species. Ireland remained unsubdued, most of the island being under the control either of the Catholic Confederates (the 'home-rule' movement descended from the rebels of 1641–2) or else the royalist Protestants. In Scotland, despite the brilliant success of the Cromwell–Lambert incursion in the autumn of 1648, regicide was rejected and denounced as a gross violation of the Covenant; relations between the two countries became more and more strained, although there was no open breach until the following year. The royalists no longer had a military footing on the British mainland and little by way of an army left even in exile, but there was a still undefeated naval squadron under the formidable Rupert, now turned admiral and operating in the name of the new King. It was made treasonable to call Charles II King in England or its dependencies. As a face-saving compromise, the Commonwealth authorities officially referred to him as 'the King of Scots' or 'of Scotland' (where he was indeed to be crowned in 1650). Meanwhile his father's alleged posthumous memoirs and religious reflections, the *Eikon Basilike*, proved in seventeenth-century terms to be a runaway best seller. It is not of great consequence how much of the text had actually been written by Charles I and how much was 'ghosted' by John Gauden, later rewarded with a bishopric. In spite of the reimposed censorship and the all-present soldiery, more imprints and editions kept appearing, and we can only suppose that they were bought and read. The Republic's spokesmen went into action against the dead King and against his living apologists, both domestic and foreign, of whom the Dutchman Salmasius seems to have been regarded as the most formidable; the pens of John Milton and John Goodwin were employed against them, the former's specifically against Salmasius.

Other writers urged acceptance of the Commonwealth and subscription to its loyalty oath, called the Engagement, on the basis of what has been accurately, if inelegantly, called '*de factoism*'. On this view, obedience is owed and allegiance due to any government which is effectively in power and affords its subjects minimal protection against external enemies and internal disorders, regardless of its rightfulness *de jure*. Such an argument for practical recognition has obvious moral as well as political implications; it seems to require the assumption that anarchy is a greater danger, a worse evil, than tyranny. It is therefore not surprising that the historian of *de factoism* has claimed Thomas Hobbes's *Leviathan* as the greatest tract in this genre.

Another important element in the propaganda of the Commonwealth was to portray the royalists and the Levellers as secret allies. Both were in turn described as the agents or dupes of the Jesuits, part of the great international popish plot. In *A Manifestation*, Walwyn (its principal author) demolished this charge with devastating irony. Yet, as with all successful propaganda, there was just enough truth in it to make the smear a plausible one. Back in 1647 Lilburne had got on close (card-playing) terms with a daring if unorthodox royalist colonel who was also in the Tower; in his pamphlets of 1648–9, while he did not defend the King and the other Cavalier leaders who were put on trial for their lives, he did denounce the arbitrary and illegal methods which were being employed against them. More remarkable still, there survives in a collection of royalist correspondence a lengthy memorandum, apparently written by Hyde for the Queen at the end of 1649, considering whether it was better for the King and his party to ally with the Presbyterians or with the Levellers, and coming out in favour of the latter. Moreover, when he was subsequently banished by the Commonwealth and in enforced exile, Lilburne was shadowed by a secret agent, and was allegedly seen and heard in private conversation with the Duke of Buckingham (Dryden's 'Zimri' of 1680). Other royalist documents provide proof of later contacts with two of the ex-Leveller leaders, Sexby and Overton, in mutually mistrustful and ineffective discussions with royalists on the Continent. Not long before the Restoration a group calling themselves Levellers offered conditional support to Charles II. On the argument of preferring the lesser evil, it is possible to see how strictly opportunist negotiations with a view to an alliance might have been undertaken from both sides. But the notion that there was a secret alliance in operation, with royalists using Levellers or vice versa, belongs in the fantasy world of conspiracy theories.

In the real world of 1649–50, it was their own ex-allies the parliamentarians, mainly but not exclusively Presbyterian in religion, who were now the most serious problem for the new regime. Various clergy wrote and preached against the Engagement and were answered by the Commonwealth's supporters. More serious than that, there were two quite widespread plots and plans for armed risings timed to coincide with external attacks. (Presumably at this stage, ex-parliamentarians had not been disarmed with the same thoroughness as ex-royalists.) The networks were penetrated by government agents, information was extorted (though not by torture); some of those implicated were tried and two executed. But the political leadership of the Presbyterian party was already broken and demoralized. Some who had been prominent in the years 1646–8 were in prison; others had escaped or been released, and of these some were in exile with the King, others had retired into private life. The most active and daring, Edward Massey, escaped from the Tower twice, which suggests either crass incompetence or treachery among those in charge. Some, who had not openly gone over to the royal cause, re-entered public life later in the 1650s, when as we shall see, this accorded with Cromwell's policy, but as a movement or party they were not to play any decisive role again until 1660. Of the parliamentary peers, three (Pembroke, Salisbury, and Howard of Escrick) obtained seats in the Commons (for this they were not required to renounce their titles). Leicester and then Northumberland limited their role to acting as guardians for those of the late King's younger children who were still in captivity. Warwick and Saye and Sele withdrew completely; both may have been more upset by the abolition of the Upper

House and of the legal privileges and immunities of peers than by the regicide and abolition of monarchy.

Ireland reconquered

So, while positive support for the Commonwealth was narrowly based, the main danger of a royalist comeback was from outside. Charles II's councillors were divided on whether to go for an Irish or a Scottish alliance, disagreeing as to which of these two countries would provide a better springboard for the invasion of England. Hyde favoured Ireland, and this was the first choice, although fortunately for him Charles II never went there, since the royalists' plans were overtaken by events. As early as March 1649 Cromwell had agreed to lead a large expeditionary force to reconquer Ireland, provided that he was given a free hand in the selection of units and their commanders and adequate provision was guaranteed for pay and supplies (mainly food and ammunition). As we have seen, the tide of war had already turned against the Confederates before Cromwell or a single soldier of his Army set foot in Ireland. But the historical legend is none the less substantially correct in portraying him as the reconqueror of the country. The massacres after the capture of Drogheda and of Wexford did not—as Cromwell hoped—succeed in terrorizing by example. Waterford, Clonmel, and Limerick were all defended with stubborn courage, and the massacres were not in fact repeated. Neither the Confederates nor the Protestant royalists could stand against the New Model in the field, and wisely neither tried to do so.

The Protestant resistance under the Marquis of Ormonde and Lord Inchiquin soon crumpled, and both the leaders went into exile. But the Catholic resistance was longer-lasting, probably because its adherents had more to lose. The war of sieges and guerrilla raids dragged on past Cromwell's recall in 1650; past the death of his successor as commander-in-chief, his son-in-law Ireton, at the end of the following year: it was carried to a final conclusion by Charles Fleetwood, the next English commander (and also about to become Cromwell's son-in-law by marrying Ireton's widow), and the memoir-writing republican Edmund Ludlow, in the course of 1652. Reviewing the twelve years of war, Sir Charles Firth wrote: 'the failure of the Irish to regain their independence was due not so much to the greater strength

and wealth of England, as to their own divisions.' One does not
lightly quarrel with a judgement in what is still, after over eighty
years, the best single biography of Cromwell. However, until the
collapse of the royalist cause, the English—in Ireland as at
home—were surely at least as sharply divided as the Irish. This
also raises the question of the Old English, or Anglo-Irish: did
they not divide both nations, even if in different ways? In the
last stages of the war, from 1649 on, it does seem to have been
largely a matter of greater military resources, although there
were disagreements and rivalries among the Confederates
themselves which had all along reduced their effectiveness.

The Commonwealth's post-war settlement of Ireland was in
theory, and to a large extent also in practice, punitively severe.
The claims of the Adventurers (from 1642 and after) and of
subsequent government creditors, likewise the outstanding pay
arrears of the army were all to be settled out of the lands of the
Catholic population and of incorrigible Protestant rebels (that
is, royalists who had not come over in time). The whole country
except the province of Connaught and the county of Clare was
to be cleared of its Gaelic Irish landowners; the rest of the native
population was to remain in order to provide the labour force
needed by the new landowners, Protestant English. This may be
seen as no more than the logical conclusion of the 'plantation'
policy pursued since the middle of the previous century, but it
was still social engineering on a hitherto unknown scale (perhaps
the nearest parallel would be what happened in England after
the Norman Conquest in 1066). As is often the case with such
ambitious schemes, it did not work out quite as intended. Many
of the English soldiers and the Adventurers did not want to settle
in Ireland, so a lively market grew up in the titles to lands which
they had been allocated. And, while there were many executions
of priests and resistance fighters (often called Tories), especially
if they were suspected of having been involved in the atrocities
of 1641–2, even Cromwell occasionally showed himself prepared
to relent in the case of some Anglo-Irish.[4] After more than a
year of intensifying 'cold war' with Scotland, he was recalled
from Ireland when the negotiation of a royalist–Scots alliance
posed the imminent threat of a real shooting war instead.

Scotland conquered

The Scots might have been thought to be a tougher nut to crack than the Irish, militarily speaking. But they were even more seriously disabled by ideological and sectional divisions than the Irish or the English themselves. Hamilton's 1648 invasion on behalf of Charles I had cut across previous royalist–Covenanter divisions; or rather it had split the Kirk and its lay supporters. In the course of 1649–50 the Remonstrants, those who had opposed the Engagement with Charles I, purged first the civil government, then the Scottish army itself of all ex-Hamiltonians, thereby removing many of the best officers and probably many trained and reliable NCOs and even common soldiers.

The English Puritans saw their forthcoming conflict with the Scots, and their intended invasion of Scotland which would result from it, in a very different light from their reconquest of Ireland. Whereas it was obvious that, as papists and rebels responsible for horrible atrocities against the English and Scottish settlers and their families, the Irish would be justly punished in the name of a righteous God, the Scottish war and most particularly a pre-emptive invasion, required a more elaborate justification. It is indicative of this that Fairfax refused to lead such an attack; he would help to defend England if the Scots invaded in the name of Charles II, but he would not undertake a war of aggression against godly neighbours (his own grandfather had been made a peer of Scotland by Charles I). Cromwell and other leading figures pleaded with him, but to no avail. So Cromwell became Lord or Captain-General of the whole Army as well as commander-in-chief of the northern expedition. The view of Cromwell as a scheming hypocrite in no way fits the facts here; the record makes clear his sincerity and the strenuousness of his attempt to persuade Fairfax to stay on and his regret at the loss of his old comrade-in-arms and superior officer since the Naseby campaign of 1645. It is also symptomatic that there were declarations justifying the English action, issued by the Rump itself, by Cromwell and the other senior officers on their way north, and by (or on behalf of) the junior officers and soldiers when the English Army had already penetrated through the Lowlands to the vicinity of Edinburgh. The last of these is more apocalyptic or millenarian in tone, but addresses itself closely to the problem of the Solemn League and Covenant, arguing that the loyalty to the King which it expressed was only a means to the ends of preserving true religion and the proper liberties of the subject, and thus that, when and if the monarch became an irreconcilable obstacle in the way of these objectives, then commitment to him was automatically abrogated. This was not exactly a rewriting but certainly a strange rereading of recent history if one looks at the text of the document as promulgated and then widely subscribed back in 1643–4. But whatever we may think of these mental gymnastics, the English Army was a tried and proven force, and absolutely united under Cromwell's leadership.

Very different was the case of the Scottish army. Its Commander-in-Chief, David Leslie, had fought beside Cromwell at Marston Moor and had won the decisive victory over Montrose in 1645; potentially he was a formidable opponent. The Scots had the advantage of fighting on home ground and of superior numbers. But many of Leslie's men were much inferior in training, discipline and equipment, and probably in morale too: worse still Leslie was not a free agent but was hamstrung by a politico-religious committee at his headquarters, whose members interfered in military decisions. Hence, while the Scots had the best of a strategic stalemate, being able to deny battle to the English who were far from home and running out of supplies, east of Edinburgh in August 1650, Cromwell was still able to seize and exploit the tactical initiative at Dunbar on 2–3 September. This was the second major battle where the losers had superior numbers and marks the New Model's peak as a purely military instrument. But, although an overwhelming victory, it was not in the event a decisive one. The English occupied Edinburgh and then Glasgow, but a war of attrition dragged on through the autumn and winter, when Cromwell himself fell seriously ill, first physically and then it seems psychologically. As for the Scots, reacting in the opposite direction after the disaster of Dunbar, they formed an 'uncovenanted' army, containing sinners, anyway royalists and Engagers or Hamiltonians, as well as saints. And at the same time politically Charles II came much nearer to being the head of his own government, to ruling as well as reigning, no longer trammelled by Argyll and the Remonstrants. National feeling

against the English Army of occupation, although it behaved
well as armies go, now told in the King's favour. Perhaps for the
first time since 1603, anyway since 1625, a Stuart King was
popular in Scotland. Once again, as before Dunbar, it was far
from clear that time was on the English side, superior in strength
as their forces were. This time it was the young King and his
Cavalier advisers who lacked the patience for a long-drawn-out
war of resistance. His own health restored, Cromwell used his
command of the sea to regain the initiative, by putting part of
his Army across the Firth of Forth and into Fife; from there
the English swept north to occupy Perth.[5] The way south was
deliberately left open for the King; and the royalists fell for the
trap, unable to resist the possibility of invading England ahead
of Cromwell. He followed them south, leaving Major-Generals
John Lambert and the stolid dependable ex-royalist George
Monck, soon to be joined by Richard Deane, who was also one
the Commonwealth's 'Generals-at-Sea' or admirals, to complete
the subjugation of Scotland.

Now was the opportunity for the Cavalier party in England to
show their loyalty and join the young King. Very few indeed did
so as Charles advanced down the western side of the country and
then into the Midlands; in fairness this may have been due to
lack of arms as well as to disinclination. Harassed by initially
inferior English forces, the invaders got as far as Worcester.
Quite what would have happened if Charles had marched
straight towards London is not clear; probably he would still
have found the way blocked by stronger forces than he could
have cut through. But simply waiting in Worcester until the
main English Army arrived was disastrous. Another remarkable
series of forced marches brought a sufficient proportion of his
total force south to give Cromwell superior numbers. Of all the
great set-piece battles, Worcester was the most predictable in
outcome, fought like Dunbar on Cromwell's birthday. Huge
numbers of prisoners were taken; the rest of the royalist army
melted away, and as a military threat they were no more. In fact
the Rump had raised considerable militia forces, some of whom
did good service in the Worcester campaign. So *de facto* support
for the Commonwealth must have been growing and cannot
have been entirely limited to the Army and the Puritan sects.
Charles II's remarkable, and as some of his supporters believed

miraculous, escape after his defeat and his eventual flight across the Channel to France obviated the need for a second regicide and meant that monarchists, at least all pro-Stuart ones, would continue to recognize him as their rightful ruler. Without Charles, they would still have had James, then Duke of York (the future James II) whose defects of character were not yet apparent or at least not widely known. Rupert's naval challenge had by this time also been overcome, and the Republic might have seemed secure at last.

Uncertainties and shortcomings

The real political challenge for the Commonwealth came after its military victory was complete. 'Peace hath her victories no less renowned than War,' as John Milton wrote in his sonnet to Cromwell of 1652; and they certainly proved harder to win. The republic rested on an unresolved paradox. The more successful that the Commonwealth regime was in overcoming its enemies and consolidating its position, the sharper the contradiction between its public professions of freedom and reformation and the realities of vested interests and immobility. This in turn was closely linked to the yet unanswered question of whether the constitutional arrangements of December 1648 to February 1649 were to continue indefinitely, or were only to be temporary. And, if the latter, by what and how soon were they to be replaced? The regime had both the strengths and weaknesses of a relatively well-knit minority. The House of Commons was eleven years old by the autumn of 1651. Although as many as two hundred MPs may have sat at one time or other after December 1648, the average attendance in the Rump was well under a hundred. Numerous constituencies had only one sitting member to represent them; many had none. The Self-Denying Ordinance, while it had never been repealed, was largely disregarded. Some of the senior judges were also MPs, though admittedly normally inactive ones. The supreme executive body, the Council of State, was elected by the Commons yearly, and almost all its active members were MPs.[6] On occasion, too, the House itself acted judicially, as it did against Lilburne after he had allegedly libelled Sir Arthur Hesilrige and the Commissioners for Compounding, accusing them of disposing corruptly of some sequestered lands in Durham, the home

county of the Lilburne family, where Hesilrige was in the
process of building up a large estate. Lilburne was sentenced to
a penal fine (far beyond his ability to pay) and in addition to
banishment on pain of death if he returned to England (or any
other of the Commonwealth's territories), all this without giving
him a hearing or right of reply; it was the nearest thing to an
attainder. On the credit side, the Rump was at last persuaded to
set a terminal date to its own existence. Not long after
Worcester, Cromwell and Oliver St John (by then a judge who
no longer sat regularly in the House) narrowly carried a vote to
this effect. Four days later it was agreed—apparently without a
division—to dissolve not later than 3 November 1654, in three
years' time or fourteen from its first election. In the event, the
Rump was not to last that long.

As an administrative and above all a money-raising machine,
it was an efficient regime. A huge amount was extracted from
the country in one or other way, whether or not called taxation:
the monthly assessment, though reduced after Worcester, was
still running at an equivalent of many pre-war subsidies a year;
the customs revenue had largely recovered from the wartime
dislocation of foreign trade; the excise, though not yet the largest
single branch of the public revenue, as it was to become later,
was levied on a wide range of goods, but its yield was buoyant
on drink, especially beer and cider. All this was not enough to
finance the wars in Ireland and Scotland and to maintain
internal security and defence at sea, and had to be augmented
by the sale of capital in the form first of Crown lands, then of
the royal family's moveable possessions, then of the cathedral
clergy's estates (a logical sequence of the earlier sale of bishops'
lands), and lastly of the Crown's fee-farm rents (lands held on
the equivalent of a low but perpetual ground rent), which in turn
had gone by 1651–2.

This was still not enough. Again under Cromwell's influence,
Parliament passed a Pardon and Oblivion Act early in 1652, as
an attempt to reconcile all the royalists except those who had
been in arms since 1648–9. But in a very contrary spirit to this,
even if not in breach of its letter, the policy of penal confiscation
of estates was resumed, three successive acts being passed, for
the seizure and sale of the lands of numerous individual
royalists. So, although the system of compounding had by then

almost come to an end, many families were faced with the outright loss of their properties and homes. Historians who have studied this question have concluded that in many, perhaps most cases, either other members of the same family, or remoter relatives, or trustees (usually personal friends) acting for them were able to buy the estates back, often at far less than the normal market price, because the land market had been glutted by the Long Parliament's prodigality, much as had happened with Henry VIII's and Edward VI's sales in the previous century. So perhaps in substance this was not so different from paying composition fines, which the sale acts purported to supersede; but it was hardly the way to conciliate people or to heal political divisions. Finally, in their by then almost frantic efforts to scrape the barrel, the Commonwealth authorities contemplated selling royal forests, though here the navy's need for the right kind of timber conflicted with cash-flow priorities. They also sold off the royal palaces and houses, reserving only Whitehall (for their own lodgings), St James's, and Hampton Court, and they considered the sale of the cathedrals for their demolition value. Admittedly some of this only arose under the Rump's successor, but it was a logical continuation of their policy. Why had the Commonwealth got into such acute financial straits?

War with the Dutch

With what seems like either wanton aggressiveness or a self-destructive urge, the Rump had scarcely disposed of its last royalist enemies within the British Isles and the colonial empire, when it became involved in a foreign war. This was not, as might well have been predicted, a conflict with Spain, the secular arm of the Counter-Reformation and so of the Catholic–papal Antichrist, nor yet with France also Catholic and absolutist and giving shelter to the exiled Stuart Court, and with whom there were also more material disputes about shipping in the Channel. The English Commonwealth offered the United Provinces, as the independent northern Netherlands were often called, a full and close alliance, little short of a kind of confederal union. When the Dutch understandably held back, the Rump began to legislate against their shipping, which was engaged in the carrying trade, a vital interest especially for the rich maritime provinces of Holland and Zealand. The Navigation Act of 1651 limited the carriage of foreign imports into England and its colonies to English ships or those of the country of origin. This was only the foremost of a series of measures. There was trouble, too, over Dutch herring busses which were netting their catches too near the English coast, and more importantly over the prestigious issue of 'striking the flag', that is forcing the Dutch and anyone else to acknowledge English sovereignty over the seas around the British Isles by lowering their ensigns and dipping their topsails whenever they passed an English naval squadron. Within a matter of months armed brushes led to exchanges of gunfire, and this rapidly escalated to full-scale naval war. It is true that the House of Orange had favoured and had tried to help the Stuarts in the Civil War (they were, after all, their in-laws as from 1641 at the Long Parliament's own prompting); but there had been no effective head of the Orange family since the death of William II in 1650 and the Amsterdam mercantile faction was strongly in the political ascendant.

Colonial, commercial, and maritime rivalry brought the two Calvinist republics into collision: in a sense they were too alike, and their interests conflicted at too many points. As with all wars, even those undertaken for economic reasons, the material interests of some sections of the community were severely damaged even if those of others benefited or were believed to do so. Charles I's ship-money fleet and what had been built or renovated since then now came into its own. The first of the three Anglo-Dutch Wars which were to be fought in the space of only twenty years, was important in helping to turn the attention of the English state outwards again after the introspective conflicts of the 1640s, towards the oceans and the non-European world as well as towards the narrow seas around Britain and western Europe. Although severely contested and at first seeming to go in favour of the Dutch, in strictly naval terms it was the most successful of the three. By the summer of 1653 the Commonwealth's navy had been brought to a pitch of efficiency and to a prestige comparable to that of its army.

All this was at a fearful price, both in material costs and political stress. The modest recovery of prosperity since the improved harvests from 1650 on was severely dented, if not reversed, by the interruption of trade, the diversion of resources,

and the reimposition of heavy taxation. Besides the wars against
the Irish and the Scots and then the Dutch, too much of the
Rump's attention was diverted away from reforms and other
desirable objectives by trivial items of business designed to
benefit individuals who were still owed compensation for war
damage or even for their 'sufferings' under the Personal Rule of
Charles I. Here was a parliament in perpetual session, meeting
four or even five days during every week of the year. What did
the Rump spend its time doing? There was too little planning of
government business; indeed that very concept was almost
unknown, and on many issues it is hard to say who constituted
the government. Some members were obviously more influential
than others but there was no official front bench. Finance—all
matters involving revenue and expenditure—had not been
delegated to the Council of State; until 1652 there was no one
committee or body of commissioners with overall responsibility
for all treasuries and branches of the revenue. Even then, the
small group of MPs appointed lacked many of the powers
needed if they were to be co-ministers of finance. Apart from the
conscientious but compliant Speaker, William Lenthall, there
was no one to regulate the conduct of business in the House
from day to day or week to week, unless influential individual
members happened to be present and seized the opportunity to
move procedural resolutions. Only occasionally in the Parliament's long life, when an appropriate committee was appointed
and its chairman empowered to report, was there anything like
a review of business in progress. And when such a report had
been made, urgent new items almost invariably intervened and
prevented the completion of an agreed programme. Hence
schemes for reform of taxation, of the law and the courts, of the
Church and the clergy, and of the parliamentary system itself
were all concurrently pursued but none was ever concluded.
Some of these require a closer look.

Compromises and reforms

Despite the political defeat of the Presbyterians, their church
settlement of the 1640s remained in being and was never
formally rescinded until 1660. One act passed by the Rump in
1650 did however substantially modify its implications. The
Elizabethan Uniformity Act of 1559 was amended in respect of

compulsory church attendance every Sunday, allowing instead the alternative of worship at home or in some other recognized place; without saying so, this abrogated any compulsory claim by the Presbyterian Church set up in 1645–8, that everybody in the country must take part in their services or else be treated as a recusant. On the other hand, shortly before this a new Blasphemy Act tightened restrictions on such as the Ranters, the few Unitarians (known as Socinians after the sixteenth-century Polish refounder of the old Arian heresy), and the soon much more numerous and alarming sect of Quakers. Further plans for the replacement or even amendment of the 1640s legislation never got beyond the stage of draft bills. Special measures were taken for Puritanizing, some would say Christianizing, what were called 'the dark corners of the land', namely Wales and the far north of England. A special commission of clergy and laymen, presided over by Colonel (soon to be promoted Major-General) Thomas Harrison, the leading millenarian in the Army, was appointed to evangelize Wales for three years early in 1650. An identical act was passed for the four northernmost English counties, also limited to three years. But in this case the commissioners were headed by two peers and seven baronets or knights, including Hesilrige in his capacity as Governor of Newcastle. Not surprisingly their activities aroused nothing like the same controversy as those of the commissioners for Wales, several of whom besides their chairman were millenarian radicals.

As regards the law, very little was done in spite of repeated heavy pressure from Cromwell personally, the Army collectively, and many other radical preachers and pamphleteers. Whether this was due to a conscious and deliberate rearguard action by lawyer MPs, or simply to the Commons' dilatory and incompetent conduct of business is unclear. At any rate, by 1652 the House recognized the strength of discontent with the slowness of its own proceedings and appointed a wholly non-parliamentary committee instead with a general brief to consider any necessary changes in the laws. Its chairman was a moderate Puritan–parliamentarian judge, Matthew Hale, later to be knighted by Charles II; however, it also included more radical figures, military and civilian, clerical and lay, as well as other conservatives like Sir Anthony Ashley Cooper, the future

Cromwellian councillor of state and (as Earl of Shaftesbury) the leader of the Whig opposition under Charles II. The committee seems to have worked quite fast, and by 1653 numerous bills dealing with many aspects of both the criminal and the civil law were ready in draft.

In administrative matters some concessions were made to critics, both supporters and opponents of the Republic. The power of county committees was reduced; sequestration and compounding business was now in the hands of local commissioners directly subordinate to the parent committee in London. In 1652 it was decided by Parliament that the chairmanship of all committees and commissions, including the Council of State itself, should rotate monthly; more important than this, several of Parliament's standing committees with administrative and quasi-judicial responsibilities were replaced by smaller bodies of salaried commissioners none of whom was an MP. Whether this last provision was a belated bow to the self-denying principle or more likely an attempt to improve attendance in the House of Commons itself remains open to argument. Besides the consolidation and concentration of financial control already mentioned, entire responsibility for the navy was entrusted to a small body of Admiralty and Navy Commissioners, two MPs who were councillors of state, two non-councillor MPs, and two non-MPs from the City. This proved to be a remarkably effective body with the younger Sir Henry Vane as its most distinguished member but by no means its head (he, like Cromwell, seems initially to have been against the Dutch War and temporarily withdrew from public business, but later threw himself into the pursuit of naval supremacy with redoubled vigour). The Rump also encouraged schemes for poor relief in London and other large towns, which were to be partly financed from a tax on sea-borne coal, a sensible idea even if slightly reminiscent of Charles's government in the 1630s. In spite of shipping losses and interruption to trade caused by the Dutch war, material conditions for the mass of the people may have been continuing to improve into the mid-1650s, though this cannot have been more than a marginal amelioration.

Deadlock and dissolution

Perhaps not surprisingly, it was over the future of Parliament itself and providing for its own replacement that the Rump finally came to grief. As early as 1649 the House was discussing a bill for 'a new representative', and before long the details were entrusted to a Grand Committee which was to meet at least weekly. It seems from the start to have been taken for granted that the bill would include quite drastic redistribution of seats and probably some modification or slight widening of the franchise. The bill thus owed a good deal to the Heads of Proposals, for the basic concepts of reform, and to the officers' *Agreement of the People*, presented to the House in January 1649, for the more detailed provisions; a little too was owing indirectly to the Levellers. Much time was spent on the constituency changes; but it became increasingly clear that the most intractable issues were the political and other qualifications (or rather disqualifications) to be imposed on voters and candidates for election to future parliaments. Since no record was kept, or at least none has survived of the Grand Committee's deliberations, it is hard to be sure how much of the bill was ready by what date. It was repeatedly put aside for more urgent business; even the vote of November 1651 for dissolution within three years seems to have done little to speed them on. A sharply worded petition from the Army officers stationed in the home counties, the contents of which were clearly known to Cromwell though he was not a signatory, was presented to the Commons in August 1652. This was a warning of growing impatience, and an indication that the developing naval war with the Dutch would not be regarded as an alibi for delaying domestic reforms as had happened with the campaigns of 1649–51. In the winter following this, Cromwell and other senior officers, who seem initially to have been less than enthusiastic for the Dutch War, were co-operating to the extent of selecting unfortunate foot-soldiers and dispatching them to help man the ships in the fleet, probably to provide extra guns' crews rather than seamen. Perhaps as an unspoken quid pro quo, the Rump at about the same time resumed work on the constitutional bill, achieving a much brisker tempo: Harrison even chaired the Grand Committee at one stage. But the professional politicians of the Rump, as it is hardly fanciful to call them by this stage in the Parliament's history, were too smart for the generals and soon got the bill back into their own hands. Because of illness or disillusion and suspicion, Cromwell stopped attending the Council of State and, as far as the evidence shows, the Commons too, for much of March and April 1653. The conviction seems to have been growing in his and other officers' minds that, whatever else was decided about the qualifications for membership of the next parliament, the Rumpers were determined to safeguard their futures by guaranteeing their own seats, that is by recruiting or filling the rest of the House and not having a totally new parliament. Lambert, who was now the recognized spokesman for one group of officers and was not himself an MP, had his own grievance against the Rump, which had deprived him of the Lord Deputyship of Ireland in 1652. Instead he had been offered the less lucrative and prestigious post of commander-in-chief which he had refused, the more compliant Fleetwood accepting it in his place. Harrison, despite his work on the reactivated bill, or maybe because of it, was also acutely disgruntled by the House's failure to renew the Committee for the Propagation of the Gospel in Wales when its three-year term came to an end—a quite gratuitous snub.

So the most dynamic leaders of what we might loosely call the gentry–republican and the populist–millenarian factions in the Army had both decided that the Rump was incorrigible. They were no longer prepared to wait for its promised demise the following year, and were alike pressing Cromwell to take decisive action. In fact, ironically, the bill which was rapidly being concluded in April provided for dissolution by that November; in the event it was the immediacy, not the remoteness, of the proposed settlement which precipitated the crisis. On the evening of 19 April Cromwell apparently attended an informal meeting of MPs and others, at the end of which he thought he had got a promise, notably from Vane, that the House would not proceed with the bill until the Army's fears, about 'recruiting' and disqualifications (to prevent a royalist majority being elected presumably), had been satisfied. Overnight it seems that Hesilrige arrived back in London from the north; and on the next day word was brought to Cromwell that the House was after all engaged on the final stages of the bill and was about to pass it into law. He stormed into the House with soldiers at his back, berated the members for their various failings both personal and political and dissolved them almost by force, or to be exact ended their sittings, likewise those of the Council of State which had been re-elected by the House the previous winter. He was clearly in breach of the May 1641 statute, unless the royalist argument was accepted that the Rump had ceased to be a true parliament since 1648–9 (if not earlier); and as Cromwell's own commission as Captain-General of the forces of the Commonwealth had been given to him by the Rump in 1650, he was hardly well placed to use this particular justification!

Since the text of the constitutional bill has not survived, we can only surmise precisely what it said. The authors of the two most recent and best studies partially disagree,[7] so what is suggested here is no more than a hypothesis. Cromwell and his closest colleagues on the Council of Officers seem to have sincerely believed that it included a self-perpetuating clause or some device to safeguard the rights of sitting members. Other-wise their Declaration issued only two days later is based on an uncharacteristically crude lie. Probably Cromwell himself had destroyed the only written text of the bill, snatched up from the Clerk's table on 20 April, when he had worked himself into such a storm of rage. It is none the less possible that the officers were more worried about the danger of a future anti-republican, anti-military parliament getting out of hand and that the recruiting issue was a convenient arguing point but not the real issue. For Cromwell, the breach with his old colleagues, including some close and tried friends, was a sad one, but not unexpected in the circumstances. Of the leading civilian MPs, St John and Whitelocke continued to serve as judges, as did one or two lesser figures including the ex-Speaker, William Lenthall, who had early on been rewarded with the Mastership of the Rolls. Most of the others either withdrew at once or else were removed from the executive posts which they held over the next month or so. For the first time, England, indeed the whole British Isles, had no civilian government, but Cromwell and the officers speedily set about altering this. Naked, undisguised military rule was most certainly not what they were after.

The republican regime of February 1649 to April 1653 did not fail through lack of talent. The Rump included a number of individuals, whose abilities, if properly harnessed and directed, would have been an asset, in some cases an ornament, to any government in any age: the younger Henry Vane, Thomas Scott,

Oliver St John, Richard Salwey, Henry Nevile, the Chaloner brothers, Algernon Sidney, Henry Marten, George Thomson, and others. Sir Arthur Hesilrige, Bt., enjoyed great prestige as the only survivor of the Five Members. Along with Cromwell and Vane he was the most prominent single political figure in the House and, except when absent in the north, more consistently active than either of them. But Hesilrige was an unperceptive, monumentally tactless blunderer, sincere and of some ability but a difficult man. As we shall see, his defects as a political leader were to be among the decisive influences in the disaster which befell the republican cause in 1659–60. As for Cromwell himself and his actions, judgement may be left to Dorothy Osborne, who came from a royalist family but had once been courted by Oliver's second surviving son, Henry Cromwell, when she wrote to her fiancé, the young William Temple: 'If Mr. Pim were alive again, I wonder what he would think of these proceedings, and whether this would appear so great a breach of the Privilege of Parliament as the demanding the 5 members?'

Having dismissed the Council of State, where Bradshaw delivered a dignified rebuke to Cromwell for his action, the officers at once began to recruit civilians to their own Council. In effect, they turned it into a new Council of State; even so, during May and June it contained a greater preponderance of military men than at any other time. What longer-term constitutional plans the officers had is another matter. The *Declaration*, already cited, which they issued on 22 April, states that 'after much debate it was judged necessary and agreed upon', but leaves unclear whether this was by themselves alone or after joint meetings with selected MPs, and then continues: 'that the supreme authority should be, by the Parliament, devolved upon known persons, men fearing God and of approved integrity, and the government of the Commonwealth committed unto them for a time . . . ' This was apparently to continue for as long as it took to implement various necessary reforms of the legal system, and until the people (presumably the potential voters) came to realize that their own interests would best be served by successive parliaments without monarchy (or Lords): a candid admission that the republican regime rested upon no more than minority support in the country as a whole. It was hinted strongly by some contemporary observers—newsletter-

writers, foreign envoys, etc.—that the statement in turn
concealed a deep division, and most historians since then have
accepted this view. Harrison and the other millenarian-inclined
officers are supposed to have wanted an Old-Testament style
'Sanhedrin' of seventy selected godly men, to begin the process
of replacing the Fourth Monarchy of this world by the Fifth
Monarchy as an interim to the next, alternatively styled the rule
of the Saints on earth. Those like Lambert who, while sincere in
religion, were not adherents of a millenarian theocracy,
favoured the temporary rule of a small select council, which was
presumably to be charged with producing a blueprint for a
future reformed parliamentary system.

The Nominated Parliament

The assembly whose members were summoned by Cromwell on
behalf of the Council in June and which met early in July would
therefore seem to represent a compromise between the two
policies. Its membership was approximately double that of the
proposed Harrisonian Sanhedrin, but it was essentially a gather-
ing of nominees, chosen by the Army leaders or by factions
among them from the more distinguished, better-known lay
members of the local Congregational and Baptist Churches,
together with a few other like-minded individuals. For the first
time a reality was given to the forcible incorporation of Scotland
and Ireland into the English Commonwealth by the presence of
nominees from both these countries, although like the rest they
were chosen by the high command of the English Army. The
relationship of this nominated assembly to the Council of State
was at first left unclear; likewise its precise responsibility with
regard to a longer-term constitutional settlement. Cromwell's
opening address to the members took place in the council
chamber in Whitehall, not down the road in Westminster where
the House of Commons normally met. The tone and content of
his speech as reported suggest a mood of great enthusiasm,
almost evidence that he had been swept off his feet by the
millenarians; in fact the fundamental contradictions between his
desire for pragmatic, limited reform and the outlook of the Fifth
Monarchists was soon to be proved unbridgeable, and this could
never have been otherwise. Cromwell now provided a new

version of the breach with the Rump and a different justification for its dissolution from that given in the earlier *Declaration*. More positively and constructively, he had in his hand while he was speaking a document which he called 'an Instrument', which seems to have been meant as their brief for a constitutional settlement with a reformed parliament. Whatever the truth of that may be, the assembly adjourned itself to the usual Commons chamber and then resolved itself to be a parliament. This was a contested vote, of about three to two, with close associates of Cromwell on both sides, so it does not look like part of a pre-arranged plan.

Known to history as the Nominated or Little Parliament, or derisorily after one of its radical members, a London Baptist businessman, simply as 'the Barebones', it at once began to act the part of a parliament. A new Council of State was elected, or rather a civilian majority was added to the existing membership. Grand committees were appointed on the normal range of topics; the drafting of bills was speedily begun on such matters as the reform of the Church and the law; grants of taxation were voted to carry on the war at sea, but tactlessly not for the maintenance of the Army at home; and a term was set to the assembly's own existence, the symbolic date of 3 November 1654 again being chosen.

The Barebones has been substantially rehabilitated by recent studies.[8] Some of its minor reforms—on the law of debt and civil marriage—were sensible and moderate; even its more radical ones—the proposed abolition of the Court of Chancery and the replacement of compulsory tithe payments by some alternative way of maintaining parish clergy—were only in line with what many reformers and supporters of the parliamentary cause had long been demanding. It was more in their priorities and the way in which they plunged into reforming measures without adequate preparation that the extremist, Fifth-Monarchy influence showed through. On some issues the Fifth Monarchists and other millenarians could muster a majority, but when a new Council of State was elected by ballot in November, Cromwell got nearly twice as many votes as Harrison, let alone any of the other radicals, and there was a comfortable non-millenarian majority including Oliver's distinctly conservative son, Henry; but by then the assembly was probably already doomed. Lambert, although co-opted as a member, never sat and was probably all along scheming for its replacement. More suprisingly Harrison also soon ceased to sit; after the Rump, parliaments were perhaps not to his taste. Cromwell never attended again after the opening ceremony. Fears that the Army would have to resort to free quarter if the assessment was not quickly voted, together with growing alarm at the apparent threat to any form of state church and salaried clergy, especially after a vote to abolish advowsons (the right of appointment to church benefices or livings), were probably the immediate causes of its downfall. The conservative majority in the House were persuaded to surrender the assembly's powers back to Cromwell as Lord-General on the grounds that he had called them together. Some of the radical minority attempted to resume sitting, but were eased out by armed soldiers even more crudely than had been done with the Rump seven and a half months before.

What the Barebones would have done given more time, if allowed its self-allotted span, remains a question mark. Cromwell subsequently spoke of it more in sorrow than in anger, yet none the less referred to the members having 'flown at liberty and property', as if he were confusing them with Levellers if not Diggers, which was plainly nonsensical. The Barebones allowed Lilburne's second trial on capital charges, for having returned to England in spite of the Rump's banishment order, to proceed unhindered, and the overlap between the Fifth-Monarchist and the Leveller programmes for reform was at most slight. Common hostility to tithes and insistence on better treatment of insolvent debtors are the only significant common elements to be discerned: with the Diggers, extinct anyway before the Barebones assembled, the overlap is even smaller.

The members did not intervene to help Lilburne who was again on trial for his life. He was acquitted for a second time by a London jury, but now he was held under arrest after the verdict; although not maltreated, he was imprisoned and then, when his health began to fail and he was converted to Quakerism, he was allowed out on a form of house arrest, he and then his widow receiving a small pension from the State. The Rump was to abrogate its own 1652 sentence against him when it returned to power in 1659; Cromwell himself had always felt ambivalent towards Lilburne, and even Hesilrige may have been a less implacable enemy than the Leveller leader believed him to be. In their abstention from the use of terror as a political weapon except in Ireland, the English revolutionaries compare favourably with many others in different parts of the world since then.

The radicals in the Barebones curiously had been the readier to continue the Dutch War. By this time it had turned decisively in England's favour, and an outright victory seemed possible by maintaining the blockade of the Dutch coast, for this was beginning to strangle the sea-borne trade on which the Netherlands' economy depended. By contrast, the moderates or future Cromwellians, whom we might be tempted to equate with commercially-minded imperialists, were prepared and even eager for a compromise peace, as was to follow in a few months' time. Possibly it was part of the millenarian scheme of things that an all-Protestant union must be created, if necessary by force, in order then to destroy the Catholic powers and the Papacy; it is hard to equate their motives with those of the materialistic Rumpers and London merchants who had engineered the outbreak of the war. This, until 1659, was the end of the Commonwealth.

7

Problems of the Protectorate

A new constitution

The new constitution was presented to Cromwell and accepted by him only four days after the demise of the Barebones. This remarkable speed, together with the great detail which it contained, is proof of careful preparation. The Instrument of Government, as it became known, was probably drafted in November, with provision at an early stage for Cromwell to be made king; at least so he himself said in a later speech and this was never refuted. When he declined, some consequential changes were obviously necessary. According to Bulstrode Whitelocke, who while full of self-justification and self-importance is not a deliberately dishonest witness, back in 1651–2 Cromwell had already, in private discussions, asked the rhetorical question of what would happen if someone took it upon himself to be king and had more directly expressed his own preference for a constitution 'with something monarchic in it'. During the summer of 1653 a rumour had circulated that he was to become emperor or generalissimo. Characteristically his choice was neither for this, with its Caesarist overtones, nor for the title of king which he himself helped to abolish less than five years earlier, but for the very traditional style of Lord Protector. In England during the fifteenth and sixteenth centuries protectors had normally acted on behalf or instead of kings who were either under age or *non compos mentis*, and while the throne was itself in dispute between rival claimants. There was a temporary *ad hoc* flavour to the title; none of its previous holders had lived out his natural life as protector. Charles I's youngest surviving son, Henry Duke of Gloucester, had been released and allowed to join the rest of his family on the Continent in 1652, so it was hardly plausible to see the new Lord Protector as a regent for a Stuart prince. Moreover, the new constitution made very specific provision for the election of Cromwell's successor after his death by the (much smaller)

Council of State, whose original members were named in the text of the Instrument; and this has led some historians to assume that Lambert, its principal author, saw himself as the successor designate.

The Instrument of Government can best be thought of as an amalgam of the *Heads of Proposals*, the officers' *Agreement of the People*, and the Rump's lost bill for a new representative. It made government by a single person and periodic parliaments its fundamental tenet, but at the same time the Council was to enjoy much greater powers than any royal privy council before or since. Up to a point this can be related to the Army's political role as an additional 'estate of the realm'; five of the original fourteen of its members can be reckoned as primarily military types and spokesmen for the Army's interests. The religious rights of the individual were more carefully safeguarded than in any previous enactment. If there had been a widespread demand for a written constitution and a general readiness to give it a fair trial, then the Instrument had much to commend it. But forms of government are workable not only on their merits; they also depend on whether enough people want them to work and are prepared to operate within the rules which a given constitution prescribes or presupposes. The new Protector and his Council had the Instrument enrolled in Chancery (itself reprieved from abolition by the fall of the Barebones), but it lacked the status and hence the authority of a parliamentary statute, and was never to be turned into one. Yet it was emphatically not a Leveller-style 'agreement', validated by mass subscription, or the product of a direct popular mandate. Its provisions allowed the Protector and Council to legislate by ordinance until the first of its prescribed triennial parliaments was to meet the following September. This in itself was unprecedented, and most unlikely to be accepted by any parliament worthy of the name; not even Henry VIII, most tyrannical of English kings, or James and Charles I had claimed the right to legislate without Parliament. As with the Rump and the Barebones, there was, therefore, a basic, underlying contradiction between the main thrust of Cromwell's own desires and priorities and the formal means and institutions with which he had to operate. It has been forcefully argued that his aim was to return to more settled ways of government and, as part of this policy, to conciliate as many as possible of the traditional ruling class: nobility, gentry, and City fathers.

Early reforms

The substance of some of the Protectorate's early measures pointed in that direction, yet the means employed to realize them contradicted it. The Commonwealth's Engagement Act was repealed by conciliar ordinance. A few members of the old governing élite were persuaded to serve on the Council: one peer, two peers' sons, two baronets. The activities of the county committees were virtually brought to an end, as was the para-legal work of the Indemnity Commission. Whereas the Rump had issued new commissions of the peace for the counties in 1650, in theory eliminating all monarchists who would not take the Engagement, additional JPs were now appointed, in some cases non-republicans, even non-parliamentarians. Yet at the same time the Protector and his Council legislated busily. Above all they levied taxes under the authority of the Instrument, a fundamental breach of the Petition of Right and of the various acts passed in 1641.

Some of the ordinances touched more basic matters than others. The bill for the full incorporation of Scotland into the English Commonwealth, for a forcible union in short, was yet another of the Rump's undertakings which had never been brought to completion; this was now implemented by ordinance, though the creation of a single state in Great Britain might be regarded (and not only by Scottish nationalists) as a fundamental change. The re-organization of financial administration under a board of Treasury Commissioners supervising a restored and reformed Exchequer on the other hand was the sort of tidying up which might not seem to require the authority of statute, though it probably would have been thought to do so under Henry VIII or Elizabeth I. The Rump's scheme for recruiting better qualified parish clergy, testing their fitness and removing unfit ones from benefices, the system which came to be known as that of the Triers and Ejectors, was perhaps somewhere half-way in between, but again would have been better left to a parliament. The reform of the Court of Chancery after its recent reprieve reflected the impatience of the Army with the legal profession. It may well be that no normally elected parliament would have broken free of the lawyers in it sufficiently to make such a measure possible; as it was, the opposition was so intense from the legal members of the government, judges, and others, that the Chancery ordinance remained inoperative for nearly another year, by which time the constitutional position of the 1654 legislation was even more problematic.

Much of what the Council did during these first eight months of the Protectorate was useful and sensible. Peace negotiations with the Dutch were brought to a successful conclusion as was fully within its powers under the Instrument; the war could have been described as a draw in England's favour and the treaty reflected this fact. Besides various minor colonial concessions, some of which proved unenforceable, the United Provinces agreed to a secret clause excluding the House of Orange from holding office in any of the signatory provinces. This could be seen as a prudent anti-Stuart precautionary measure, but it committed England to a particular alignment of political forces inside the Netherlands which in the longer run was unwise. In a sense the clause remained operative not only while the Dutch observed the Treaty, but for as long as the regents' regime (the mercantile ruling élite of Holland) continued in power and was able to keep the Orangists out.

The Western Design

At about the time when the treaty was being concluded, the Council held a discussion on what to do with the navy, and there was a second debate on the same question a little later, during the early summer. The rational decision would have been to pay off a large number of ships' companies and lay up the vessels, keeping a sufficient fleet in being to protect normal commercial and shipping interests and to prevent any possible foreign-sponsored royalist invasion. Instead it was decided to attack Spain in the Caribbean by mounting a full-scale amphibious expedition. English merchants and their agents or factors and the crews of English merchant ships had genuine grievances against Spain or rather against the Spanish authorities: they were often molested and sometimes arrested and imprisoned by the local officers of the Inquisition simply for being Protestants, or allegedly for proselytizing among the local population.

Furthermore, the continued attempt by Spain to maintain a monopoly of trade with her American empire, left hopelessly unclear by the terms of the peace made in 1604, was another chronic source of trouble. Here the English were technically in the wrong, but a small, if vocal, lobby argued for positive action, to establish a base in the western Caribbean (the English so far only held a few of the small islands further east, notably Barbados) and thus to force an entry for English trade with the Spanish 'main'. As against this, trade with Spain itself and the Spanish-held parts of Italy might well be threatened by any such move. And it was Spain's enemy, France (the two monarchies were still at war) that currently sheltered the royalist *émigrés*; there was more maritime rivalry with the French, as with the Dutch, than with the Spaniards. On the other hand, the geographical position and military strength of France argued for an alliance, or at least for using English neutrality as a bargaining counter to prevent the French from helping the Stuart exiles. If the French government would guarantee this, or better still would expel the cavaliers from their territories altogether, this might well be worth the price of a breach with Spain, and would certainly be more substantial than anything that the Spanish government could offer by way of concessions on the Indies or the Inquisition. From the very unusual record (informal notes kept by one of Cromwell's councillors) of the two successive debates, it is not clear whether these issues were all weighed up against each other; the arguments focused rather on the pros and cons of an attack on the Spanish Indies and its probable repercussions in Europe. The Protector and some of his colleagues may have been under the illusion that they could conduct a naval and colonial war with Spain in the Americas and still remain at peace in Europe. It has been suggested that this was a kind of atavistic throwback to an Elizabethan dream world, or at least that it arose from a folk memory of the privateering war of the 1570s–80s before England and Spain were officially at war. This error of judgement proved an extraordinarily expensive one.

The Western Design, as it came to be known, went badly wrong. The land and sea commanders of the expedition were given over-rigid secret orders with an ill-defined division of responsibility between them; faulty or unsuitable equipment, the wrong kind of supplies, lack of proper medication, inadequate training, and low morale combined to help produce a situation where only exceptionally good luck, exceptional incompetence on the part of the enemy, or both, could have led to a successful outcome. It is small wonder that the English were ignominiously repulsed from San Domingo (the island now divided between Haiti and the Dominican Republic), more surprising that they captured and, despite appalling losses from dysentery and other tropical diseases, managed to hold the island of Jamaica. Although in the long run its possession was to be valuable for England and to serve as a springboard for illicit trade with the surrounding Spanish possessions, this in no way compensated at the time for the losses suffered by English merchant shipping from privateers in European waters, and for the economic damage done by the interruption of trade with Iberia and the Mediterranean. Some Spanish treasure ships, bringing silver back from the Americas, were intercepted and captured; Robert Blake and other admirals made England's naval strength felt both in the Mediterranean and around the coasts of Spain and Portugal (itself still at war with Spain). Blake in fact managed to advance the techniques of naval blockade by remaining at sea off the enemy's coast for unprecedented lengths of time; but overall the sea war was an expensive failure, at least in financial and economic terms. By the late 1650s the navy was costing more than ever and the public debt was assuming alarming proportions. The seamen's pay was shockingly in arrears; either state bankruptcy or a collapse of credit, and thus of naval morale, seemed the likeliest outcome.

A sterile Parliament

At home, the Protectorate maintained itself, but its position got no better. For example the Protector's firm line, when the Portuguese ambassador's brother had killed an innocent man, seems to have won him genuine popularity with ordinary Londoners. The plea of diplomatic immunity was rejected (on strong but not absolutely irrefutable grounds); the trial proceeded and the defendant, having been found guilty, was eventually executed. At the same time two out of three convicted royalist conspirators were also executed. Ironically one of the them was the very man whom the Portuguese nobleman had been seeking, to avenge an earlier insult, when he picked the wrong victim. In this case the crowd's sympathy appears to have been with the condemned royalists.

The first parliamentary elections were held under the provisions of the Instrument during the summer of 1654. There were to be 400 MPs for England, Wales, the Channel Islands, and Berwick-on-Tweed (only the Isle of Man and the Scillies remaining disfranchised), and thirty each from Scotland and Ireland. The main differences from the traditional system were a massive transfer of seats from small and decayed boroughs to the larger and more populous counties and a uniform suffrage for all seats of £200-worth of property, real or personal (in contemporary reckoning this was equivalent to an income of £10 a year). The prevalence of multi-member constituencies (ten or more seats for some undivided counties) seems to have led, as a practical necessity, to voting on paper and the use of marked lists. The members from Scotland were little more than nominees of the English military government. By this time George Monck had been put in sole charge of the Army there, after taking a prominent part in the naval war against the Dutch, and was in the process of suppressing another royalist rising in the Highlands. Scotland had been quiescent since the completion of English conquest in 1652. Montrose's abortive attempt to stage a comeback in 1650 had already led to his capture and execution without any attempt by Charles II to intervene on his behalf. In Ireland, by contrast, the MPs were chosen variously by the Dublin government, by this time under Fleetwood, who was soon to be promoted to the Lord Deputyship, assisted by a group of civil commissioners, together with the Army and some of the New English settlers.

The English elections of 1654 were probably as free as any in the century. There were, however, complaints against electioneering by local garrison commanders and an undertone of hostility towards courtiers, as the Cromwellians were now coming to be called. Some categories of royalists were still excluded from voting and from standing for election. Whatever the extent of government interference, the new parliament contained numerous ex-Presbyterians or moderate parliamentarians who had opposed the Commonwealth, probably a good many neutrals and even some royalists too young to have fought in the civil wars and thus not formally disqualified. There was also a significant group, vocal out of all proportion to their actual numbers, of republicans, erstwhile members or other supporters of the Rump who refused to recognize the legality of the Protectorate. And, in spite of what was clearly stated in the Instrument, the House began almost at once to challenge the very basis of the constitution on which it had been called together.

Between Cromwell's opening speech—conservative but optimistic—on 4 September and his second eight days later, his mood changed abruptly. All his suspicions and resentments towards his one-time allies and collaborators from the years before 1653 came bubbling out. Subscription to yet another test or loyalty oath was made a condition of MPs being allowed to continue sitting. At first only about a hundred signed; eventually nearer three hundred. Over a hundred, including the Protector's most implacable opponents, were thus excluded from the House. Yet the Parliament still conspicuously failed to validate the Instrument by statute; instead MPs embarked on its virtual replacement by a new constitutional bill of their own devising. If ever completed, this measure would have kept within the letter of the Instrument and the new 'engagement', in accepting that government should be by a single person and periodic parliaments; but it would have greatly reduced the powers and prerogatives of the Protector, have downgraded the role of his Council, and have increased the powers of the Commons. The bill also seemed likely to narrow religious liberty as enshrined in the Instrument; at the same time the House was doing nothing about voting vitally necessary taxes for the upkeep of the armed forces. Cromwell therefore decided not to allow them to complete and pass their own constitutional measure; the Instrument gave him only a suspensive twenty-day veto except of bills contrary to the Instrument itself. Once more his patience ran out and he dissolved the Parliament after five lunar rather than five calendar months, the minimum length of session prescribed by the Instrument. Here indeed was an 'addled' if not exactly a short parliament, with not a single act added to the statute book.

Conspiracies

There were other reasons, too, for the peremptory dissolution. The Protectorate was threatened by conspiracy, secret plans for royalist risings and simultaneously republican plots to overthrow the Government and even to remove Cromwell by kidnapping or assassination. As is frequently the case, those responsible for security tended to exaggerate the danger. In spite of the defeat at San Domingo, the Cromwellian Army was still overwhelmingly loyal to its commander-in-chief and on home ground was still an invincible fighting force. On the republican side, it is hard to take seriously the notion of a single master-minded conspiracy. There was an ill-assorted alliance of ex-Levellers, notably John Wildman—most formidable of the radical debaters and pamphleteers of 1647, but without Lilburne's mass following—Fifth-Monarchy men in opposition since the end of the Barebones, republican army officers who were unhappy with the semi-monarchical idea of a Lord Protector, and even some ex-members of the Rump. If anything there were more like two or three separate but overlapping plots, none of which came to much. Three colonels were implicated, of whom only one was regarded as a serious menace although two lost their commissions; a Major-General stationed in Scotland was cashiered and imprisoned; other republicans were put under varying forms of house arrest; Wildman himself and another ex-Leveller, the brilliant polemical pamphleteer Richard Overton, may have become secret agents for the Government as the price of being allowed to remain at large.[1]

The royalist plans went equally awry though with more outwardly spectacular consequences. A small local rising took place in Salisbury, led by Colonel John Penruddock, but no mass action developed and it was all over in a few days. Another rising planned to take place in Yorkshire at the same time was nipped in the bud and merely resulted in preventive arrests. Short of Cromwell's removal by death or assassination, coinciding with a foreign invasion led by Charles II, it is hard to imagine the Protectorate having been overthrown by force of arms, and such an invasion might easily have failed even if Cromwell had been removed; it is not clear how many ex-Cavaliers and other potential enemies still had weapons and ammunition and were ready to use them. Countermeasures

were at once taken by Cromwell's efficient if politically limited
Secretary of State, John Thurloe, who was in charge of internal
security. The Protector's Council over-reacted, but with a
curious kind of delayed effect like men suffering from shock.[2]

The legal position of the revenue system was unclear,
following the first Protectorate Parliament. Under the
Instrument, the Protector and his Council no longer had the
power to legislate by ordinance and they did not attempt to do
so, although the Chancery reform ordinance was at last
implemented; this led to the resignation of Whitelocke and one
of the other two senior judges (Lords Commissioners for the
Great Seal), but they were prepared to compromise by remaining
in office as salaried Treasury Commissioners and although
Lenthall grumbled, he stayed on as Master of the Rolls. As
regards taxes, another clause of the Instrument appeared to
guarantee a sufficient revenue for the army and navy, over and
above a lesser, fixed amount for the civil government, and stated
that this could only be altered or removed by act of parliament.
So the position of those branches of the customs, likewise the
monthly assessment, which had been granted for a fixed period
of time in earlier acts and ordinances, was now thoroughly
ambiguous. One test case arose out of a refusal to pay the
monthly assessment; another, from the refusal of a merchant,
George Cony, to pay customs on some of his goods, gained
more publicity, perhaps because it was so similar to the cases of
Bate, Chambers and Rolle under the monarchy. No wonder that
Chief Justice Rolle, the brother of the merchant MP who had
refused to pay tonnage and poundage not voted by Parliament
back in 1628, should have resigned from the bench as a result of
Cony's case. Of the three main taxes, the excise was clearly the
most unpopular, but no single comparable case arose; even the
Indemnity Commissioners under the Commonwealth had by no
means always upheld excise officials who appealed to them for
protection or redress when local magistrates took the side of
those evading or resisting payment.

Perhaps what is most astonishing, looking at the situation as
a whole, is the amount raised in taxes and the paucity of
sustained opposition to their collection. To this the cynic might
reply that it was only collected at the point of the sword, with
the reality or threat of armed forces ever present. In fact the

Army normally kept in the background. If this was a military dictatorship, it was a reluctant and exceptionally legalistic one. It may be significant, too, that the commissioners responsible for assessing people's wealth and then overseeing the collection of direct taxes on property and income were normally local men; by contrast, the excise officials were often not, and were directly answerable to a central body of commissioners in London. And this, besides the inherent nature of the tax and what its enforcement inevitably involved, may help to explain its greater unpopularity. In the customs service, the republican period probably saw the origin of 'rolling' officials, that is posting them on from one seaport to another, so that they would not become pillars of local society susceptible to improper pressures and blandishments. Here, as in other respects, it is necessary to distinguish between those features of government under both Commonwealth and Protectorate that won these regimes some measure of popular acceptance and security, and those that anticipated later developments or were to serve as precedents, if not at once then later, after the return of monarchy.

The Major-Generals

The Council's remedy for royalist sedition and other subversive activities seems to have been Lambert's brainchild. Immediately after Penruddock's rising at Salisbury, Cromwell's brother-in-law, Major-General John Disbrowe, had been put in charge of all the south-western counties and given authority over the militia as well as over units of the regular army stationed in those counties. But he seems to have exercised no other powers beyond that. At one level the system which has become known to history as the rule of the Major-Generals could be represented as no more than an extension of this arrangement for the south-west to the whole of the country. It has also been argued that the intervention in local government and civil affairs generally by garrison commanders and other officers in charge of military detachments stationed around the country had been constant ever since the mid- or later 1640s, and that what was done in 1655 arose naturally from this, indeed that its significance has been exaggerated. None the less the commissions to the Major-Generals, first issued in August and then elaborated and reissued in October from when they took full effect, were novel and distinctive. The country was divided into eleven or twelve districts; and, since two of the Major-Generals (Lambert, and Fleetwood who was now recalled from Ireland, where he was effectively succeeded by Henry Cromwell) were allowed to have deputies, in practice there were more like fourteen. Each of them, together with specially appointed commissioners for securing the peace (not to be confused with the JPs) in every county, were to raise and train a new select militia; this was to be paid for out of a tax to be levied at the rate of 10 per cent on all royalists worth over £100 a year, hence its colloquial name the decimation tax. To these and other responsibilities for security were added duties connected with the overseeing of local government, especially with regard to 'the reformation of manners', including the suppression of various sports and pastimes and control over alehouses. As Disbrowe and others pointed out, this was going to be very difficult unless they were also put on the ordinary commission of the peace in their respective counties, as in fact followed.

The full system was in operation for something over a year, from the autumn of 1655 until the mid-winter of 1656–7. It is clear, both from their surviving correspondence with the Protector and his Secretary of State and from local government records where these are available, that some of the Major-Generals were more active than others; some were tenderer towards royalists in their handling of the decimation tax, others took less part in local government as JPs and left alehouses and cruel sports to the ordinary magistrates in their counties. But their unpopularity was not an invention of post-Restoration royalist propaganda, as is evident from what happened in the next parliament. Most of them were outsiders to the areas where they were in charge, and a large proportion of them were self-made men below the social status and landed wealth of those who would normally have been JPs in most counties. Above all the decimation tax, whatever its intentions and whatever its justification in ex-Cavalier support for Penruddock's and other plots, looked like a return to the penal taxation of the 1640s and a breach of the 1652 Pardon and Oblivion Act. That the experiment was, in itself, fatal to Cromwell's policy of conciliating the hereditary upper classes seems less likely. If anything there was more co-operation between the Protectorate

Government and members of those classes in the years 1657–9 than there had been in 1654–5; so this case still remains unproven. Ashley Cooper had already resigned from the Protector's Council; other individual peers and landed gentlemen continued either to marry into the Cromwell family, hold office in the Protector's household, or co-operate at a political level. An example of those who had been purged back in 1647–8 but who were again prepared to play a part in public life was Sir Richard Onslow, MP for Surrey; another was Sir John Trevor who sat for Flintshire. As agents of central government in the localities, the Major-Generals were perhaps more analogous to the assize judges, who were not normally sent to the counties where they lived or had their own estates, rather than to the JPs or the Lord and Deputy Lieutenants, who under the monarchy were responsible for the county militias. Their unpopularity may have been due less to their having been geographical 'outsiders' than to the other reasons which have been suggested here.[3]

Another parliament

The second parliament of the Protectorate, called in 1656, though in some respects like a repeat of the first, was in other vital ways very different. The elections were held a year before they were required under the Instrument, because the Government was desperately short of money and wanted extra taxes voted for the Spanish War, now officially extended to Europe with a French alliance under negotiation. To that extent the circumstances seem more reminiscent of the 1620s or even the 1580s and 1590s than of the years 1640–53. Having received a characteristically verbose but powerful address from the Protector, in which he spoke with a distinctly weary tone, comparing himself to a parish constable, something like a hundred out of the 460 MPs were then summarily prevented from taking their seats, on the grounds that they were unfit persons, disqualified from being elected or sitting under the terms of the Instrument. This reflected the elections, when, in spite of much more active intervention by the Major-Generals and other agents of the Government than in 1654, there was stronger Country feeling against the establishment, as witness the emotive slogan, whether coined by a republican or a royalist does not really matter: 'No swordsmen, no decimators!' So the

House was garbled from its very beginning. Those so excluded seem to have been mainly republicans rather than Cavaliers, and those who were allowed to sit evidently included a large number of would-be monarchists, even if not many active adherents of the exiled Stuarts. When it did begin business, the House of Commons showed not the least eagerness to consider the Spanish War or to vote supplies. In spite of the existence of the official journal and the fact of two successive diaries having been kept by individual MPs, it is something of a mystery how the members occupied their time for the first two and a half months of the session. It is tempting to conclude that this was a conscious design by a group who saw that the House would gain a stronger hold over the executive with the passing of time, and hence dragged its feet on trivial matters.

The session suddenly came to life, in a rather ugly way, over the case of James Nayler. The Quakers had already been in trouble with local magistrates and several had been imprisoned in various parts of the country. As much as their doctrines, it was the violence of their speech, with denunciations and noisy interruptions of church services, which aroused the most hostility. Cromwell had already granted an interview to one of their leaders, George Fox, and there is some evidence that he took a more tolerant view than JPs and others and was readier to leave them alone. Nayler, an ex-quartermaster from Lambert's regiment, had recently entered Bristol in what was held to be a blasphemous parody of Jesus's entry into Jerusalem on Palm Sunday. His case raises several questions of historical interest. It has been powerfully argued that the Quakers were indeed a more militant threat to the social order and to Church and State than their later history and their modern image would suggest; that they were revolutionaries in the tradition of Levellers, Diggers, and Ranters, not pacifists or quietists at all, and more powerful than any of these because more numerous than the Diggers and better organized than the Ranters. Closely related to this is the further contention that Fox was by no means their accepted leader in 1656, and that Nayler if anyone, was nearer to being a national figure and popular hero than he was; indeed that Fox may not have been too heartbroken to see his rival come to grief. In short, orthodox Quaker historiography has distorted the whole Nayler episode, in the interests of their later respectability and Fox's subsequent dominance in the movement.[4] Secondly, it was not clear why, if Nayler had offended against the Rump's 1650 Blasphemy Act, or even against the relevant clause in the Instrument itself which denied religious liberty to anyone who might 'hold forth and practise licentiousness', he was not brought to trial in the ordinary way. If a case was considered too serious for the JPs to deal with at quarter sessions, the normal procedure was to refer it to the assize judges or even direct to the criminal side of the Court of Upper Bench in Westminster. However two influential local magistrates from Bristol and Exeter, both also MPs, were so alarmed at the progress of Quakerism in the south-west that they incited Parliament to intervene. The Instrument was silent as to Parliament's judicial powers, and it could therefore be argued that this left the Commons' jurisdiction exactly as it had been before; but the absence of the Lords, crucial as the judges in impeachment procedure, might have suggested that the Commons' jurisdiction was meant to be restricted to cases of disputed elections, parliamentary privilege, and the conduct of members. As it was, not only did the House devote a great deal of time and energy to the unfortunate Nayler, but the Protector himself clearly became disillusioned with its proceedings and therefore readier to consider a proposal for major constitutional change.

Scarcely was Nayler consigned to flogging, branding, tongue-boring, and solitary imprisonment, than the military party in the House went on to make one of those errors of political tactics which turn out to have far-reaching results. Whether in order to safeguard themselves from possible future legal retaliation in their capacities as Major-Generals, or simply to square their activities with the letter of the law, they introduced a bill giving statutory approval to the decimation tax. Once started, the debates rapidly developed into a trial of strength and a general contest over the legality of the whole system and on the standing of the military in civil affairs. All the other factions in the Commons, including some of the leading civilian members of Cromwell's own government, seem to have united against the bill, which was resoundingly defeated. Always a pragmatist who waited on providences, Cromwell now became further disillusioned with his military colleagues. Whereas in his speech at the opening of this parliament he had gone out of his way to defend and to praise the rule of the Major-Generals, by the spring of 1657 he was ready to imply that it had all been foisted on him by others, as—he also suggested—had been the calling of the parliament itself.

Kingship

The House had by then been sitting for over four months and still had little to show, and the time was ripe for a new initiative if there was anyone to take it. Some of those supporters of the Protectorate who had helped to defeat the decimation tax bill, together with some of the non-party representatives of both Country and City, had clearly been at work in secret, preparing a new constitution. This was unveiled by one of the London MPs, an ex-Lord Mayor, under the style of 'A Remonstrance from the Parliament . . .', and included a clause which would have made Cromwell king. From late February until into May 1657 the whole political scene was dominated by this document which, in its revised form, came to be known as 'The Humble Petition and Advice', and in particular by the question whether Cromwell would or would not accept the crown. The pressures on him were heavy, from both directions. Until very late in the proceedings, the protagonists of the Humble Petition argued that it was an all or nothing package, that without the kingship the whole offer would lapse, though this must have been partly bluff. The Protector's family, notably his son Henry who had become Lord Deputy of Ireland in place of Fleetwood (who was regarded as what we should call a fellow-traveller with anabaptist republicans), the influential Lord Broghill, recently returned from helping Monck to reorganize the civil side of government in Scotland, and the ever faithful Thurloe, probably a majority of his Council and certainly a large majority of the Commons were all pressing Cromwell to accept. On the other side was opinion in the Army and the sectarian church congregations, which was overwhelmingly against. Not only Lambert, who seems to have felt a proprietory interest in the Instrument of Government and perhaps also to have seen his own chances of the succession fading, but also Fleetwood and Disbrowe threatened to resign their commissions and retire into private life if Cromwell made himself king; the opposition in the middle and lower ranks might not have stopped at that but have extended to direct action, even an attempted coup against the Protector.

Those of the puritan clergy who had most influence with Cromwell were divided, but the majority were anti-monarchist. John Owen, his favourite preacher who had been made Vice-Chancellor of Oxford University, seems to have been against the kingship, but Thomas Goodwin, who had led the moderate Congregationalist opposition in the Westminster Assembly during the 1640s, was probably in favour; Philip Nye, one of the Protector's main advisers on Church questions, and the volatile (in all likelihood manic depressive) Hugh Peter, were certainly against. The attitude of his other personal chaplains, Nicholas Lockyer and Peter Sterry, is unclear. These men were the nearest that the Protectorate came to having an unofficial guiding body on religious affairs, although Peter's influence was in decline by the later 1650s. The more consistently radical (but also more stable) John Goodwin, for whom even the Triers and Ejectors represented an Erastian encroachment on true religion, was outside this group. He and the Fifth-Monarchist preachers, who had been in opposition to Cromwell since 1653, were certainly against kingship.

There has been much debate among historians and among Cromwell's biographers as to his own preferences. The likeliest answer seems to be that he was instinctively against accepting the Crown; merely repealing the Engagement of 1649–50 in 1654 had not turned him into a crypto-monarchist. But he might well have been persuaded into acceptance against his personal inclination if there had been something nearer to a consensus in favour. To that extent the Army's opposition may indeed have been decisive; less because Cromwell was actually frightened of a military revolt than because a split with his old comrades in arms was a pointer against the kingship being a dispensation of divine providence. After a series of interviews between the Protector and committees and delegations sent on Parliament's behalf and after he had made several speeches in which he seemed to be playing for time, putting off what was bound to be an unpopular and controversial decision, Cromwell came out against. However, with a few minor modifications he accepted the rest of the Humble Petition, and its authors and supporters had to settle for this; so there was a new form of government, but Cromwell remained Lord Protector. In practice, however, the stability and endurance of the regime depended more on Cromwell's health than on his title. His survival for a few more years would have done far more to increase the Protectorate's chances of outliving him than if his eldest son had succeeded as King Richard IV, rather than as His Highness Richard the Lord Protector. The end of his second Protectorate Parliament was to prove that the political contradictions remained as profound as ever and as far from solution, but that Cromwell's capacity for sudden, decisive action had not deserted him.

A revised constitution

In a general sense the new constitution was more parliamentary than its predecessor. First and foremost this was so because the Humble Petition and the postscript, usually called the Additional Petition and Advice, were statutes enacted by Parliament in a way that the Instrument of Government had not, and perhaps never could have been. It was made clear that, except where the new constitution itself positively provided otherwise, common and statute law were to be observed and no additional powers were to be assumed by government. There were to be triennial parliaments (or more frequent ones if occasion so required) with two Houses, the members of the new 'Other' or 'Upper House' being nominated by the Protector. Instead of revenue being raised for an army and a navy of a certain size, a fixed amount of money was now allocated for the armed forces as well as for the civil government. This was apparently to be raised by customs and excise only, and not by a land tax except in time of war. The reason for the much reduced assessment being continued at all was perhaps so that the Spanish War could be carried on; in peacetime, it would have come to an end. The two Houses in future parliaments were to have a veto over the Protector's appointment of councillors. Generally speaking the Council was downgraded by comparison with its place under the Instrument. Religious freedom was still prescribed, but its limits were more strictly drawn; scope for the Protector to intervene on behalf of such as John Biddle, the Socinian, or the Quakers was diminished. Acts and ordinances not contrary to the act embodying the Humble Petition itself were to remain in force; but this seems to have been regarded as ambiguous in relation to non-parliamentary enactments, and another separate act was passed validating several of the ordinances of 1654 and omitting others which were to lapse with the next session of the present parliament. The financial provision for the naval war was quite inadequate, and was granted at the price of a massive cut in the monthly assessment, which would in turn entail either a drastic reduction in the Army's strength or, once more, the danger of arrears, free quarter, and state indebtedness leading to bankruptcy. So, fiscally speaking, the downward spiral continued.

The new constitution was eventually accepted by all the existing councillors of state and general officers of the Army except Lambert. He refused to give his allegiance as required and was finally stripped of his offices and commissions. Like Ireton he was a republican but at the same time a political conservative in the context of Levellers and millenarians, a sincere Congregationalist but also a religious liberal. A man of some sensibility with artistic interests, Lambert was the most talented of Cromwell's surviving generals, but he lacked Ireton's reputation and his personal influence with Cromwell: it is too easy to say that his character was flawed by ambition, for so to some extent is that of everyone who gets to the top in any human situation or institution. But some people's ambitions are cruder, more corrupting and disfiguring than others'. Politically Lambert's ability was limited in a way that was to prove fatal to the whole republican cause, but this was not because he was vicious or dishonest. Only one other man, another Yorkshireman of lesser rank though a skilful administrator, followed him into the political wilderness of opposition. Many of the other senior officers who had expressed doubts about the new constitution and had vigorously opposed the kingship were rewarded with life peerages in order to fill the 'Other House', which was to number between forty and seventy of the Protector's nominees.

After an adjournment of over six months, a new session was called, presumably in the hope of getting more money. Despite the military–civilian split, dating from the previous winter (of 1656–7), the Court's or Government's potential support was inevitably weakened by the removal from the Commons of the new peers. An even more serious development arose from another provision of the Humble Petition coming into operation. The legal grounds on which the hundred or so, mainly republican, members had been excluded back in September 1656 was now held to have lapsed along with the rest of the Instrument of Government, so they were all able to take their seats. This wholly altered the balance of political power. It resulted in a parliament, which had been recalled to grant extra supplies for carrying on the war, at once challenging the very basis of the new constitution by querying the right of the 'Other House' to exist, at least to be a valid part of a true parliament. At the same time, Cromwell became increasingly alarmed that some kind of opposition alliance was being forged between the republican MPs, millenarian and other radicals in London, and disgruntled officers in the Army. In scenes very reminiscent of his dismissal of the Rump and his dissolution of the first Protectorate Parliament, he made a short, outspoken, self-justificatory speech dissolving the Parliament; he then went on to cashier the second-in-command and five other captains in his own cavalry regiment, giving the Army radicals generally a piece of his mind at the same time. Now if ever, one might have thought, was the moment for a military uprising against him. Once more, as with Harrison in 1653–4, the major-general and three colonels in 1654–5, and Lambert in 1657, this kind of selective purging proved efficacious. At least while he lived, Cromwell's hold on the loyalty and even the affections of the Army was little impaired. But it was a very different force from the Army of 1647–9, even from that of 1651–3.

In Ireland, Henry Cromwell was becoming more and more like a traditional viceroy. This was true both in his personal style of life and in his policy of balancing the interests of the various sections and trying to play them off against each other. The upheavals of the land settlement had more or less come to an end and the beginnings of economic and demographic recovery were discernible. In Scotland, George Monck, a truly professional soldier, proved an extremely efficient commander-in-chief, but Broghill did not return to Scotland after the Parliament ended; and, although Monck kept the army there loyal to the Protectorate and Scotland subdued, there was no longer any creative element in English rule and nothing save the passing of time to reconcile more of the Scots to the forced union. At home, Cromwell's son-in-law Fleetwood was now the second-in-command of the Army, but it was increasingly assumed that the Protector would be succeeded by his eldest son Richard. With Lambert out of the running, there was little choice; both Henry Cromwell and Monck would have been better choices in the sense of having greater ability and tougher personalities, but neither would have been acceptable to the Army in England or indeed to most civilian supporters of the regime.

Financial necessity once more pointed towards the calling of another parliament in 1658. Neither the fleet nor the army was quite on the brink of mutiny through the lack of pay, and the force which had been landed in Flanders as part of the alliance agreement with France against Spain soon proved its worth. An Anglo-French army utterly defeated a Spanish-royalist one, and Dunkirk was handed over to England as part of the price France had to pay. But all this cost more money and did not help to provide supplies; even the capture of more Spanish treasure ships only went a very small way towards what was needed. So to say that the Cromwellian regime was winding down before the Protector's death is debatable; it can neither be proved nor disproved. The Republic's prestige in Europe had never stood higher and there had never appeared to be less serious danger from either royalist or radical dissent at home. Cromwell's health had been deteriorating for some time; the change in his signature on official documents between 1654 and 1658 is shocking enough evidence of this. The death of his favourite daughter from cancer in August led to a rapid collapse which, given the state of medical knowledge and treatment, proved fatal within two weeks. Allegedly he nominated his eldest son Richard as his successor before he died; others said that he had named Fleetwood; possibly he failed to utter any name at all until it was too late. Richard, however, was duly proclaimed Lord Protector and, for the time being, accepted as such.

Cromwellians, old and new

Who were the Cromwellians or, to give them a more accurate but less expressive name, the Protectorians? As with the Caesarist party at the end of the Roman republic[5] and the Bonapartists around 1800, they included diverse elements but they were certainly more than a mere gang of ambitious adventurers. There were the members of Oliver's own family and his connections by marriage as well as descent. These included his two surviving sons, Richard and Henry, his successive sons-in-law Henry Ireton and Charles Fleetwood, and, married to younger daughters, the less important civilians John Claypole, Thomas Belasyse, Lord Fauconberg, and Robert Rich, grandson of the Earl of Warwick, and the Protector's brothers-in-law John Disbrowe and Valentine Walton (or Wauton), though the latter opposed the Protectorate. There were cousins too; but here one has to be even more careful than with in-laws not to make too much of such associations or to assume that relatives are necessarily political allies. Cromwell and John Hampden were cousins, but so were Hampden and King Charles I.

Then there were the Protector's clients, servants, dependants and junior military colleagues. Some of these had been with him since the early 1640s, while others had attached themselves or been recruited to his service at some stage in his career, either in the Eastern Association or the New Model, or later when he was successively Lord-General and then Lord Protector. John Thurloe the Secretary of State (previously a client of Oliver St John), John Maidstone and Nathaniel Waterhouse his household managers, John Blackwell his military paymaster and John Owen his favourite chaplain, his successive personal secretaries Robert Spavin (who ended in disgrace) and William Malyn, his various physicians especially Jonathan Goddard, his favourite ambassador the Scot Sir William Lockhart, and the Anglo-Irish ex-Agitator John Reynolds (drowned when commander of the English forces in Flanders)—these are a selection of names, to which others could easily be added. Then there were political allies and more senior military colleagues who stuck with Cromwell throughout their careers but were not dependants in the same sense: for example the civilian politicians and later councillors of state, Walter Strickland and Sir Gilbert Pickering, the aristocrats on his Council the Earl of Mulgrave and Lord Lisle (the Earl of Leicester's eldest son), and in the armed forces such as Robert Blake, Edward Montague, and indeed George Monck. Harder to classify are those who were intimate as friends or allies but who broke with Oliver at some stage along the way from 1647 to 1657: the younger Sir Henry

Vane is the pre-eminent example here; Thomas Harrison and John Lambert two others. Then there were Bulstrode White-locke and Oliver St John, who remained in high office during the Protectorate but ceased to play an active political role and can hardly be called Cromwellians; by contrast William Pierrepont, purged in December 1648, was out of politics until February 1660 but appears to have remained on friendly personal terms with Cromwell and his family.

It may be an indication of growing conservatism that none of the Protector's councillors was a regicide. In some cases this was simply a matter of age and the passing of time. By the later 1650s several men had risen to prominence who had been too young or too obscure to have fought in the civil wars or to have been named to the High Court of Justice. Then there were the ex-neutrals, ex-Presbyterians and, as some said, the ex-royalists—notably Charles Howard (the future Earl of Carlisle) and Monck himself. What might be called the non-ideological element among them included some who were moderate by conviction and others who were mere opportunists, or careerists in the worst sense. The longer Oliver lived and his regime lasted, the larger this element in it became. Not that he could ever have broken with all his old colleagues of civil war days. His own beliefs may be characterized as commitment to a broadly Congregationalist Puritan church with toleration for other non-episcopalian Protestants, and in politics to a mixed constitution, with a single person, a council, and periodic parliaments. But it is hard to say that all the so-called Cromwellians even had that much in common with their leader, though all but the most cynical must have shared at least some of these beliefs.

Many historians have seen the various constitutions of 1649–57 and even that of 1657–9 as no more than facades, to conceal the reality of military rule. It is tempting to identify the Cromwellian Army with the one-party rule of modern dic-tatorships and so-called totalitarian states, but this can be no more than a half-truth. Like most such single parties in the modern world, the Army was itself divided in its religious and political attitudes, if not into organized factions. And it is more plausible to see it as an exceptionally powerful sectional vested interest or an additional estate of the realm. By 1657–8 the Cromwellians were deeply divided between the predominantly military and civilian wings (there were of course exceptions on both sides) and to some extent also on generational lines between the older and younger men. This partly explains their undoing within eight months of Oliver's death.

Richard Cromwell

The new Protector had many attributes of a successful modern constitutional monarch, even down to his interest in horses and field sports. But given the realities of 1658–9 this was irrelevant. Once more it was decided to call a parliament, again to provide money. The old Protector's funeral was a very elaborate expensive affair, but it was foreign relations and the consequent naval and military involvements which were chiefly responsible for the Government's financial problems. The victory won in Flanders and the acquisition of Dunkirk should have reduced the shipping losses from privateers and at least have stabilized the cost of the expeditionary force there, but this was slow to take effect. Dunkirk was also meant to act as a deterrent to the Dutch, with whom relations were again deteriorating, this time mainly due to rivalries in the Baltic and over control of its entrance through the Sound. The kingdom of Denmark (which then included Norway) was a tributary ally, indeed almost a client state of the United Provinces at this time, whereas England was allied with Sweden, although not committed to the extent of a defensive military treaty. In the Dano-Swedish wars of the later 1650s it was in England's interest to prevent the defeat of the Swedes by Dutch intervention on the Danish side, but to limit the completeness of a Swedish victory.

Oliver Cromwell's Baltic policy, like his West Indian adventure and his war with Spain, has been severely criticized. He is said to have neglected strategic and mercantile interests in favour of the religious, semi-crusading quest for Protestant unity and the defeat of the Habsburgs and destruction of the Roman Church. Maybe he never totally discarded his millenarian hopes, but since Denmark, Sweden, and the Netherlands were all Protestant powers, and France as well as Spain Catholic, this could at most be a remote aspiration, not the basis of diplomacy or foreign relations. And the foremost authority on seventeenth-century Swedish history has at least partially rehabilitated

Cromwell's Baltic policy.[6] In the winter of 1658–9 English interests were held to require the dispatch of a large war fleet, which was to act as a deterrent against Dutch intervention and, if possible, not to get involved in the fighting; even so, this was a major added expense on top of the still mainly naval war with Spain. It should have been feasible to make peace there too on some sort of compromise terms, as the French indeed were to demonstrate when they discarded their respective allies (England, the Catalan rebels against Spain, and Portugal) and ended a twenty-four-year conflict with Spain in the spring of 1659. Whether Spanish recognition of the loss of Jamaica would have entailed the handing back of Dunkirk is not clear; it did not do so when peace was made a few years later, though Spain still refused to concede free entry for English merchants into her American empire. In fact, not long after ending the war with Spain, the restored royal Government sold Dunkirk to France, a much more debatable action. Subsequent criticism of Cromwell for having helped to build up the power of France to the detriment of English national interests seems like typical wisdom after the event, and in any case is more applicable to the policy of Charles II than to that of the Protector. French strength depended far more on internal factors, notably the power and ambitions of the monarch, than on the niceties of English foreign policy. In spite of the death of Blake, the most famous if not always the most successful of the Republic's naval commanders, after his blockade of the Spanish coast in 1657, the English State was beginning to use sea-power selectively as an 'instrument of (national) policy'.[7]

The Parliament called by the new Protector and his Council was the first since the Humble Petition and Advice had come into operation. Unlike the Instrument of Government, this constitution had said nothing about constituencies or the franchise; Richard Cromwell and his advisers seem to have felt that it required a return to the old (pre-1654) system in both respects, so this was put into effect for England and Wales. Somewhat incongruously, Ireland and Scotland, or rather the rulers of these two countries, were directed to send their thirty members each as under the Instrument. Their anomalous position and recognition of the 'Other House'—Cromwell's Lords—were to occupy much time and effort during the sitting of Richard Cromwell's Parliament. The composition of this body might be described as being like that of the 1656–8 Parliament, only more so: a Court or Government following, in turn split between military and civil, old and new Cromwellians, a strong and highly articulate republican faction, and a large number of independent, uncommitted gentlemen and others, many of them Presbyterian, neutral, or even crypto-royalists in their private sympathies and convictions, almost all of them opponents of military rule and the burden of taxation needed to maintain the Army at its present strength. As the session proceeded and little was achieved, suspicion and mutual mistrust grew between the Protector's circle and the leaders of the Army. During the course of March and April 1659 many of the officers became persuaded that the civilian and other more conservative Protectorians were forming a secret alliance with the 'Country' element in the House, preparatory to attacking their vital interests—the Army's strength and independence. Although the evidence is imperfect, they seem to have been partly tricked into this belief by the republicans both inside the Commons and outside. These were led by the loquacious, self-important Hesilrige, who made one three-hour speech providing a complete resumé of public events, as he saw them, since 1640!, the more workmanlike Thomas Scott, and the subtler if often increasingly obscure and apocalyptic Vane. The Army's suspicions culminated in the coup of 21 April when, under the threat of military action, the Protector was compelled to dissolve the Parliament.

The next two and a half weeks formed a kind of constitutional twilight, very different from the Oliverian take-over six years before. Some historians have supposed that Fleetwood and Disbrowe wanted to keep Richard, their brother-in-law and nephew by marriage respectively, in office and to manipulate him in their own way; but they seem to have had no idea how to go about this. And a strong current of opinion among the middle-ranking and junior officers—the source of which is unknown, but both Ludlow and Lambert were probably involved—persuaded the generals instead into restoring the Rump Parliament, that is the surviving MPs from April 1653. As a result of this, Richard Cromwell resigned and retired into private life, and the Protectorate was replaced by a restored Commonwealth; the Army in England was to be commanded by

Fleetwood, although it was probably taken for granted that a place would again be found for Lambert. On hearing the news, Henry Cromwell resigned his viceroyalty in Ireland and was shortly replaced by commissioners as in 1651–3, Ludlow again being prominent among them. Perhaps more surprisingly, Monck accepted the restored Long Parliament as the legal government and was therefore naturally confirmed as Commander-in-Chief in Scotland. As was soon to emerge, all this was but an appearance of strength and unity.

Contemporary verdicts on the Protectorate relate almost exclusively to Oliver, not Richard, Cromwell. For Clarendon, writing over ten years' later, he was 'a brave, bad man' whose 'greatness at home was but a shadow of the glory he had abroad'. Most modern historians and biographers have seized on the conflict between his conservative, traditionalist instincts and inclinations and his commitment to the Army and the Puritan sects. And it is often implied that the Protectorate was therefore inherently unstable and impermanent. This of course is said with the advantage of hindsight. If Cromwell had lived ten, or even five, years longer, if he had had a more adequate successor (both of which are logical possibilities), then it might all look very different. As to the quality of the regime, the Protectorate achieved more by way of limited, practical re-form than the Commonwealth had done; and the leadership was less self-indulgent. It was no more harsh than most other governments of its time. Revolutionary regimes which fail to gain *de jure* recognition are inherently more likely to be forced into taking repressive measures. But, as Clarendon tacitly conceded, Cromwell was not inhumane or bloodthirsty enough to pursue a policy of mass liquidation. And, in so far as unregenerate royalists were members of the traditional ruling class of peers and upper gentry, his object was to convert, or at least to conciliate, rather than to destroy them. Only convicted conspirators were executed. For the mass of the population, too, the Protectorate was certainly no worse than most other governments, arguably better than many. Its most damaging feature arose from excessive military and naval expenditure, although even in taxation there was some amelioration by comparison with the years 1642–53. A description of the Protectorate as a mere military dictatorship is inadequate; the rule of Oliver Cromwell was both more and less than that.

8
Decline and fall

The Commonwealth restored

The course of events from the death of Oliver Cromwell to the return of Charles II, a year and eight months later, seems to proceed with inexorability. Was the Restoration inevitable? It may be that some great events in human history are the result of a myriad of contingent, coincidental conjunctures as well as longer-term preconditions, as has been suggested in this book was the case with the upheavals of 1640–9. Yet it is not necessarily inconsistent to suggest that other major events can have more straightforward explanations. Those of 1659–60 obviously would not have occurred as they did without the whole pattern of preceding developments, from the defeat of Charles I in the Civil War, through his execution, the rule of the Rump Parliament, the transition to the Protectorate, and the succession of Richard to Oliver Cromwell. The republican collapse which led to the Restoration was not literally fratricidal; there was very little fighting and few killings. It was much more a process of moral and political failure and disintegration: an object lesson in what has been called the dissidence of dissent. Given the divisions and weaknesses among the Cromwellians and republicans, a Stuart restoration was probably unavoidable from September 1658. On the other hand, the precise time and manner of Charles II's return was by no means inevitable until much nearer to the event, arguably not before February–March 1660.

As we have seen, the events of 1653—first in April and then in December—had alienated many of Oliver Cromwell's one-time allies and supporters. This was very clear when the Rump reassembled under the Army's auspices in May 1659, and at once began behaving as if the intervening six years since its dismissal had been an illegal usurpation, for which all those who had participated in it would have to seek an official parliamentary pardon. It was soon made clear that the Parliament was going to take a very active and positive interest

Decline and fall

in the composition of the Army, at any rate the officer corps. A special joint committee of senior officers and MPs was appointed to grant commissions, really to sift and winnow their holders, although all recommendations then came to the floor of the House. Many of those who had been promoted by either Protector or brought in to replace republicans, at any time since 1653 but especially over the previous two years or so, were now in turned purged. Almost all those who had resigned on grounds of principle or had been dismissed, including Lambert but not Harrison, were now reinstated, and in some cases given more senior commands than before. At first the officers and politicians seem to have worked in harmony together, but the very fact of all regimental appointments having to gain parliamentary approval irked the military; and, even when the exercise had been more or less completed, it left an atmosphere of suspicion and resentment. In any case Fleetwood's authority as the new commander-in-chief did not extend to the armies in Scotland and Ireland; Monck in fact held the rank of full General and Fleetwood did not do so. No doubt an argument could be made for not having a single Lord or Captain-General for the whole army everywhere, over all the land forces of the Commonwealth; but again, in the circumstances of 1659 when the Rump owed its resurrection so completely to the Army's action and its continuance to their good will, even this kind of negative interference or downgrading was unwise.

In other ways the members of the restored Rump did seem to have learnt some lessons from 1649–53, in the priorities which they now gave to different types of business. Quite early on they voted to dissolve not later than 7 May 1660, giving themselves in effect exactly a calendar year to settle the affairs of the country and to find their own replacement. Less time was spent on private business in the interests of members and their friends than had been before; and a grand committee on a new representative soon commenced weekly meetings. But to judge from contemporary comment and such memoir material as bears on this, they were soon back in the familiar deadlock, how to have successive parliaments with anything approaching free elections and yet to prevent a monarchist come-back. There was also pressure for a new kind of upper house, a select senate, perhaps to give tacit recognition to the Army's special position.

A fresh wave of pamphleteering had begun even before the end of April, during the interval between the end of Richard's Parliament and the Rump's recall. Measured by the contents of Thomason's collection and copies surviving in other libraries, 1659 might be be called one of the vintage years for radical tracts, both in the sheer volume of output and the interest of their contents; nothing like it had been seen since the late 1640s. Besides Vane and Milton, who seem from somewhat different viewpoints to have favoured a select senate, the strongest arguments for a bicameral system reflecting the balance of different social classes, measured in terms of landownership, came from James Harrington and the so-called Harringtonians, of whom Henry Nevile (a late recruit to the Rump) had already figured actively in Richard's Parliament. There was even an incipient Leveller revival, but without any effective political focus; it is claimed that Agitators re-appeared in the Army, but the evidence seems slight and there was certainly nothing like the General Council of 1647. In a sense this radical recrudescence made it harder for the more conservative civil and military republicans to reach any kind of agreed settlement.

A royalist invasion, of which there was much talk, might paradoxically have pulled the regime together and been the saving of it, for a time at least. As it was, the pro-royalist Presbyterian rising of Sir George Booth in Cheshire was put down by Lambert with almost laughable ease, so much so that this helped to precipitate the next crisis. Lambert and the other officers in his force began petitioning for more senior military appointments and for the high command to have a freer hand, while the confidence born of apparent military supremacy made the Rump politicians all the more obstinate as well as suspicious. Between Lambert and Hesilrige there seems to have been a mutual mistrust almost as intense as that between John Pym and Charles I in 1641–2. Only along these lines can the apparent idiocy of what happened in October be explained in any rational way. It was not a simple civil–military split. When the Army redissolved the Rump after only just over five months, some units were ready to defend the Parliament and there was nearly a battle in Westminster and Whitehall. Moreover, after it had been done (the members were kept from entering the chamber rather than being turned out of it), some civilian politicians proved willing to co-operate and act with the Army. A committee of safety was appointed instead of a council of state and another new body to press on with constitution-making. Of this indeed there was a veritable orgy. But the most important development was Monck's refusal to accept this latest coup, news of which reached London quite quickly; it also became known that he was beginning to make threatening military preparations.

At this stage Monck's distinctiveness as a commander-in-chief was twofold. He was extremely thorough, indeed personally painstaking, in purging his own army in Scotland of all radical officers, be they inclined to Fifth-Monarchism, Quakerism, republicanism, or whatever; he even got rid of some potential trouble-makers in the ranks too. Was he merely following in Cromwell's footsteps? It has been suggested that known political opponents of the high command were deliberately chosen for service away from the centre earlier—in Ireland in 1647–9, in Scotland and Ireland again in the 1650s, in the West Indies from 1654 on, and finally in Flanders in 1657–8. In short, it is argued that, once they had got firm control of the Army, having forced out the Presbyterian and other more conservative officers in 1647, Cromwell and his allies embarked on a successive series of purges against those more radical than themselves. On the whole there seems to have been less of this than might be supposed; several ex-Agitators of 1647 rose to commissioned rank and some, unlike the colourful Sexby who eventually died in the Tower after planning Cromwell's assassination, were still in post at the end of the 1650s. There is no doubt that Monck was far more thorough and systematic about this than ever Cromwell was. His second characteristic was an apparently sincere belief that the military should always be subordinate to the legitimate civil government and should, so far as possible, keep out of politics. Attempts that have been made to portray him as a crypto-royalist all along have foundered from lack of evidence; indeed what there is points the other way. Even as late as the spring and summer of 1659 there is nothing to suggest it. Nor is it entirely sensible to call him a non-political general; whatever that may mean today, it was a contradiction in terms for the 1650s. A senior commander might be politically ineffective and could then retire like Fairfax in

1650; that was certainly not Monck's line, and he is better thought of as political but in a different way from the other Cromwellians and republicans of his time. His role in events was to be unique and decisive, also constructive in ultimately presiding over the Army's withdrawal from politics and then its peaceable disbandment after thirteen years of constant political activity.

The rule of the Army

The autumn of 1659 was the first occasion since April 1653 when the country had no legal civil government. There the similarity in the two situations ended. Whereas Cromwell had both commanded sufficient following and respect to enable the processes of government (tax collection, law enforcement, local administration, etc.) to continue, and had successfully set about giving his rule a civilian base in the Council of State and then the Nominated Parliament, his would-be successors had neither the political skill nor the moral authority to repeat this achievement. In other ways, too, the situation was unlike 1653, and if anything nearer to that of 1647–9. Some leading figures in the restored Rump and other civilian politicians—Vane, Salwey, the Scottish zealot Johnston of Warriston, even the archetypal trimmers St John and Whitelocke—went along with what had been done, and accepted positions under the interim regime or took part in its constitution-drafting procedures. Although Lambert was abler and more determined and decisive than Fleetwood, there is no evidence that he was scheming to be made commander-in-chief, let alone protector. That was part of the trouble: the Army had no single undisputed head and leader.

Once more the atmosphere seems to have been conducive to argument and speculation, rather than to practical compromise. As during the spring and summer, discussions about a new form of government, also the increasingly frigid negotiations with Monck in Scotland, were conducted against a background of intense radical pamphleteering and, in the famous Rota Club, of Harringtonian debates. The importance of this may well have been negative; none of the many schemes put forward had any real likelihood of gaining general acceptance, or enough support from those with the power to put them into practice. As in the early and again in the late 1640s, the threat of a possible popular upheaval, the apparent danger of social revolution, may well have pushed many members of the propertied classes in town and country back in a more conservative direction. This has recently been argued particularly in relation to the widespread Quaker activities, agitation, and even entry into public affairs, which is evident in 1659. Whether or not they actually did threaten the whole established order—ecclesiastical, political, and social—the Quakers were believed by many people to do so.[1]

But the crucial factor in the situation was the weakness of the Army leaders and of their few civilian allies. They could neither reach an acceptable compromise with Hesilrige and the majority of the civilian republicans, nor put themselves at the head of a popular radical reconstruction, nor destroy their opponents while they still had the upper hand. They were both too scrupulous and too inept to survive. As the autumn went on, Lambert prepared to lead a force north to confront Monck, or at least to prevent him from entering England, and by December when he had marched as far as Yorkshire there seemed a real prospect of renewed civil war. In his absence Lambert's colleagues lost their nerve. The fleet was now commanded by a Baptist professional seaman, John Lawson, the Cromwellian Edward Montague having been set aside earlier in 1659. The Navy came out for the Rump Parliament against the Army, and Portsmouth was recovered with its citadel and magazine, the Tower of London nearly so. Rather than take drastic military action—mass arrests, exemplary executions, etc.—Fleetwood and company allowed the Rump to reassemble for the second and, as it turned out, the last time in late December. When news of this débâcle reached the north, Lambert's army there, never adequately supplied or properly paid, rapidly began to disperse and had soon virtually disintegrated. Monck crossed the Tweed at Coldstream with his lifeguard to enter England, thus bypassing Berwick, and he was welcomed into Yorkshire a little later by none other than Lord Fairfax, now father-in-law to the disreputable but influential royalist Duke of Buckingham.

What followed showed the resilience of the English landed classes and urban élites. A tremendous campaign began through petitions, meetings and declarations in favour of a 'free parliament', by which was clearly meant one that would restore the King, although this of course was still not openly stated. While royalist agents no doubt played their part both on orders from the exiled court and on their own initiative, most of this activity was spontaneous, and reflected almost universal disillusionment with those who had been in power but had been failing to govern, since the death of Oliver or at least since the fall of his son. On his arrival in the south, Monck at first refused to accept these demands and began to co-operate with the Rump which sent plenipotentiaries to meet him on his way. As in the previous May, he appears to have accepted them as a genuine legal authority. At what stage this became a political gambit is again a matter for argument. The Parliament was still committed to dissolving itself by early May; but, as in 1652–3 and again in the summer of 1659, the question was what provision would the members of the Rump make for what kind of future parliament to succeed themselves? With a modicum of political skill they might still have dissolved themselves in favour of a parliament from which known monarchists were to be strictly excluded, and for all that we can tell Monck might have collaborated in enforcing this. But Hesilrige and his following displayed truly monumental ineptitude. Owing as they did so much to him, they fatally alienated Monck by forcing him into a confrontation with the growing anti-military feeling in London.

Opinion in the city had by now changed decisively. London as a whole had sustained the parliamentary cause steadfastly ever since the winter of 1641–2. Admittedly there had been support for the Presbyterian opposition to the Army in 1647, and the city had had to be coerced into accepting the revolutionary events of 1648–9. But there had never been any question of Londoners in general abandoning a broadly Puritan–parliamentarian standpoint; and active, articulate royalists had never been more than a small minority. By the end of 1659 many Londoners, including almost all those with influence in civil affairs, were so incensed with the cost and other excesses of military rule that they had been reconverted to royalism. There was at least one quite serious street battle between soldiers and apprentices. And many now wanted the King back, even at the cost of sacrificing parliamentary government and a Puritan church.

Monck and the Long Parliament

At this stage the thesis that Monck was a non-political general breaks down. Within about five weeks of his arrival in the capital he had evidently decided that the Rump was an incorrigible body with which to deal and compelled the sitting members to allow the re-entry of those secluded since Pride's Purge. Of course not all had survived from December 1648 and some were in exile or in prison, but enough were alive and available to alter the balance of power in the House immediately and decisively. Hesilrige and the republicans were now in a minority. A new Council of State was at once elected with a monarchist, though not yet openly pro-Stuart, majority. Monck was made Captain-General of all the land forces of the Commonwealth; Montague was restored to the fleet, he and Monck being made co-admirals and Lawson vice-admiral under them. The House of Commons put the county militias and the collection of taxes into the hands of those similarly inclined and prepared for its own legal demise. Writing in 1900, C. H. Firth saw Monck's greatest achievement not as the restoration of the monarchy, which he believed to have been inevitable by 1659–60, but its return without another civil war. But if one considers the commanding position which the parliamentarians and Puritans still occupied, their control of Church, State, local government, if not also the armed forces, as late as March 1660, it is perhaps equally remarkable that Charles II was to return almost unconditionally.

On some issues the men of 1646–8 now restored to political predominance could act in alliance with their old opponents, the survivors of the Commonwealth. When the Rump had been restored for a second time at the end of 1659, swift action had at once been taken against the leading figures in the usurping military regime of the preceding autumn. Vane and Salwey, Fleetwood, Disbrowe, and Lambert and some others were all banned from holding any office or from sitting in any parliament. With the return of the Secluded Members in late February and Monck's consequent appointment as commander-in-chief of all the armies, this was rapidly extended to become a general purge of known republicans from commissions in the Army (and to a lesser extent the Navy) and from posts in the civil administration. Pamphlets and printed petitions now began to be published calling openly for a royalist restoration, for the return of the King if not also of the bishops and the House of Lords. The latter's position was equivocal, since it had of course been after the removal of the Secluded Members that it had been abolished; and the Long Parliament remained unicameral to the end of its days, numbered as these now were, perhaps because any reassembled Lords would have been too openly royalist for this to be politic. Meanwhile Lambert was arrested and put in the Tower. Those now working for a return to monarchy, who included a majority of sitting MPs and councillors of state and the present commanders of the armed forces, were correct to regard him as their most dangerous enemy, indeed as the only person who might still stand in the way of their design.

Who else was there? Vane had now become a millenarian seeker, and seems to have had only a small, if devoted, personal following. Ludlow had returned from Ireland, where control had passed to Broghill and other openly professing monarchists; he too was isolated and lacked an effective power base. Quakers and Harringtonians posed no real threat to anybody. Hesilrige and the other civilian republicans had been partially discredited and wholly out-manoeuvred. Milton's defiant defence of republicanism, which he now believed must be based on an avowedly oligarchic constitution, was eloquent and courageous, but it evoked no response. Even the bravest and most high-principled had no body of armed men at their disposal, who might resist Monck. Lambert escaped from the Tower and did rally a small force of republican officers and soldiers behind him in the Midlands, declaring for the Good Old Cause and the preservation of the republic. When a strong detachment sent by Monck caught up with him, most of Lambert's officers and men fled or surrendered without fighting; he was retaken, and, after trial in 1662, was to remain a prisoner of state for the rest of his life. As during the previous winter when he had tried to oppose Monck's entry into England, even Lambert could no longer arouse sufficient enthusiasm and commitment among members of the Army, junior officers let alone ordinary soldiers, to fight and risk dying for the Good Old Cause. Indeed, so thorough had the process of purging been by this time that it would have been more a question of raising ex-officers and ex-soldiers, if they had had the weapons, horses, etc., necessary for such an undertaking. The English republic therefore expired through its own inanition and above all due to its adherents' conflicts and mutual distrust: a lesson for other would-be revolutionaries.

The Long Parliament had come to the end of its long life. As with any institution which remains in being for many years, not only did its composition change, so too did the relations between its individual members. Of those who had been most prominent and active, or most often referred to as leaders, back in 1640–2, death and political disqualification had already removed all but a few even before the rifts of 1647–8. Those who had sat continuously since November 1640 and were still figures of consequence included: among the more conservative parliamentarians, only Denzil Holles and John Glyn (or Glynne), Steward of Westminster, Recorder of London and later Chief Justice of Upper Bench; among those more in the centre, Sir Walter Erle from Dorset, Sir John Evelyn of Wiltshire, and the lawyers Oliver St John, Bulstrode Whitelocke, and John Wilde (or Wylde); and finally on the radical side Sir Arthur Hesilrige, the younger Sir Henry Vane, and Cromwell himself. By the time that we reach 1649–53, the list reduces itself to Cromwell, Hesilrige, and Vane, with St John, Whitelocke, and Wilde functioning mainly as judges. When the Long Parliament reassembled in 1659, it was these same men, less Cromwell. Correspondingly, some recruiter MPs, who had only entered the House during the mid- or later 1640s, had eclipsed most of the remaining original members: for example Thomas Scott, Thomas Chaloner, Richard Salwey, Henry Nevile. The only thoroughgoing republican of all those elected in 1640, Henry Marten, had been excluded by the House itself for his outspoken anti-monarchist views in the mid-1640s but returned to achieve prominence in the Rump.

There is one less tangible but important distinction to be drawn. That is, between those who were busy and useful in the House and on its committees but were not necessarily in the first rank politically, and those who spent less time on matters of parliamentary or administrative routine but carried more weight as national figures, Cromwell himself being the outstanding example. The intellectually most distinguished of all the members, the great historical and antiquarian scholar John

Selden (who died in 1654), had taken a very active part in the parliaments of the 1620s; indeed he was one of those imprisoned after the end of the disorderly 1629 session. He seems to have normally been heard with respect but, despite denouncing the King's commissions of array in 1642 as illegal and unconstitutional, he became increasingly conservative. He stood up for the privilege of universities, colleges, and schools, to be exempt from taxation, and opposed the theocratic tendencies in the Presbyterian Church programme of the 1640s; so much so that he was for a time referred to as the leading Erastian in the House, but this was an intellectual rather than a political label. And, in spite of his opposition to Presbyterianism, Selden was no friend to military intervention in politics; he was secluded in December 1648 and did not sit again.

It is tempting to say that the Long Parliament was more than the sum of its parts. Corporate bodies do often develop an ethos distinct from that of the individuals comprising them. But in this case we are talking about a parliament which changed its character and composition so much over the nineteen years of its existence as scarcely to be the same body except in a formal institutional sense. During the last few weeks of its life, among the original parliamentarian leaders, Denzil Holles returned to resume his earlier role, as did a few others in the second rank such as William Pierrepont and Sir William Waller. It might therefore seem that the moderate or Presbyterian party had triumphed over the radical or 'war-party' Independents, later republicans, typified by Hesilrige and Vane. But this is at most a half-truth, or rather a minor aspect of a wider, more general phenomenon. No one defeated the English republicans; they destroyed themselves.

The return of the King

In one sense the letter of the law was observed. The Long Parliament duly dissolved itself in mid-March 1660 as laid down in the Act of May 1641, though in the absence of king or Lords many had long ceased to regard it as a true parliament. The Council of State was entrusted with responsibility for overseeing the conduct of the elections which were to take place a few weeks later, for a new parliament to decide on the settlement of the country's affairs, though there could be little doubt what form such settlement would take. During this interval the text became known of the declaration which Charles II had issued from the Dutch town of Breda where he was now staying. Almost certainly drafted by Hyde, this paper, with appropriate covering letters to the various public bodies and authorities, put the whole onus of settlement on to the new parliament. It was to decide who should be excepted from the general pardon which the King now promised to extend to all his father's ex-enemies; how to provide religious liberty for tender consciences (thus ironically borrowing Cromwell's terminology of the 1640s); likewise to sort out the question of titles to lands which had been confiscated and sold; and not least to work out how the Army was to have its pay arrears settled and then to be demobilized. This was an astute document, even if everything did not work out exactly as the Declaration implied that it should after the King's return. We may take our story as ending when the new 'Convention' House of Commons, so-called because of the lack of royal writs of summons, declared that the government of the country was properly in the King, Lords, and Commons, and shortly after this invited the new, or rather restored, monarch to come and resume his rightful position. Not everything fell neatly into place; history is not like that.

The Convention Parliament was itself a deeply divided body, especially on religion. Its other measures could be called reasonably constructive, except for its deplorably vindictive pursuit of republicans and other radicals, besides the regicides who had signed the death warrant or approved the sentence on Charles I. Only with the next elections of early 1661 do we find in the so-called Cavalier Parliament an overwhelming episcopalian–Anglican as well as ultra-royalist majority in the House of Commons. The restored House of Lords had, understandably enough, at least a working majority in that direction from the start. To call Charles II's Government a coalition is perhaps anachronistic, but it was certainly a mixture. Edward Hyde, soon to be Earl of Clarendon, was Lord Chancellor and the recognized chief minister; and a majority both of councillors and of major office holders were ex-Cavaliers, but there was a significant ex-parliamentarian, even ex-Cromwellian element.

All the traditional methods and institutions of government came back, except those which had been removed or altered by

statute in 1641. Of the measures to which Charles I had given the
royal assent, only the act to remove the bishops from the House
of Lords and to disqualify all clergy from holding civil offices
was repealed. Of those passed as ordinances or later as acts
without the royal assent, the abolition of the Court of Wards
and Liveries and of the so-called feudal dues were re-enacted;
likewise the excise tax on drinks was granted to the King, half
for his reign and half in perpetuity, to make good the loss of
revenue; the Navigation Act of 1651 was actually extended to
cover exports, which were also to be carried only in English
ships. The forced union with Scotland was unscrambled, and
that country brought back under royal rule, soon also with a
restored Episcopalian Church. Ireland remained firmly under
English rule with the Protestant royalists among the Old and
New English effectively in control; the land settlement there
took far longer than the equivalent in England, and at the end
of it the massive transfer of property away from Gaelic Catholic
Irish to Protestant English, Scots, and Anglo-Irish was only
slightly modified and in no way reversed. In England and Wales
all confiscated lands were restored to the Church and the Crown
and to individual royalists, and the property of the regicides and
others who were attainted was in turn confiscated even if it had
not been so acquired. Private sales of land, in order to pay war
debts or composition fines, could only be reversed by private
acts of Parliament; this was done in the case of some peers and
other influential individuals, but was beyond the reach of the
ordinary rank and file Cavalier gentry and freeholders. This
gave an irredentist edge to the politics of the next generation, as
did the deplorably petty, revengeful attitude and behaviour of
the Anglican clergy towards the Puritan dissenters.

The Restoration and after

Some would see the underlying cause of the Restoration as the
ineradicable passion of the English people for monarchy and for
traditional ways in general. Enough has already been said here
about the impossibility of measuring or assessing public opinion
in the seventeenth century to suggest scepticism on that score. A
great many people turned out to cheer Charles II on his arrival
and then at his state entry into London, and this may tell us that
there was disillusionment with the Republic and with the Army,

perhaps with the Puritan churches and sects, but how widely and deeply such feelings went is a matter of guesswork. The Restoration can, however, be characterized as a successful reaction. If in some respects it seems like a return to the *status quo ante* of 1641, in others it was to bring an actual strengthening of the established order and of the traditional pillars of State, Church, and social hierarchy, with the removal of any serious radical threat from Puritans and republicans, let alone from Levellers or other species of revolutionary. Without disputing this, it is also necessary to try to distinguish the institutions which were restored and the policies which were then pursued from the underlying assumptions in people's minds which might in certain circumstances again lead them to take revolutionary action. This can clearly be seen in the reigns of both Charles and James II. Those who wished to exclude James from the succession on the grounds of his Catholicism in 1679–81, the first Whigs, were defeated in large part because people feared a return to 1641–2; William and Mary were installed as joint monarchs in place of James (and on definite conditions) in 1689, after the so-called Glorious Revolution of 1688, because people feared the equally terrifying opposite possibility—which would be as if Charles I had won the Civil War with Catholic Irish help.

Once again we must be careful in saying that people wanted this or that, felt something or other. Public opinion was no more measurable at the end of the century than at the beginning; it can only relate to those who, at a given time, had the means of expressing themselves, who participated in the political process as peers, MPs, voters, judges, jurors, magistrates, constables, churchwardens, clergymen, and so on. Publishing was again subject to censorship, this time in the royalist–Anglican interest, with brief intervals, from 1660 until the 1690s. So at most we are speaking of an articulate minority, mainly those with some share in government at whatever level, when we try to assess 'public opinion'. To set against the crowds who turned out to cheer Charles II, there had been huge crowds to see Strafford executed and to cheer Lilburne's two acquittals. There is contemporary evidence for the terrible groan which went up when Charles I was beheaded, and perhaps this does tell us something, if only negatively. Not enough of the English people would rally to Charles for him to defeat his enemies, but most of them were not revengeful towards him and still felt the primitive awe of monarchy. There was also something primitive, almost atavistic, about the exhumation of the dead, of Cromwell, Ireton, Bradshaw, and Pride, and the decapitation, quartering, and public exhibition of their corpses.[2] This was particularly repulsive when supported by men who had served under Cromwell or had been defeated by him but had profited from his clemency.

So much of what happened in England, not to say in the British Isles and beyond, during the years from 1645 or 1647 to 1658 is bound up with Oliver Cromwell that it is impossible to imagine what these years would have been like without him. An alternative leader might conceivably have emerged, for instance if either Hampden or Rainsborough had survived the wars and Cromwell had not. As it was, his qualities and limitations are inseparable from the history of the country and from the impact of England outside its own boundaries, in Ireland, Scotland, and the world beyond. The unresolved contradictions between his social conservatism and his reliance on radical military and religious support led almost unavoidably to the disasters which followed his death.

Rebellion and revolution

Without entering into a sterile argument about definitions, we must return to the title of this book. As has already been suggested, if a revolution is taken to entail a new, or radically different economic order and social structure, then mid-seventeenth-century England did not experience one. A rebellion, on the other hand, is normally taken to mean an armed uprising against an established order, without its necessarily being replaced by anything fundamentally new or different. And the political and religious changes which took place between 1640 and 1660 were surely too drastic and thoroughgoing to be adequately so described. Nor do rebellions usually have the traumatic effect on national consciousness which can fairly be ascribed to the Civil War and its aftermath. Despite the wide disagreement among historians as to the consequences of these events in subsequent English history and on the wider world scene, no one can doubt their massive and continuing psychological and emotional impact. On one narrow point of some topical interest today, it is not surprising that the House of Lords was abolished in 1649, granted its sorry decline since 1641. But in no way can the years that followed be said to provide a good advertisement for government by a single-chamber parliament. The very fact that there has not been a civil war in England since the mid-seventeenth century probably causes that conflict to loom larger in our historical conscious-ness than would otherwise be the case. In 1660 the traditional upper classes regained control of the country, and they were not to lose it again until the twentieth century and then so far without bloodshed. There had indeed been a 'great rebellion'. There had also, if only temporarily and partially, been a middle-class as well as a Puritan revolution

Notes

Introduction

1. There is even a 'genetic' interpretation. See C. D. Darlington, *The Evolution of Man and Society* (New York, 1969; paperback edn. London, 1971), pp. 493–4.

Chapter 1. Reform

1. It is not necessary to have read the whole of his correspondence in the FitzWilliam Manuscripts, deposited in the Sheffield City Library, to be persuaded that—whatever his defects of character—he was a man of very high ability. For a printed selection, see W. Knowler (ed.), *Letters and Dispatches of the Earle of Strafford . . .* (2 vols., London, 1739).
2. Including my own: see *The Struggle for the Constitution 1603–1689* (London, 1963; last edn. 1975; also published in the USA as *A Short History of Seventeenth-Century England*), p. 101.
3. See Edward Hyde, Earl of Clarendon, *The History of the Rebellion . . .* ed. W. D. Macray (6 vols, Oxford, 1888), Book III, section 3 (this judgement appears in the first draft of 1646–7 and in the revised one of 1668–73). About 320 of the original 550 or so MPs, elected in November 1640, had sat in April–May; at least another dozen who were elected or allowed to take their seats by June 1642 had also been in the Short Parliament (M. F. Keeler, *The Long Parliament, 1640–1641* (Philadelphia, 1954), p. 16; P. Hasler, for the History of Parliament Trust, typed list of all MPs, 1640–1660. I am extremely grateful to Mr Hasler and the Trust for making this List available to me).

Chapter 2. Rebellion

1. Curiously A. M. Everitt, *The Community of Kent and the Great Rebellion 1640–1660* (Leicester, 1966), which has justly been described as 'the seminal work on the county communities', does not discuss this possibility. On the Kentish gentry, see also the pioneering article by P. Laslett in *The Cambridge Historical Journal*, 9 (1948); P. Clark, *English Provincial Society from the Reformation to the Revolution* (Hassocks, 1977), and D. Hirst, 'The Defection of Sir Edward Dering, 1640–41', *Historical Journal*, 15 (1972).
2. Edward Hyde, Earl of Clarendon, *Life of Himself* (Oxford, folio

edn. 1759), p. 67; see article by C. C. Weston in *English Historical Review*, 75 (1960) for the interpretation which is questioned here.

3. The earliest work on this is B. S. Manning, 'Neutrals and Neutralism in the English Civil War', (Oxford D. Phil. thesis submitted 1955, deposited 1957). Professor Manning's published works do not reflect the substance or the originality of his thesis.

4. Of the twenty-three peers with gross rentals of over £6,600 per annum in 1641, only seven were parliamentarians (the Earls of Bedford, Clare, Manchester, Northumberland, Pembroke and Montgomery, Rutland, Salisbury): see L. Stone, *The Crisis of the Aristocracy 1558–1641* (Oxford, 1965), Appendix VIII, p. 761, correlated with C. H. Firth, *The House of Lords during the Civil War* (London, 1910). Since Bedford and Clare were side-changers, only five were consistent anti-royalists.

5. A. Fletcher, *The Outbreak of the English Civil War* (London, 1981), p. 407.

6. See C. Holmes, 'The County Community in Stuart Historiography', *Journal of British Studies*, 19 (1980). When published, Professor Holmes's Waynflete Lectures, delivered in Oxford during 1984, will deal much more thoroughly with the whole subject.

Chapter 3. War

1. If possible Professor J. H. Hexter's thesis, 'The Rise of the Independent party' (Harvard Ph.D. 1936) should be consulted, and I am grateful to him for having lent me a copy back in about 1969; a revised version of the earlier part appeared as *The Reign of King Pym* (Cambridge, Mass., 1941). Of the numerous more recent studies, David Underdown, *Pride's Purge* (Oxford, 1971) remains outstanding; see also his article, 'Party Management in the Recruiter Elections, 1645–1648', *English Historical Review*, 83 (1968).

2. See B. S. Manning, 'Parliament, "party" and "community" during the English Civil War, 1642–6', *Historical Studies*, 14 (1983), criticizing Hexter and others; for the other, more drastic reinterpretation, see M. Kishlansky, *The Rise of the New Model Army* (Cambridge, 1979), and his articles in *Past & Present*, 81 (1978), *The Journal of British Studies*, 20 (1981), *Historical Journal*, 22 (1979), *Journal of Modern History*, 49 (1977).

3. This is one of the few cases when the system of royal wardship actually worked, in changing someone's religion permanently, and did not just serve as a financial racket for the benefit of royal officials and middlemen.

4. I am grateful to Dr M. D. G. Wanklyn for pointing out, in an article in *Southern History*, 3 (1983), the inadequacy of what I had written

in my own textbook on the war at sea, though I must not make him responsible for what is said here.

5. Alas, these are now available for consultation only on microfilm (which is often hard to read) because over-use has become a threat to their physical survival.

6. Walker's first publication, *The Mystery of the Two Juntoes Presbyterian and Independent* (1648) was written from a kind of 'cross-bench' viewpoint and implied a conspiracy between the two groups of opposing leaders, but it was only a prologue to his virulently partisan *History of Independency*. For all those named here see the *Dictionary of National Biography* and various of the suggestions under Further Reading.

Chapter 4. Revolution

1. There has been some disagreement as to whether or not Cromwell was present. The official report to Parliament, written by Rushworth immediately after the event, only mentions Fairfax; nor does Fairfax's own letter to the Speaker of the House of Lords refer to Cromwell's presence. A royalist newsletter and later accounts by opponents of Cromwell would not in themselves carry enough weight to contradict this. After reporting favourably to the Commons on the state of the Army, Cromwell was thanked by the House for his part in the proceedings at the rendezvous (*Commons Journals*, V, 364, 19 Nov. 1647). Since the word 'rendezvous' is both singular and plural, this could refer to all three meetings collectively, or even to one other than that at Ware. However, a deposition submitted to Cromwell six years later by the one-time pro-Leveller officer John Reynolds, against a soldier from one of the regiments concerned, refers unambiguously to his having been at Ware (Public Record Office, State Papers Additional, SP46/97, fols. 71 et seq. I am extremely grateful to Dr D. P. Massarella of Chuo University, Tokyo, for allowing me to cite this reference).

2. The case is excellently argued by J. S. Morrill; see 'The Army Revolt of 1647' in *Britain and the Netherlands*, VI, *War and Society*, ed. A. C. Duke and C. A. Tamse (The Hague, 1977). See also his article in *Past & Present*, 56 (1972) and entries in Further Reading under Gentles and Kishlansky. The troops paid off seem to have been additional or 'supplementary' units put under Fairfax's command in 1647, and not from the New Model itself.

Chapter 5. The quality of life

1. I am grateful to Professor J. P. Kenyon for having first encouraged me to look at this excursus; it is currently being redated by Professor Austin Woolrych.

2. For the composition and chronology of Clarendon's *History*, see C. H. Firth, 'Clarendon's *History of the Rebellion*', *English Historical Review*, 91 (1904), and compare B. Bandinel (ed.), *The History of the Rebellion and Civil Wars in England* . . . (8 vols. Oxford, 1826), Vol. I, 'Advertisement', pp. i–vii, Preface to Vol. I of the first edn. (1702), pp. 1–32, and W. D. Macray (ed.), *The History of the Rebellion* . . . (6 vols. Oxford, 1888), Vol. I, pp. v–xiv. For a recent attack on Clarendon's accuracy, if not truthfulness, see R. Hutton, 'Clarendon's *History of the Rebellion*', *English Historical Review*, 97 (1982). Neither the original (incomplete) *History* written in 1646–8, nor the *Life* (first published separately in 1759 and republished in 1857) has ever been reissued in an adequate modern edition, though both are drawn upon in the composite editions of Bandinel and Macray. As historians walk past the Clarendon Building on their way into the Bodleian Library from Broad Street, the Earl's statue looks reproachfully down upon them. The Oxford University Press enjoys a perpetual copyright in his works; alas, it is his dreadfully difficult handwriting which is largely to blame for this otherwise shameful neglect.

3. Whitelocke's account of his embassy to Sweden in 1653–4 is a livelier work and in some ways of greater interest. See *The Memorials of the English Affairs* . . . (4 vols. Oxford, 1853), the least unsatisfactory edition; compare *A Journal of the Swedish Embassy* . . ., ed. L. Morton (2 vols. London, 1772); and ed. H. Reeve (2 vols. London, 1855). Dr Ruth Spalding, his latest biographer, is preparing a new edition of the *Memorials* based on a collation of all his auto-biographical remains.

4. See A. B. Worden (ed.), *A Voyce from the Watch Tower, part Five: 1660–1662*, Camden 4th Series, Vol. 21 (1978), Preface, pp. vii–x, Introduction, especially pp. 1–39, and compare C. H. Firth (ed.), *Memoirs of Edmund Ludlow* (2 vols. Oxford 1894), Vol. I, Editor's Introduction, pp. vii–lxix. Unfortunately the surviving manuscript of the *Memoirs*, which Ludlow called 'A Voyce from the Watch Tower' and which has been so skilfully edited by Dr Worden, only begins in 1659, so the extent of Toland's tampering before that can only be surmised.

5. C. Hill, *The Century of Revolution 1603–1714*, Nelson's New History of England (Edinburgh, 1961), pp. 184–5, 301; (rev. edn. paperback, Walton-on-Thames, 1980), pp. 158, 257–8.

6. M. Spufford, *Small Books and Pleasant Histories* (London, 1981); see the review by P. Clark in *English Historical Review*, 99 (1984), pp. 621–2, suggesting that chapbooks may have been less widespread before 1640.

7. The phrase is Sir John Summerson's. See his *Architecture in Britain*

1530–1830, Pelican History of Art (Harmondsworth, 1953), pp. 89–97.

8. E. A. Wrigley and R. S. Schofield, *The Population History of England 1541–1871* (Cambridge, 1981), especially pp. 4, 11, 19–20, 24–5, 27, 31–2, 83, 153, 232, 681.

9. The *Novum Organum*, Book II, Aphorism lii, does indeed suggest that a partial recovery or restoration may be possible; but this work was only available in Latin until the eighteenth century.

Chapter 6. The contradictions of the Commonwealth

1. David Underdown, *Pride's Purge* (Oxford, 1971), p. 220, and Appendix A, pp. 361–98, classifies all the members still eligible to sit on the eve of the Purge according to their fate then and subsequent attitude; his category of 'revolutionaries', i.e. those positively in favour of what happened from December to February, includes only 71. A. B. Worden, *The Rump Parliament* (Cambridge, 1975), Appendix A, pp. 387–94, classifies those who sat in the Rump at any time from 1648 to 1653 according to the estimated levels of their activity in the House, on its committees, etc.; his three top categories number 61, with a mere 35 appearing in both lists. The overlap between Worden's busiest Rumpers and Underdown's revolutionaries is, therefore, 49.3 and 57.4 per cent respectively.

2. C. V. Wedgwood, *The Trial of Charles I* (London, 1964), published in the USA as *A Coffin for King Charles*, p. 88.

3. I am grateful to Dr Paula Gregg, the biographer of Lilburne, for this suggestion. It can, however, only have been an afterthought, or they would not have needed to go as far north as the Thames crossings, where they turned in a westerly direction.

4. See W. C. Abbott, *The Writings and Speeches of Oliver Cromwell* (4 vols. Cambridge, Mass., 1937–47), vol. III, pp. 631–2, the case of Sir Andrew Aylmer of Donadea.

5. Confusingly known as St Johnston's in most of the contemporary sources.

6. The most striking exception was John Bradshaw, President of the High Court of Justice for the King's Trial, and then President of the Council, 1649–52.

7. Contrast A. B. Worden, 'The Bill for a New Representative: The Dissolution of the Long Parliament, April 1653', *English Historical Review*, 86 (1971) and *The Rump Parliament*, chs. 15–17, with A. Woolrych, *Commonwealth to Protectorate* (Oxford, 1982), chs. I–III.

8. Notably by Professor Woolrych in his *Commonwealth to Protectorate*, chs. VI–IX.

Chapter 7. Problems of the Protectorate

1. The evidence is less clear in Overton's case than in Wildman's; it is, of course, possible that both were acting as double agents, pretending to serve the Protectorate's interests but secretly still working for its overthrow.
2. It has recently been pointed out that Thurloe's staff was weak in cryptanalysts, many intercepted royalist letters apparently remaining undeciphered or undecoded; and from 1655 he may have had a royalist 'mole' on his own staff.
3. It is probably exaggerated in my own book, *The State's Servants* (London, 1973), pp. 48–9, but see pp. 312–14 for a more qualified view.
4. Contrast C. Hill, *The World Turned Upside Down* (London, 1972), ch. 10, and *The Experience of Defeat* (London, 1984), ch. 5, with the standard account in W. C. Braithwaite, *The Beginnings of Quakerism* (2nd edn. Cambridge, 1955). G. F. Nuttall, *James Nayler: a revaluation* (London, 1954), and H. Barbour, *The Quakers in Puritan England* (New Haven, 1964) represent more limited revisions of Braithwaite, independent of Hill's.
5. R. Syme, *The Roman Revolution* (Oxford, 1939).
6. M. Roberts, 'Cromwell and the Baltic', *English Historical Review*, 75 (1960), reprinted with additions in his *Essays in Swedish History* (London, 1967).
7. The phrase is the late Admiral Sir Herbert Richmond's; see his *The Navy as an Instrument of Policy, 1558–1727* (Cambridge, 1953).

Chapter 8. Decline and fall

1. See article by Barry Reay in *History*, 63 (1978), and his chapter in J. F. McGregor & B. Reay (eds.), *Radical Religion in the English Revolution* (Oxford, 1984).
2. There is some doubt whether the order took effect in Pride's case; he was not buried in Westminster Abbey. Of those who had been, twenty-one including Blake and Pym were ordered to be disinterred and reburied in a common grave outside the church; in one case this was not carried out (that of another Commonwealth admiral). Fourteen surviving regicides and other leading republicans were executed in 1660–2; only Vane was beheaded, rather than being hanged, drawn, and quartered.

Table of events

In the military column, d = drawn or indecisive battle; p = parliamentarian victory; r = royalist victory; d.p = draw in parliament's favour; d.r = draw in the King's favour.

Date	Political	Military
1640		
12 Jan.	Wentworth = Earl of Strafford	
19 Jan.	Strafford = Lord-Lieut. of Ireland	
3 Feb.	elder Sir Henry Vane = Sec. of State	
23 Mar.	Irish Parlt opens	
13 Apr.–15 May	Short Parlt	
May	Lambeth riot, two executions	
June	second session of Irish Parlt	
July–Sept.		second Bishops' War
24 Sept.–28 Oct.	Great Council of peers at York	skirmish at Newburn
2–26 Oct.	Ripon negotiations	
3 Nov.	opening of Long Parlt	
10 Nov.	Strafford's impeachment moved	
18 Dec.	Archbishop Laud impeached	
1641		
16 Feb.	Triennial Act	
23 Mar.	Strafford's trial opens	
Mar.–Apr.		first Army Plot
2 May	Orange marriage (William = Mary)	
3 May	The Protestation; Army Plot revealed	
9 May	death of Bedford	
10 May	Strafford Attainder Act; Act against Dissolution	
12 May	Strafford's execution	
May–June		second Army Plot
24 June	The Ten Propositions	
5 July	Act abolishing Star Chamber	
19 July	first proposal of a Militia Bill	
13 Aug.	King leaves for Scotland	
9 Sept.–20 Oct.	recess	
23 Oct.		Irish Rebellion breaks out
30 Oct.	second Army Plot revealed	

Date	Religious	Cultural	External
1639–48			Shah Jahan moves capital of Mughal Empire from Agra to Delhi:
1640		1st English edn. of Machiavelli's *Prince*, Francis	builds the Red Fort, Catalan and Portuguese
May	Southern Convocation votes taxes and passes new Canons	Bacon, *Of the advancement and proficiencie of learning*, IX Bookes. translated	revolts against Spain
Nov.	'Root and Branch' Petition	Thomason begins his collection	
1641		Censorship breaks down; Sir Robert Naunton's *Fragmenta Regalia*; [Gabriel Plattes] *Macaria*; Sir Richard Baker, *A Chronicle of the kings of England*	
July	Abolition of High Commission 'Root and Branch' bill introduced		
1 & 9 Sept.	Commons' and Lords' resolution on innovations		

Date	Political	Military

1641 (cont.)

Date	Political	Military
1 Nov.	news of Irish Rebellion reaches London	
4 Nov.	Impressment Bill (for soldiers to Ireland)	
22 Nov.	Grand Remonstrance passed	
25 Nov.	King re-enters London	
28 Nov.	idea of a Militia Bill reintroduced	
1 Dec.	Grand Remonstrance presented to the King	
7 Dec.	first Militia Bill moved	
15 Dec.	decision to print and publish Grand Remonstrance	
30 Dec.	impeachment of twelve bishops	

1642

Date	Political	Military
3 Jan.	impeachment of Lord Mandeville and five MPs	
4 Jan.(p.m.)	attempt to seize the Five Members	
10 Jan.	King leaves London	
Feb.	Militia Bill passes both Houses	
5 Mar.	Militia Ordinance	
23 Apr.		King denied entry to Hull
1 June	The Nineteen Propositions	
9 June	Ordinance for Money, Plate, and Horses	
11 June		King's Commissions of Array
18 June	King's Answer to Nineteen Propositions	
4 July	Committee of Safety appointed	
11 July		King again denied entry to Hull
12 July		Essex = Lord-General
15 July		first bloodshed at Manchester
22 Aug.		King raises his standard at Nottingham
23 Oct.		Battle of Edgehill (d)
12 Nov.		Brentford (r)
13 Nov.		Turnham Green (p)
Nov.	King sets up HQ in Oxford	

1643

Date	Political	Military
1 Feb.–14 Apr.	Oxford negotiations	
24 Feb.	Ordinance for 'weekly pay'	
27 Mar.	first Sequestration Ordinance	

Date	Religious	Cultural	External
1642		Dr Thomas Browne, *Religio Medici*; Sir	
13 Feb.	Bishops' exclusion and Clergy Disqualification Act	Edward Coke, *Second Part of the Institutes of the Laws of England*; Thomas Hobbes, *De Cive*; Thomas Fuller, *The holy state and the profane state*	death of Cardinal Richelieu; Cardinal Mazarin succeeds
2 July		Henry Parker, *Observations upon some of his Majesties late Answers*	
2 Sept.		closing of theatres	
22 Sept.	suspension of episcopacy		
1643			Swedish attack on Denmark
4 May			d. Louis XIII; Louis XIV, aged five

Date	Political	Military
1643 (cont.)		
Mar.–May	'Waller's Plot'	
24 June	d. John Hampden	
30 June		Adwalton Moor (r)
5 July		Lansdowne (r)
13 July		Roundway Down (r)
22 July	First Excise Ordinance	
26 July		fall of Bristol (r)
3 Aug.	Lords' peace resolutions	
7 Aug.	Commons reject same	
8–9 Aug.	women's peace riot	
16 Aug.	seven peers desert Parlt	
5–8 Sept.		relief of Gloucester (p)
15 Sept.	first Irish 'cessation'	
20 Sept.	d. Lord Falkland	first Newbury (d.p)
25 Sept.	alliance with Scots (Solemn League and Covenant taken in Commons)	
11 Oct.		Winceby (Cromwell's first victory)
8 Dec.	d. John Pym	
Dec.–Jan.	Sir Basil Brooke's Plot	
1644		
19 Jan.		Scots army enters England
22 Jan.	'Oxford Parlt' meets	
25 Jan.		Nantwich (p)
25 Jan.	Committee of Both Kingdoms	
29 Mar.		Cheriton (p)
11 Apr.		Selby (p)
16 May		Rupert enters Lancs.
22 May	renewal of Cttee of B.K.	
June		York besieged
29 June		Cropredy Bridge (r)
2 July		Marston Moor (p)
14 July	Queen leaves England	
16 July		surrender of York (p)
1 Sept.		Tippermuir (Montrose's first victory)
2 Sept.		Lostwithiel (r)
27 Oct.		second Newbury (d.r)
23 Nov.	'new modelling' first moved	
9 Dec.	'Self-Denial' first moved	

Date	Religious	Cultural	External
1643 (cont.)			
9 May			Rocroi (French defeat Spanish army)
24 May		Philip Hunton, *A Treatise of Monarchy*	
14 June		attempt to reimpose censorship	
1 July	Assembly of Divines opens		
1 Aug.		Milton's first divorce pamphlet	
20 Sept.	No one to hold a command under Parliament without taking the Covenant		
25 Sept.	Assembly takes Covenant		
1644			
19 Jan.		Coke, *Third* and *Fourth Institutes* [Richard Overton], *Mans Mortallitie* [William Walwyn], *The Compassionate Samaritan*	Revolution in China: Ming overthrown and beginning of Manchu dynasty
24 Mar.		[Henry Robinson], *Liberty of Conscience*	
15 July		[Roger Williams], *The Bloudy Tenent of Persecution*	
13 Sept.	'Tender Consciences' resolution in Commons		
24 Nov.		Milton, *Areopagitica*	

Date	Political	Military
1645		
10 Jan.	Execution of Archbishop Laud	
29 Jan.–22 Feb.	Uxbridge negotiations	
Feb.	King's commission to the Earl of Glamorgan	
17 Feb.	New Model Army Ordinance	
12 Mar.	further commission from the King to Glamorgan	
3 Apr.	Self-Denying Ordinance	Fairfax C-in-C of New Model
30 May		Leicester (r)
14 June		Naseby (p)
10 July		Langport (p)
23 July		Bridgwater (p)
15 Aug.		Kilsyth (Montrose's last victory)
25 Aug.	Glamorgan's treaty with Irish Confederates (second Irish 'cessation')	
10 Sept.		Bristol (p)
13 Sept.		Philiphaugh (defeat of Montrose)
24 Sept.		Rowton Heath (p)
20 Dec.	second Glamorgan Treaty	
1646		
24 Feb.	Court of Wards and Liveries abolished	
2 Mar.	Prince of Wales leaves for Scillies	
21 Mar.		Stow-on-the-Wold (p)
16 Apr.	Prince to Jersey	
27 Apr.–5 May	King flees to the Scots	
6 May		surrender of Newark (p)
5 June		Benburb (Irish victory over Ulster Scots)
13 July	Newcastle Propositions	surrender of Oxford

Date	Religious	Cultural	External
1645		Edmund Waller, *Poems*	Treaty of Brömsebro
4 Jan.	Ordinance for Directory of Worship	Gresham College group of scientists formed	
23 Apr.	Preaching ministers in the north to be maintained out of cathedral revenues		
2 May	first English translation of works by Jacob Boehme		
19 Aug.	first Ordinance for Presbyterian Church Government		
10 Oct.		John Lilburne, *England's Birthright Justified*	
Dec.		John Milton, *Poems*	
1646	Thomas Edwards, *Gangraena* (3 parts)		
14 Mar.	further Ordinance for Presbyterian Church Government	Thomas Browne, *Pseudodoxia Epidemica* (= 'Common & Popular Errors') Henry Vaughan, *Poems*	
9 June	Commons order enforcement of Presbyterian Ordinance	Richard Overton, *Remonstrance of Many Thousand Citizens*	
9 Oct.	abolition of episcopacy		

Date	Political	Military
1646 (cont.)		
1 Aug. 1646–12 May 1647	King's answers to the Propositions	
16 Sept.	d. Earl of Essex	
7 Oct.	Commons resolution to continue New Model for six months (only)	
1647	sale of bishops' lands	
30 Jan.	Scots hand over the King	Scottish army leaves England
16 Feb.	King arrives at Holmby House	
18–19 Feb.	Proposals in Parlt for reduction of the Army	
21 Mar.	Saffron Walden meeting of MPs and officers	
26 Mar.	*An Apologie of the souldiers*	
15 Apr.	parlty commissioners again at Saffron Walden	
16 Apr.	Ordinance for city militia committee	
28 Apr.	three Agitators at bar of House	
4 May	parlty authority given to city militia nominees	
7 May	third Saffron Walden meeting	
16 May	*The Declaration of the Army*	
18 May	vote to disband those not going to Ireland	
19 May	circular letter from the Agitators	
20 May	Commons' vote to burn Large Petition	
25–7 May	disbandment scheme passes both Houses	
31 May–1 June	failure to disband Fairfax's regmt	
June	secret meeting at Cromwell's house	
May–June	first and second Indemnity Ordinances	
3 June		Joyce arrives at Holmby
4 June	King moved to Newmarket; Cromwell joins Army there	
5 June	*The Solemn Engagement*	
11 June	Commons' resolutions for a rival army	
15 June	*The Declaration of the Army*	
16 June	Army's charge against the Eleven MPs	Army moves to Uxbridge
24–6 June	Houses give way; the Eleven withdraw	

Date	Religious	Cultural	External
1647		Thomas May, *History of the Parliament* . . . Jeremy Taylor, *Liberty of Prophesying* [William Petty], *The Advice of W. P. to Samuel Hartlib. For the Advancement of . . . Learning* further ordinance against theatres and plays	
31 Mar.		Ralph Cudworth, *A Sermon preached before the House of Commons*	

Date	Political	Military

1647 (cont.)

Date	Political	Military
June–July	King moved to Windsor	Army HQ moved to Reading
15 July	The Reading debates	
17 July	The 'Heads of Proposals' before the General Council	
18 July	Heads referred to a committee	
23 July	Heads submitted to the King	
26 July	the forcing of the Houses	
30 July	withdrawal of the Speakers and Independant minority	
1 Aug.	Heads of Proposals	
6–7 Aug.		Army enters London
8 Aug.		Dungan Hill (Michael Jones defeats the Confederates)
mid-Aug.	seven of the Eleven MPs abroad; one in prison, three in the country	
20 Aug.	ordinance nulling all votes passed 26 Jul.–6 Aug	
7 Sept.	Propositions submitted to the King at Hampton Court	
8 Sept.	two more of the Eleven in prison; seven peers impeached	
7,9,16 Sept.	discussions in General Council at Putney	
22 Sept.	Marten and Rainsborough move No Addresses motion in Commons; defeated	
25–28 Sept.	Independent take-over of City's government	
8 Oct.		Rainsborough first appointed Vice-Admiral
14 Oct.	further Army Council meeting	
15 Oct.	*The Case of the Army truely stated*, presented to Fairfax	
28 Oct.	the first *Agreement of the People*	
28 Oct.–1 Nov.	the Putney debates	
30 Oct., 2–6 Nov.	committee meetings	
8 Nov.		officers and Agitators ordered to their quarters
9, 11 Nov.	new committee of officers only	
11 Nov.	King's escape from Hampton Court	
13 Nov.	King arrives Isle of Wight	
15 Nov.		Corkbush Field 'mutiny'
8 Dec.	*Humble Representation* (of the Army to Parlt)	

Date	Religious	Cultural	External

1647 (cont.)

17 July   Richard Overton,
*An Appeale from
the degenerate
Representative
Body . . . to the
free people*

Date	Political	Military
1647 (cont.)		
14 Dec.	the Four Bills passed	
22 Dec.	Army's prayer meeting at Windsor; unity restored	
24 Dec.	Four Bills presented to the King	Rainsborough reapptd V-A
26 Dec.	the 'Engagement' signed (King and Scots)	
28 Dec.	King rejects the Four Bills; tries to escape and fails	
30 Dec.	[John Wildman], *Putney Projects*	Sir Arthur Hesilrige = Governor of Newcastle-upon-Tyne
1648		
3 Jan.	Vote of No Addresses; Cttee of B.K. becomes Derby House Committee	
17 Jan.	Lords accept No Addresses	
11 Feb.	Commons *Declaration* justifying same	
23 Mar.		Revolt in Pembrokeshire (beginning of Second Civil War)
21 Apr.	escape of Duke of York	
24 Apr.	meeting of Agitators at St Albans	riot at Norwich
29 Apr.	second Windsor prayer meeting	
1 May		Cromwell leaves for S. Wales
8 May		St Fagan's (p)
12 May		riot at Bury St. Edmunds
24 May	Commons resolve to reopen negotiations with the King	
21–6 May		rising in Kent
27 May		revolt of the fleet
1 June		Maidstone (p)
8 June		rising in Essex
13 June		royalists occupy Colchester
8 July		Hamilton invades England
10 July		St Neots (p)
11 July		surrender of Pembroke
17–19 Aug.		Preston and Warrington (p)
24 Aug.	repeal of No Addresses	
25 Aug.		Hamilton surrenders at Uttoxeter
27 Aug.		surrender of Colchester
11 Sept.	*Humble Petition* (of Levellers)	

Date	Religious	Cultural	External
1647 (cont.)			
1648		Francis Bacon, *Remains*	
19 Jan.	further Ordinance for Presbyterian Government	Robert Herrick, *Hesperides*	
31 Jan.		[Sir Robert Holborne], *Freeholder's Grand Inquest*	
		John Wilkins, *Mathematical Magick*	
		John Wilkins's scientific group founded in Oxford	
19 Apr.		Sir Robert Filmer, *Anarchy of a Mixed Monarchy*	
2 May	Blasphemy Ordinance		
17 June		Richard Hooker, *Of the Laws of Ecclesiastical Politie*, Books VI & VIII	
28 July		Anthony Ascham, *A Discourse: wherein is examined what is . . . lawfull during the confusions and revolutions of Government*	Fronde revolt breaks out in France

Date	Political	Military

1648 (cont.)

Date	Political	Military
18 Sept.	Newport negotiations begin	
4 Oct.		Cromwell and Lambert enter Edinburgh
7 Oct.		Cromwell leaves Scotland
29 Oct.	d. Thomas Rainsborough	
16 Nov.	*Remonstrance of the Army*	
20 Nov.	*Remonstrance* presented to Parlt	
27 Nov.	Newport commissioners leave the King	
30 Nov.	*Declaration of the Army*	
1 Dec.	King moved to Hurst Castle	
2 Dec.		Army re-enters London
4–5 Dec. (a.m.)	debate in Commons on removal of the King and on his replies; adjournment carried 144–93; King's replies a ground for proceeding carried 129–83	
5 Dec. (p.m.)	meeting of officers and some MPs	
6 Dec.(a.m.)	Pride's Purge	
6 Dec.(p.m.)	Cromwell arrives in London	
10 Dec.	*Foundations of Freedom* (= second Leveller Agreement)	
23 Dec.	King brought to Windsor	

1649

Date	Political	Military
1 Jan.	first ordinance for High Court of Justice passes Commons; rejected by Lords	
3 Jan.	second HCJ Ordinance thro Commons	
4 Jan.	Commons assume sole legislative power	
6 Jan.	HCJ set up by act of parlt	
15 Jan.	officers' *Agreement*	
20 Jan.	officers' *Agreement* presented to Parlt	
20–27 Jan.	trial of the King	
23 Jan.	Act of Classes in Scotland (Engagers purged)	
30 Jan.	King executed	
5 Feb.	Charles II conditionally proclaimed in Scotland	
6 Feb.	Commons resolve to abolish House of Lords	
7 Feb.	Commons resolve to abolish kingship	
8 Feb.	first printing of *Eikon Basilike*	

Date	Religious	Cultural	External
1648 (cont.)			
29 Aug.	final Ordinance for Presbyterian Government		
			Peace of Westphalia (end of Thirty Years War)
1649		Gerrard Winstanley, *New Law of Righteousness* Milton, *The Tenure of Kings and Magistrates*	
13 Feb.		Robert Sanderson, *A Resolution of conscience . . .* Lord Herbert of Cherbury, *Henry VIII* Descartes, *A Discourse of Method* (first English version) Richard Baxter, *The Saints Everlasting Rest*	

Date	Political	Military
1649 (cont.)		
10 Feb.–6 Mar.	HCJ for trial of Hamilton, Holland, and co.	
14–15 Feb.	first Council of State chosen	
22 Feb.	Charles II's commission to Montrose Engagement for Councillors of State	
9 Mar.	execution of Hamilton, Holland, and Capel	
17 & 19 Mar.	Acts abolishing kingship and House of Lords	
28 Mar.	arrest of Leveller leaders	
30 Mar.	Cromwell accepts command in Ireland	
1 Apr.	Diggers begin communal cultivation in Surrey	
	sales of Crown lands begun	
27 Apr.	execution of Agitator, Lockyer	
1 May	mutinies; third Leveller *Agreement*	
14–15 May		mutineers defeated at Burford
19 May	Act declaring England a free Commonwealth	
2 Aug.		Rathmines (Jones defeats Ormonde)
15 Aug.	Cromwell lands in Ireland	
11 Sept.		sack of Drogheda
11 Oct.		sack of Wexford
25–6 Oct.	Lilburne's first trial for treason	
1650		
2 Jan.	The Engagement Act	
Mar		Montrose lands in Orkneys
26 Mar.	third High Court of Justice set up	
27 Apr.		Carbisdale (Montrose defeated)
8 May	Marchmont Needham's *Case of the Commonwealth of England stated*	
21 May	Montrose executed	
26 May	Cromwell leaves Ireland; Ireton = Lord Deputy	
11 June	Treaty of Heligoland (Charles II and Scots)	
23 June	Charles II takes Covenants	
26 June		Fairfax resigns; Cromwell = Lord-General
Aug.		invasion of Scotland

Date	Religious	Cultural	External
1649 (cont.)			
		John Hall, *An humble motion to the Parliament, concerning the Advancement of Learning*	
		stricter censorship of the press	
14 Apr.		[William Walwyn], *A Manifestation*	
25 Apr.		[Francis Rous], *The lawfulness of obeying the present Government*	
21 June		Richard Lovelace, *Lucasta*	
Aug.		*Tyranipocrit* (? Rotterdam)	
27 Aug.		[? Anthony Ascham], *The Bounds and Bonds of Publique Obedience*	
30 Oct.		Nicholas Culpeper, *A Physicall Directory*	
1650			
10 Jan.		[? George Bate], *Elenchus Motuum nuperorum in Anglia* (Paris)	
21 Feb.		Hobbes, *Humane Nature . . .*	
22 Feb.	Act for Propagation of Gospel in Wales		
14 Mar.		Henry Hammond, *Of the Reasonableness of Christian Religion*	

Date	Political	Military

1650 (cont.)

Date	Political	Military
3 Sept.		Dunbar
25 Oct.	Legal Proceedings Act	
25 Nov.		destruction of Rupert's squadron by Blake in Mediterranean

1651

Date	Political	Military
1 Jan.	Charles II's coronation in Scotland	
2 Jan.	Scottish Act of Classes repealed	
15 July		English forces cross into Fife
16 July	first Act for sale of royalists' lands	
20 July		Inverkeithing
1 Aug.		Charles II starts for the south
2 Aug.		capture of Perth; Cromwell follows
22 Aug.	execution of Christopher Love	
28 Aug.	capture of Scottish Committee of Estates (and public records) at Alyth	
3 Sept.		Worcester
25 Sept.	vote to introduce a bill to set a term to present Parlt	
9 Oct.	Navigation Act	
14 Oct.	bill for new representative committed	

Date	Religious	Cultural	External
1650 (cont.)			
6 Apr.		Milton's reply to Salmasius	
10 May	Adultery Act		
22 May		Jeremy Taylor, *The Rule of Holy Living*	
		James Ussher, *Annales Veteris Testamenti* (*The Annals of the World*, Part 1)	
9 Aug.	Blasphemy Act		
27 Sept.	Amendment of Uniformity and Recusancy Acts		
1 Oct		Sir Anthony Weldon, *The Court & Character of King James*	
17 Oct.	'Remonstrance' of anti-Engager clergy in Scotland		
27 Oct.			d. William II of Holland
4 Nov.			b. William III
1651			
Jan.		John Cle(a)veland, *Poems*	
		William Davenant, *Gondibert*	
2 Feb.		[Sir Henry Wotton], *Reliquiae Wottonianae*	
7 Mar.		Francis Glisson, George Bate & A. Regemorter, *A Treatise of the Rickets*	
17 Mar.–20 June			Oliver St John's and Strickland's mission to the Netherlands
Apr.–May		Hobbes, *Leviathan*	
6 Aug.		William Lilly, *Monarchy or No Monarchy in England*	

Date	Political	Military
1651 (cont.)		
15 Oct.	execution of Earl of Derby	Commonwealth fleet reaches Barbados
16 Oct.	Charles II escapes to France	
27 Oct.		surrender of Limerick
7 Nov.	d. Henry Ireton	
14 Nov.	agreed (by 49–47) to set a term to present Parlt	
18 Nov.	resolved not to sit beyond 3 Nov. 1654	
26 Nov.	monthly rotation of chairmanship of Council and all committees	
1652		
Dec–Jan.	non-parliamentary committee on reform of law set up	
15–30 Jan.	proceedings against Lilburne (£7,000 fine + banishment)	
13 Feb.	first offer of incorporation to the Scots	
24 Feb.	Pardon and Oblivion Act	
12 Mar.	act for impresting seamen	
12 & 19 Mar.		Virginia and Maryland submit to Commonwealth
13 Apr.	second reading of Union Bill	
May-June		Rupert in the Caribbean
7 May	grand committee revived on bill for new representative	
19 May		first battle with Dutch in Channel (Blake vs. Tromp)
9 July	Charles Fleetwood = C-in-C Ireland	
2 Aug.	officers' petition	
12 Aug.	Settlement of Ireland Act	
13 Aug.	officers' petn presented to Parlt	
16 Aug.		battle off Plymouth (De Ruyter vs. Ayscue)
27 Aug.		English squadron defeated off Elba
28 Sept.		battle off Kentish Knock (Blake vs. de Witt)
18 Nov.	further confiscation and sale of lands bill introduced	
30 Nov.		Blake defeated by Tromp off Dungeness
6 Dec.	Admiralty and Navy Commissioners appointed	
17 Dec.	Sale Act passes	

Date	Religious	Cultural	External

1652

Date	Religious	Cultural	External
4 Feb.		Robert Burton, *Anatomy of Melancholy* (edn with author's last corrections)	Sexby's mission to the *Ormée* (or radical *Fronde*)
		Elias Ashmole, *Theatrum Chemicum Britannicum*	
10 Feb.	John Owen's and other congregnlist ministers' scheme submitted to Parlt		
20 Feb.		Gerrard Winstanley, *The Law of Freedom in a Platform*	
5 Sept.			French forces surrender Dunkirk to Spaniards
11 Oct.			Louis XIV re-enters Paris

Date	Political	Military
1652 (cont.)		
21 Dec.	France recognizes the Commonwealth	
1653		
6 Jan.	Harrison i/c bill for New Representative	
11 Feb.	Duke of Gloucester sent to France	
18–20 Feb.		battle from off Portland Bill to Beachy Head; Tromp defeated
14 Mar.		further English defeat in Mediterranean
20 Apr.	Cromwell dissolves the Rump (and the Council of State)	
22 Apr.	first *Declaratioin* of the officers	
29 Apr.	new Council of State	
2–4 June		battle off Gabbard (Deane killed, Dutch defeated)
8 June	writs sent out for nominated assembly	
15 June	Lilburne returns to London	
17 June	Dutch commissioners arrive	
4 July	opening of nominated assembly	
6 July	the Barebones declares itself a parliament	
13–16 July	Lilburne's second trial on capital charge	
15 July	immediate abolition of tithes defeated	
31 July		Monck defeats Dutch off the Texel (Tromp killed)
5 Aug.	vote to abolish Chancery	
19–20 Aug.	conclusion of Lilburne's trial	
20 Aug.	committee appointed to codify the law	
21 Aug.	Lilburne transferred to the Tower	
24 Aug.	Marriages and Civil Registration Act	
16 Sept.	Joyce (now Lieut-Col) cashiered	
26 Sept.	Satisfaction Act (on allotting Irish lands)	
1 Nov.	new Council of State elected	
17 Nov.	resolution to abolish advowsons	
21 Nov.	fourth High Court of Justice set up	
2 Dec.	report of committee on tithes	
10 Dec.	1st clause of report on Ejectors defeated	

Date	Religious	Cultural	External
1653		Henry Hammond, *A Paraphrase... upon . . . the New Testament* Arthur Wilson, *A History of Great Britain Being the Life & Reign of King James I*	
23 Jan.		Dr William Harvey, *Anatomical Exercises*	
27 Jan.		first work by George Fox and James Nayler	
8 Feb.		James Shirley, *Six new playes*	
20 May		Isaac Walton, *The Compleat Angler*	
20 May		Richard Brome, *Five New Playes*	
10 June		Francis Bacon, *The . . . history of winds*	
15 June		Sir Thomas Urquhart, translation of Francois Rabelais's works, Parts I and II	
20 July			surrender of Bordeaux (*Fronde* at an end)
Aug.–Sept.			discussions with Dutch on scheme to divide the world
29 Aug.		Nicholas Culpeper, *The English Physitian, enlarged*	
1653–4			Bulstrode Whitelocke's mission to Sweden

Date	Political	Military
1653 (cont.)		
12 Dec.	resignation by majority in Barebones; minority evicted	
15–16 Dec.	Instrument of Government accepted; Oliver Cromwell installed as Lord Protector	
21 Dec.	Major-General Harrison cashiered	
1654		
19 Jan.	Engagement repealed	
Jan.–Feb.	Sealed Knot first formed	
8 Feb.	[?M. Needham], *A True State of the Case of the Commonwealth*	
Mar.	Henry Cromwell's first mission to Ireland	
20 Mar.	Ordinance for Triers	
5 Apr.	Anglo-Dutch peace treaty	
12 Apr.	Ordinance for Union with Scotland	
19 Apr.	Treaty ratified by Lord Protector	
June		rising in the Highlands
July–Sept.		rising put down by Monck
10 July	Anglo-Portuguese treaty	
July–Aug.	Anglo-Spanish negotiations break down	
18 Aug.	Commissioners appointed for 'Western Design'	
21 Aug.	Chancery reform ordinance	
22 Aug.	Fleetwood = Lord Deputy of Ireland	
28 Aug.	Ordinance for Ejectors	
3–4 Sept.	opening of first Protectorate Parlt.; Protector's first speech	
12 Sept.	the 'Recognition' imposed	
18 Oct.	the three Colonels' petition	
13 Dec.	Commons vote to imprison John Biddle (Socinian)	
1655		
3 Jan.	Major-General Robert Overton arrested by Monck	
4–5 Jan.	Col. John Birch's report on public finances	
16 Jan.	Major-General Robert Overton in the Tower	
22 Jan.	Parlt dissolved	
29 Jan.		fleet arrives at Barbados
10 Feb.	arrest of John Wildman	
12 Feb.	arrest of Lord Grey of Groby	
16 Feb.	Harrison and other millenarians arrested	

Date	Religious	Cultural	External
1653 (cont.)			
31 Oct.		*Cabala, Mysteries of State*	
19 Dec.		John Webster, *Academiarum examen*	
1654		James Ussher, *Annales Novi Testamenti* (*Annals of the World*, Part 2)	final Dutch withdrawal from Brazil abdication of Queen Christina
20 Mar.	system of Triers to choose clergy		
24 Apr.			Exclusion Act (against House of Orange) passed in Holland
	Richard Baxter's first Voluntary Association		
26 May		S. Ward and J. Wilkins, *Vindiciae Academiarum*	
28 Aug.	system of Ejectors for removing clergy		
1655		Thomas Fuller, *Church History of Britain* William Dugdale (with Roger Dodsworth), *Monasticon Anglicanum*	

Date	Political	Military

1655 (cont.)

Date	Political	Military
12–16 Mar.		Penruddock's rising
14 Apr.-4 May		unsuccessful campaign in San Domingo
3 May	two judges dismissed	
12 May		landing in Jamaica
May-Nov.	royalist–Leveller negotiations	
28 May	Cony's case in Upper Bench	
6 June	resignation of Whitelocke and Sir Thomas Widdrington as commissioners of Great Seal	
7 June	C. J. Rolle resigns	
28 June–19 Dec.	government interference in Colchester corporation	
9 July	Henry Cromwell back to Ireland as Major-General and Councillor	
9 July	Edward Montague = co-Admiral with Blake	
9 Aug.	first ten Major-Generals named	
22 Aug.	first Instructions to Major-Generals	
Sept. 1655– Sept. 1656	Roger Boyle, Lord Broghill i/c civil government of Scotland	
6 Sept.	Fleetwood returns to England	
21 Sept.	commission to Major-Generals and county commissioners for securing the peace	
Oct.	Lilburne moved to Dover	
11 Oct.	revised commission of instructions to Major-Generals	
24 Oct.	Anglo-French treaty	
26 Oct.		war with Spain formally begins
1 Nov.	Richard Cromwell added to Trade Committee	
2 Nov.	Major-Generals begin work in localities	
25 Nov.	summary execution of Henry Manning, Thurloe's spy with royalists	
4–18 Dec.	discussions on readmission of the Jews	

Date	Religious	Cultural	External
1655 (cont.)			
26 Feb.	George Fox's first meeting with Cromwell		
31 May		Sir Richard Fanshaw, translation of Camoens, *Lusiad* Edmund Waller, *A Panegyrick to my Lord Protector*	
2 July		Sir Henry Vane, *Retired Man's Meditations*	

Date	Political	Military
1656		
5 Mar.	Protector's speech to aldermen and citizens of London	
22 Mar.	Harrison released	
2 Apr.	Spanish treaty with royalists	
26 June	elections announced; Wildman released	
10 July		successful attack on Malaga
29 July	Vane summoned before the Council	
1 Aug.	Ludlow and Bradshaw before the Council	
4 Sept.	Vane imprisoned on Isle of Wight	
9 Sept.		naval victory off Cadiz
17 Sept.	opening of second Protectorate Parlt	
22 Sept.	House accepts exclusion of opposition MPs	
6–16 Dec.	Debates on Nayler's case	
11 Dec.	Vane released	
25 Dec.	forthcoming militia bill and decimation tax bill announced	
1657		
7–29 Jan.	debates on militia and decimation bills	
8–9 Jan.	Sindercombe's Plot	
23 Feb.	The 'Remonstrance' presented to Parlt	
27 Feb.	The Protector's meeting with the officers	
13 Mar.	Anglo-French alliance	
31 Mar.	'The Humble Petition and Advice' presented to the Protector	
3 Apr.	Cromwell's first refusal of the Crown	
9 Apr.	abortive Fifth-Monarchist rising in London	
20 Apr.		Blake's victory at Santa Cruz (in the Canaries)
8 May	[Edward Sexby and Capt. Silas Titus], *Killing No Murder* (advocating Protector's assassination)	
9–16 May		English troops arrive in Flanders
25 May	Humble Petition accepted without kingship	

Date	Religious	Cultural	External
1656		William Dugdale, *The Antiquities of Warwickshire* John Bunyan's first published work William Drummond of Hawthornden, *Poems*	
12 May		Sir Henry Vane, *A Healing Question*	
18 July		Richard Baxter, *Gildas Salvianus; the Reformed Pastor*	
20 Sept.		William Davenant, *The Siege of Rhodes* (the first English opera)	
Nov.		James Harrington, *Oceana*	
1657		(Bishop) Brian Walton and others, *Biblia Sacra Polyglotta* Robert Sanderson, *Fourteen Sermons*	
May			Danes declare war on Sweden
4 May		Henry King, *Poems*	

Date	Political	Military

1657 (cont.)

26 June	Additional (or Supplementary) Humble Petn; Protector's second installation	
16 July	Lambert stripped of his commissions	
24 July	arrest of Sexby	
27 Aug.	d. Robert Blake	
30 Aug.	d. John Lilburne	
2 Oct.		English take over Mardyke
30 Oct.		Spanish counter-attack in Jamaica defeated
16 Nov.	Henry Cromwell = Lord Deputy of Ireland	

1658

13 Jan.	d. Edward Sexby (in the Tower)	
20 Jan.	Parlt reassembles	
4 Feb.	Parlt dissolved	
6 Feb.	Cromwell's speech to the officers	
11 Feb.	Major Packer and five captains cashiered	
28 Mar.	revised treaty with France	
27 Apr.	last High Court of Justice set up	
8 June	Sir Henry Slingsby and Dr John Hewitt executed	
14 June		Anglo-French victory over Spanish–royalist army in battle of the Dunes
24 June		final Spanish defeat in Jamaica
25 June		surrender of Dunkirk; English occupy it
7 & 9 July	last three royalists executed	
6 Aug.	d. Cromwell's daughter, Elizabeth Claypole	
21 Aug.	Cromwell's final illness	
3 Sept.	d. Oliver Cromwell, Richard proclaimed Lord Protector	
9 Nov.	Cromwell buried	
23 Nov.	Cromwell's funeral procession	
3 Dec.	decision to call a parliament	

Date	Religious	Cultural	External
1657 (cont.)			
3 Nov.			Swedish king (Charles X)'s victory in Jutland
1658 Jan.–Feb.		Sir Walter Ralegh, *The Cabinet Council* (ed. Milton) Francis Osborne, *Historical Memoires . . .*	further Swedish conquests in Denmark
27 Feb.			Treaty of Roeskilde (between Danes & Swedes)
May		Dr Thomas Browne, *Hydrotaphia, Urne Buriall*	
18 July		[Richard Allestree], *The Practice of Christian Graces, or The Whole Duty of Man*	Leopold I = Holy Roman Emperor (and ruler of Austrian Empire)
early or mid- Aug.	Cromwell's second (and last) meeting with George Fox		
14 Aug.			German Princes form League of the Rhine
15 Aug.			Charles X resumes war in Denmark
29 Sept.–12 Oct.	meetings of clergy at the Savoy; *Declaration*		

Date	Political	Military
1659		
27 Jan.	Parliament meets	
15 Feb.	pro-republican petition presented	
21 Feb.	foreign affairs debate	
1 Mar.	Charles II's commission to 'the Trust'	
28 Mar.	vote to transact business with the 'Other House'	
2 Apr.	Council of Officers recommences meeting	
6 Apr.	Officers' petition to the Protector	
18 Apr.	Commons vote against such meetings	
21 Apr.	last sitting of the Parlt	
22 Apr.	Richard forced to dissolve	
6–7 May	reassembly of the Rump	
12 May	Fleetwood = C-in-C; committee of seven to nominate officers to commissions, Army petition to House	
19 May	new Council of State	
6 June	vote to dissolve by 7 May 1660	
15 June	Henry Cromwell's resignation	
7 July	Commissioners appointed to govern Ireland; Ludlow = C-in-C	
12 July	Act of Pardon and Indemnity (for actions since 19 Apr. 1653)	
31 July		Sir George Booth's rising in Cheshire
2 Aug.		Booth occupies Chester
16 Aug.		Lambert defeats Booth at Northwich
21 Sept.	petition from the officers at Derby	
later Sept.– early Dec.	Monck remodels his army	
5 Oct.	further Army petition	
11 Oct.	Act against all grants since 19 Apr. 1653	
12 Oct.	nine officers' commissions revoked; committee of seven i/c of the Army	
13 Oct.	Rump's sittings again ended	
15 Oct.	Committee of Ten set up	

Date	Religious	Cultural	External
1659		John Rushworth, *Historical Collections* (Vol. I, from 1618 to 1629) Edmund Waller, John Dryden, Thomas Sprat, *Three Poems on the death of the Lord Protector*	
Jan.		Richard Brome, *Five New Playes*	
Feb.		Francis Osborne, *A Miscellany*	
Mar.–Apr.			English fleet sent to the Sound
1 May			Franco-Spanish truce
25 May			preliminary Treaty of the Pyrenees
13 July		John Hales, *Golden Remaines*	
July		Richard Baxter, *A Holy Commonwealth*	
24 Aug.			Montague brings fleet back from the Sound

246 Table of events

Date	Political	Military
1659 (cont.)		
25 Oct.	Council of State ceases to sit	
26 Oct.	Committee of Safety	
1 Nov.	constitutional committee appointed	
3 Nov.		Lambert leads large force north
23 Nov.		Lambert at Newcastle
3 Dec.		Portsmouth gained by Hesilrige and co.
5 Dec.	anti-Army riot in London	
8 Dec.		Monck at Coldstream
13 Dec.	fleet under Vice-Admiral Lawson declares for Rump	
13 Dec.	Irish army decides for the Rump	
13 Dec.	Army Council's Seven Fundamentals	
23 Dec.	Army Council's Ten Articles	
26 Dec.	Rump reassembles; new Council of State	
1660		
1 Jan.		Monck enters England
2 Jan.		Fairfax rendezvous on Marston Moor
2 Jan.	Army remodelled by Rump	
3 Feb.	Monck enters London	
9–11 Feb.	Monck forced to act against the City	
11–24 Feb.	Fleetwood again C-in-C; five army commissioners, not including Monck	
18 Feb.	Act passed for a new parlt.	
21 Feb.	readmission of the Secluded Members; new Council of State; Monck = C-in-C	
6 Mar.	Lambert in the Tower	
15–16 Mar.	Act for new elections; Long Parlt dissolves itself	
23 Mar.	Montague rejoins the Fleet (with Pepys as his secretary)	
Apr.	parliamentary elections	
4 Apr.	King's letters and Declaration from Breda	
10 Apr.	Lambert escapes from the Tower	
22 Apr.		Lambert defeated and recaptured in the Midlands
25 Apr.	opening of the Convention Parliament	
5 May	government of the country voted to be in King, Lords, and Commons	

Date	Religious	Cultural	External
1659 (cont.)			
28 Oct.			final Treaty of the Pyrenees
1660			
Nov. 1659– Feb. 1660		meetings of the Rota Club	
1 Jan. 1660		Samuel Pepys begins his diary	death of Charles X; Baltic War ends
Jan.		Richard Brome, *Five New Playes* John Ray, *Catalogus Plantarum*	
Mar.	steps to restore Presbyterian church government	Milton, *Readie & easy way to establish a free Commonwealth*	

Table of events

Date	Political	Military

1660 (cont.)

Date	Political	Military
7 May	pro-monarchist address to Monck from army in Ireland	
11 May	Parlt to send representative to the King	
14 May	King proclaimed in Dublin	
25 May	King lands in Kent	
29 May	King enters London	

Further Reading

Anything short of a full bibliography, unsuitable for this series, is bound to be so selective as to seem arbitrary in its choice of what is included. I have tried to provide a range of works written between the 1640s and the 1980s, representative of different viewpoints as well as covering different aspects of the subject. The place of publication is London unless otherwise indicated.

Primary and secondary sources

It is easy to say that historians should, wherever possible, rely on the testimony of contemporaries. Yet such evidence is often suspect and contradictory. One example may suffice. Sir Philip Warwick (1609–83) and Edward Hyde, later Earl of Clarendon (1609–74) were both royalists and MPs, sitting in the early years of the Long Parliament. Although Warwick was less senior in the King's councils than Hyde came to be, he was an official and presumably moved in well-informed circles; he was certainly no backwoodsman. Both wrote histories, so far as we know entirely independently of each other; neither's work was published until early in the next century, long after their respective deaths. Whereas Hyde describes John Hampden as a member of the inner core of the parliamentarian leadership and, in one passage, even suggests that his political importance was greater than John Pym's, he none the less portrays Pym as the key figure in the House of Commons, and the central figure in what he calls 'the factious party'. Warwick, by contrast, although he writes at some length about Hampden, scarcely mentions Pym. What are we to make of this: a sheer lapse of memory (he was writing the relevant section in exile during the 1650s), or a deliberate omission for whatever reason, or has Pym's importance been exaggerated partly thanks to Clarendon's pre-eminence among contemporary historians of the rebellion, as Sheila Lambert would appear to argue; see her article in *Historical Journal*, 27 (1984)?

I Bibliographies

Annual Bibliography of British and Irish History (Royal Historical Society, Brighton) for 1975 and after.
Annual Bulletin of Historical Literature (Historical Association).

G. E. Aylmer and J. S. Morrill (eds.), *The Civil War and Interregnum, Sources for Local Historians* (1979).

G. K. Fortescue (ed.), *Catalogue of the pamphlets* (etc.) . . . *collected by George Thomason, 1640–1661* (2 vols. 1908). Bibliographically faulty but entries are arranged by date.

M. F. Keeler (ed.), *Bibliography of British History: The Stuart Period, 1603–1714* (Oxford, for R.H.S. and Am. Hist. Assocn. 1970), supersedes G. Davies (1928). See Review by J. P. Cooper, in *Eng. Hist. Rev.*, 80 (1975).

J. S. Morrill, *Seventeenth-Century Britain 1603–1714* (Folkstone and Hamden, Conn. 1980).

II Works of reference, mainly biographical

The Complete Peerage (rev. edn V. Gibbs and others, 14 vols. 1910–59).

The Dictionary of National Biography (originally published 1885–1900; reprinted, Oxford, 22 vols. 1908–9; now available in *Compact Edition* 2-vol. microprint 1975). Many of the relevant lives are by C. H. Firth, a few by S. R. Gardiner.

C. H. Firth and G. Davies, *Regimental History of Cromwell's Army* (2 vols. Oxford 1940).

M. F. Keeler, *The Long Parliament: A Biographical Dictionary* (Philadelphia, 1954). See also Brunton and Pennington (VI below).

A. G. Matthews, *Calamy Revised* (Oxford, 1934), for Puritan clergy expelled 1660–2.

A. G. Matthews, *Walker Revised* (Oxford 1948), for Anglican clergy expelled in the 1640s and 1650s.

P. R. Newman, *Royalist Officers in England and Wales: A Biographical Dictionary* (New York, 1981).

III Sources (modern collections and reasonably accessible editions of older works)

W. C. Abbott, *Writings and Speeches of Oliver Cromwell* (4 vols. Cambridge, Mass., 1937–47). Supersedes Carlyle, but scarce to obtain; also a biography.

G. E. Aylmer (ed.), *The Levellers in the English Revolution* (1975).

Richard Baxter, *Autobiography* (shortened text, ed. N. H. Keeble, Everyman Library, 1974).

Slingsby Bethel, *The World's Mistake in Oliver Cromwell* (1668; reprint by The Rota, Exeter, 1972), a republican critique of Cromwell's foreign policy.

Thomas Burton, *Diary* . . . (ed. J. T. Rutt, 4 vols. 1828; repr. New York, ed. I. Roots, 1974), covers the parliaments of 1654–9 though that for 1654–5 is not by Burton.

Thomas Carlyle, *Letters and Speeches of Oliver Cromwell* (2 vols. 1845;

best edn by S. C. Lomas, 3 vols. 1904), out of print but many copies
around; see Abbott above.

Clarendon, Edward Hyde, Earl of, *History of the Rebellion* (ed. W. D.
Macray, 6 vols. Oxford, 1888, but in print); several other edns.

——*Selections* (ed. G. Huehns, Oxford World's Classics series), now
out of print.

John Evelyn, *Diary* (ed. E. S. de Beer, 6 vols. Oxford, 1955); older edn
has additional royal correspondence.

A. M. Everitt (ed.), *Suffolk and the Great Rebellion 1640–1660*
(Suffolk Rec. Soc., III, 1960). See also Cambridgeshire (VIII below).

The Fast Sermons of the Long Parliament, ed. R. Jeffs, (The English
Revolution, I, reprints, 34 vols. 1970–1).

Robert Filmer, *Patriarcha* (etc.) (ed. P. Laslett, Oxford, 1949).

C. H. Firth and R. S. Rait (eds.), *Acts and Ordinances of the
Interregnum* (3 vols. 1911); these are not in other edns of Statutes.

S. R. Gardiner (ed.), *Constitutional Documents of the Puritan
Revolution 1625–1660* (3rd. rev. edn Oxford, 1906; repr. 1980), large
overlap with Kenyon, which does not quite supersede it.

W. Haller (ed.), *Tracts on Liberty 1638–47* (3 vols. New York, 1934,
repr. 1965).

W. Haller and G. Davies (eds.), *The Leveller Tracts 1647–53* (New
York, 1944): see Wolfe below.

Political Works of James Harrington, ed. J. G. A. Pocock (Cambridge,
1977).

C. Hill (ed.), *Winstanley's Law of Freedom* (etc.) (Pelican, 1973;
Cambridge, 1983). See also Sabine below.

C. Hill and E. Dell (eds.), *The Good Old Cause* (1949; repr. 1969).

Thomas Hobbes, *Leviathan* (ed. C. B. Macpherson, Pelican, 1968 and
reprints); many other edns but most are out of print.

Lucy Hutchinson, *Memoirs of the Life of Colonel John Hutchinson*
(best edn J. Sutherland, Oxford 1973).

D. A. Johnson and D. G. Vaisey (eds.), *Staffordshire and the Great
Rebellion* (Staffs. C.C. 1964 or 5).

Ralph Josselin, *Diary 1618–1683* (complete text ed. A. Macfarlane,
Oxford, 1976).

J. P. Kenyon (ed.), *The Stuart Constitution 1603–1688* (Cambridge,
1966; new edn forthcoming). See Gardiner above.

W. Lamont and S. Oldfield (eds.), *Politics, Religion and Literature in
the 17th century* (1975).

Edmund Ludlow, *Memoirs . . .* (2 vols. ed. C. H. Firth, Oxford, 1894).

——*A Voyce from the Watch Tower* (ed. A. B. Worden, Camden, 4th
ser. XXI, 1978). See Chap. 5, n. 4 above.

Andrew Marvell, *Poems* (any reputable edn).

Mercurius Politicus 1650–1659, ed. P. Thomas (English Revolution reprints, Newsbooks 5, 19 vols. 1971–2).

John Milton, *Complete English Poems* (Oxford World's Classics edn, or others if available more easily).

——*Selected Prose* (ed. C. A. Patrides, Penguin, 1974); other one-volume selections in Everyman and World's Classics series.

Sir John Oglander, *A Royalist's Notebook* (ed. F. Bamford, 1936).

The Oxford Book of Seventeenth-Century Verse, eds. H. Grierson and G. Bullough (Oxford, 1934); many other anthologies and edited collections of verse are obtainable; this is the most comprehensive.

Oxford Royalist, ed. P. Thomas (English Revolution reprint, Newsbooks 1, 4 vols. 1971).

D. H. Pennington and I. Roots (eds.), *The Committee at Stafford 1643–1645* (Staffs. Rec. Soc., 4th ser. I, Manchester, 1957).

Samuel Pepys, The Diary of (eds. R. Latham and W. Matthews, 11 vols. 1970–83).

G. H. Sabine (ed.), *The Works of Gerrard Winstanley* (Ithaca, New York, 1941). See Hill above.

A. Sharp (ed.), *Political Ideas of the English Civil Wars 1641–1649* (1983).

J. Thirsk and J. P. Cooper (eds.), *Seventeenth-Century Economic Documents* (Oxford, 1970).

D. M. Wolfe (ed.), *Leveller Manifestoes* (New York, 1944; repr. 1967), some overlap with Haller and Davies above.

A. S. P. Woodhouse (ed.), *Puritanism and Liberty* . . . (1938; 2nd edn. 1974), the most accessible full text of the Putney and Whitehall debates.

IV   Classic narrative histories

S. R. Gardiner, *History of England* . . . *1603–1642* (10 vols. 1883–4).

——*History of the Great Civil War, 1642–9* (3 vols. 1886–91, or 4 vols. 1893).

——*History of the Commonwealth and Protectorate* [1649–56] (3 vols. 1894–1901; 4 vols. 1903).

C. H. Firth, *Last Years of the Protectorate, 1656–8* (2 vols. 1909).

G. Davies, *The Restoration of Charles II* [1658–60], (San Marino, Cal. 1955).

V   General histories and introductory surveys (priority given to those believed to be in print)

R. Ashton, *The English Civil War: Conservatism and Revolution 1603–1649* (1978).

T. C. Barnard, *The English Republic 1649–1660* (Longman's Seminar Series 1982).

D. C. Coleman, *The Economy of England 1450–1750* (Oxford, 1977).

B. Coward, *The Stuart Age 1603–1714* (Longman's History of England, 1980).

C. Cross, *Church and People 1450–1660* (Fontana History of England, 1976).

C. Hill, *The Century of Revolution 1603–1714* (Nelson's History of England, Edinburgh, 1961; rev. edn paperback, Walton-on-Thames, 1980).

D. Hirst, *Authority and Conflict 1603–58* (Arnold's New History of England, 1985).

J. R. Jones, *Country and Court 1658–1714* (Arnold's New History of England, 1978).

D. M. Loades, *Politics and the Nation 1450–1660* (Fontana History of England, 1974).

I. Roots, *The Great Rebellion 1642–1660* (1966; repr. edn 1979), in fact covers 1629–1660.

C. Russell, *The Crisis of Parliaments . . . 1509–1660* (Oxford, 1971).

Alan G. R. Smith, *The Emergence of a Nation State, 1529–1660* (Longman's Foundation of Modern Britain Series, 1984).

J. Thirsk, *The Restoration* (Longman's Seminar Series, 1976).

C. V. Wedgwood, *The King's Peace, 1637–41* (1955).

——*The King's War, 1641–7* (1958).

C. H. Wilson, *England's Apprenticeship, 1603–1763* (Longman's Economic and Social History of England, 1965).

A. Woolrych, *England without a King 1649–1660* (Lancaster Seminar Series, 1983).

K. Wrightson, *English Society 1580–1680* (Hutchinson's Social History of England, 1982).

VI Other secondary works (published in this century)

M. Ashley, *Financial and Commercial Policy under the Cromwellian Protectorate* (Oxford, 1934, repr. London, 1962).

——*The Greatness of Oliver Cromwell* (London and New York, 1957).

——*General Monck* (1977).

R. Ashton, *The Crown and the Money Market 1603–42* (Oxford, 1960).

——*The City and the Court, 1603–43* (Cambridge, 1979).

T. Aston (ed.), *Crisis in Europe, 1560–1660* (1965).

G. E. Aylmer, *The King's Servants . . . 1625–42* (1961; rev. edn 1974).

——(ed.), *The Interregnum . . . 1646–1660* (1972; rev. edn paperback, 1974).

——*The State's Servants . . . 1649–1660* (1973).

T. C. Barnard, *Cromwellian Policy in Ireland, English Government and Reform 1649–1660* (Oxford, 1975).

R. S. Bosher, *The Making of the Restoration Settlement: the Influence of the Laudians, 1649–62* (1951).

J. Bossy, *The English Catholic Community 1570–1850* (1975).

K. S. Bottigheimer, *English Money and Irish Land: The 'Adventurers' in the Cromwellian Settlement of Ireland* (Oxford, 1971).

H. N. Brailsford, *The Levellers and the English Revolution* (1961).

D. Brunton and D. H. Pennington, *Members of the Long Parliament* (1954). See also Keeler (II above).

D. Bush, *English Literature in the Earlier Seventeenth Century* (Oxford History of English Literature, rev. edn 1962); in fact covers 1603–60.

J. Cannon, *Parliamentary Reform 1640–1832* (Cambridge, 1973).

B. Capp, *The Fifth Monarchy Men* (1972).

——*Astrology and the Popular Press* (1979).

P. Clark and P. A. Slack (eds.), *Crisis and Order in English Towns 1500–1700* (1972).

J. T. Cliffe, *The Puritan Gentry* (1984).

J. P. Cooper, 'The Fall of the Stuart Monarchy', Ch. xviii in *The New Cambridge Modern History*, vol. IV, *1609–48/59*, ed. J. P. Cooper (Cambridge 1970); also other chapters for European and general background.

P. Crawford, *Denzil Holles 1598–1680* (1979).

F. D. Dow, *Cromwellian Scotland 1651–1660* (1979).

A. Everitt, *The Local Community and the Great Rebellion* (Historical Association booklet, G.70, 1966), concerned mainly with Leics and Northants; see also section VIII.

C. H. Firth, *Oliver Cromwell and the Rule of the Puritans in England* (1901 and many later edns, including the World's Classics).

——*Cromwell's Army* . . . (1902; 3rd edn 1921, and later reprints).

F. J. Fisher (ed.), *Essays in the Economic and Social History of Tudor and Stuart England: presented to R. H. Tawney* (Cambridge, 1961).

A. Fletcher, *The Outbreak of the English Civil War* (1981), covers 1641–2 in great detail.

J. Frank, *The Levellers* . . . (Cambridge, Mass., 1955; repr. New York, 1969).

——*The Beginnings of the English Newspaper 1620–1660* (Cambridge, Mass., 1961).

I. Gentles, arts. on land sales and the army in *Econ. Hist. Rev.*, 2nd ser. 26 (1973); *Agric. Hist. Rev. 19 (1971)*; *Hist. Jnl.* 26 (1983).

P. Gregg, *Freeborn John* (1961); Life of Lilburne.

H. J. Habakkuk, arts. on public finance and land sales in *Econ. Hist.*

Rev. 2nd ser. 15 (1962), 18 (1965); *Trans. Roy. Hist. Soc.*, 5th ser. 28 (1978), and *Welsh Hist. Rev.*, 3 (1967).

A. R. Hall, *The Scientific Revolution 1500–1800* (1954 and 1962).

W. Haller, *The Rise of Puritanism 1570–1643* (New York, 1938).

——*Liberty and Reformation in the Puritan Revolution* (New York, 1955), covers 1638–49; weighted towards Milton and the Levellers.

P. Hardacre, *The Royalists During the Puritan Revolution* (The Hague, 1956).

J. H. Hexter, *The Reign of King Pym* (Cambridge, Mass., 1941), mainly 1640–3.

——*Re-appraisals in History* (1961).

C. Hill, *Economic Problems of the Church from Archbishop Whitgift to the Long Parliament.* (Oxford, 1956).

——*Puritanism and Revolution* (1958 and later reprints), collected essays and articles.

——*Society and Puritanism in Pre-Revolutionary England* (1964).

——*Intellectual Origins of the English Revolution* (Oxford, 1965).

——*God's Englishman: Oliver Cromwell and the English Revolution* (1970).

——*Antichrist in Seventeenth-century England* (Oxford, 1971).

——*The World Turned Upside Down* (1972).

——*Change and Continuity in Seventeenth-century England* (1974), more collected essays and articles.

——*Milton and the English Revolution* (1977).

——*The Experience of Defeat: Milton and Some Contemporaries* (1984).

D. Hirst, *The Representative of the People? Voters and Voting in England under the Early Stuarts* (Cambridge, 1975).

W. G. Hoskins, *Provincial England* (1963).

E. W. Ives (ed.), *The English Revolution 1600–1660* (1968).

M. James, *Social Problems and Policy during the Puritan Revolution: 1640–1660* (1930); and 'The Political Importance of the Tithes Controversy', *Hist.*, 26 (1941–2).

W. J. Jones, *Politics and the Bench: The Judges and the Origins of the English Civil War* (1971).

W. K. Jordan, *The Development of Religious Toleration in England* (4 vols. 1932–40; repr. Gloucester, Mass. 1965); vols. 3 and 4 cover 1640–60.

——*Philanthropy in England 1480–1660* (1959), and other volumes on particular regions.

M. Judson, *The Crisis of the Constitution . . . 1603–1645* (New Brunswick, N. J., 1949).

——*From Tradition to Political Reality . . . 1649–1653* (Hamden, Conn., 1980).

256 Further reading

256 Further reading

256 Further reading

256 Further reading

256 Further reading

256 Further reading

256 Further reading

256 Further reading

256 Further reading

M. A. Kishlansky, *The Rise of the New Model Army* (Cambridge, 1979), and arts. in *Past & Present*, 81 (1978), *Histl. Jnl.*, 22 (1979), *Jnl. of Brit. Studs.*, 20 (1981), *Jnl. of Mod. Hist.*, 49 (1977).

W. Lamont, *Marginal Prynne 1600–1669* (1963).

——*Godly Rule . . . 1603–60* (1969), on millenarian ideas.

——*Richard Baxter and the Millenium* (1979).

K. Lindley, *Fenland Riots and the English Revolution* (1982).

H. Lloyd–Jones, V. Pearl, and A. B. Worden (eds.), *History and Imagination: Essays in honour of H. R. Trevor-Roper* (1981), chs. by S. Katz, V. Pearl, K. M. Sharpe, A. B. Worden, and others.

A. Macfarlane, *Witchcraft in Tudor and Stuart England . . .* (1970), based on a close study of particular Essex villages.

J. F. McGregor and B. Reay (eds.), *Radical Religion in the English Revolution* (Oxford, 1984), chs. by the editors, G. E. Aylmer, B. Capp, C. Hill, and B. Manning.

C. B. Macpherson, *The Political Theory of Possessive Individualism* (Oxford, 1962).

——*Democratic Theory* (Oxford, 1973); collected papers, some replying to criticisms of the previous work.

B. S. Manning (ed.), *Politics, Religion and the English Civil War* (1973); chs. by the editor, J. C. Davis, S. Higgins, and K. Lindley.

——*The English People and the English Revolution 1640–1649* (1976).

O. Millar and M. Whinney, *The Oxford History of English Art 1625–1714* (Oxford, 1957).

T. W. Moody and others (eds.), *A New History of Ireland*, Vol. III, *1534–1692* (Oxford, 1976), esp. chs. IX–XIV.

J. S. Morrill, *The Revolt of the Provinces . . . 1630–1650* (1976; rev. edn. 1980).

——(ed.), *Reactions to the English Civil War 1642–1649* (1982).

A. L. Morton, *The World of the Ranters* (1970).

G. F. Nuttall, *Visible Saints: the Congregational Way 1640–1660* (Oxford, 1957).

R. H. Parry (ed.), *The English Civil War and After 1642–1658* (1970).

C. A. Patrides and R. B. Waddington (eds.), *The Age of Milton* (Manchester and Totowa, N.J., 1980).

R. S. Paul, *The Lord Protector* (1955).

V. Pearl, *London and the Outbreak of the Puritan Revolution 1625–43* (Oxford, 1961).

D. H. Pennington and K. Thomas (eds.), *Puritans and Revolutionaries* (Oxford, 1978), chs. by the editors, A. M. Johnson, B. Manning, V. Pearl, I. Roots, D. Underdown, and others.

J. G. A. Pocock, *The Ancient Constitution and the Feudal Law* (Cambridge, 1957).

Further reading 257

——*Three British Revolutions: 1641, 1688, 1776* (Princeton, 1980), chs. by G. E. Aylmer, C. Hill, and L. Stone.

Barry Reay, *The Quakers and the English Revolution* (1985) and 'Quaker Opposition to Tithes', *P & P*, 86 (1980).

R. C. Richardson, *The Debate on the English Revolution* (1977).

I. Roots (ed.), *Cromwell: a profile* (1973).

——*Into Another Mould: Aspects of the Interregnum* (Exeter, 1981).

I. Roy, arts. in *War & Society* (eds. M. Bond and I. Roy) I (1977); *Bull. Inst. Histl. Res.*, 35 (1962), *Trans. Roy. Hist. Soc.*, 5th ser., 28 (1978).

C. Russell (ed.), *The Origins of the English Civil War* (1973).

W. A. Shaw, *History of the English Church during the Civil Wars and the Commonwealth* (2 vols. 1900).

W. Schenk, *The Concern for Social Justice in the Puritan Revolution* (1948).

J. A. Sharpe, *Crime in Seventeenth-Century England: A County Study* (Cambridge, 1983); also on Essex.

V. Snow, *Essex the Rebel* (Lincoln, Neb. 1971).

L. F. Solt, *Saints in Arms* (Stanford, Cal., 1959).

M. Spufford, *Contrasting Communities* (Cambridge, 1974); on the people of three Cambridgeshire villages.

D. Stevenson, *The Scottish Revolution 1637–44* (Newton Abbot, 1973).

——*Revolution and Counter-Revolution in Scotland, 1644–1651* (1977).

L. Stone, *The Crisis of the Aristocracy 1558–1641* (Oxford, 1965).

——(ed.), *Social Change and Revolution 1540–1640* (1965).

——(ed.) *The Causes of the English Revolution 1529–1642* (1972).

J. Summerson, *History of Architecture in Britain, 1500–1830* (Pelican History of Art, Harmondsworth, 1953).

J. Thirsk (ed.), *Agrarian History of England and Wales*, Vol. IV, *1500–1640* (Cambridge, 1967) and Vol. V *1640–1750* (Cambridge, 1985) and arts. on land sales in *Econ. HR*, 2nd ser., 5 (1951–2) and *Jnl. Mod. Hist.*, 26 (1954).

K. Thomas, *Religion and the Decline of Magic* (1971; paperback edns Harmondsworth, 1973 and later) and ch. in K. C. Brown (ed.), *Hobbes Studies* (1965).

H. R. Trevor-Roper, *Archbishop Laud 1573–1645* (1640; 2nd edn 1962).

——*Religion, the Reformation and Social Change* (1967; 2nd edn 1972).

D. E. Underdown, *Royalist Conspiracy in England 1649–1660* (New Haven, Conn. 1960), and 'The Chalk and the Cheese: contrasts among the English Clubmen'. *P & P*, 85 (1979).

——*Pride's Purge* (Oxford, 1971).

D. Veall, *The Popular Movement for Law Reform 1640–1660* (Oxford, 1970).

E. K. Waterhouse, *History of Painting in Britain, 1500–1800* (Pelican History of Art, Harmondsworth, 1953).

C. Webster (ed.), *The Intellectual Revolution of the Seventeenth Century* (1974).

——*The Great Instauration: Science, Medicine and Reform 1626–1660* (1975).

C. V. Wedgwood, *Thomas Wentworth, First Earl of Strafford: A Revaluation* (1961).

——*The Trial of Charles I* (1964).

M. Whinney, *The History of Sculpture in Britain, 1530–1830* (Pelican History of Art., Harmondsworth, 1964).

A. Woolrych, *Penruddock's Rising 1655* (Histl. Assoc. Booklet G.29, 1955).

——*Commonwealth to Protectorate* (Oxford, 1982).

A. B. Worden, *The Rump Parliament* (Cambridge, 1975).

K. Wrightson and D. Levine, *Poverty and Piety in an English Village: Terling Essex 1525–1700* (1979).

P. Zagorin, *A History of Political Thought in the English Revolution* (1945; repr. New York, 1966).

——*The Court and the Country: The Beginning of the English Revolution* (1969); covers mainly 1629–42.

VII Military and naval

M. Ashley, *The English Civil War: a Concise History* (1974).

A. H. Burne and P. Young, *The Great Civil War* (1959), o.p. but still arguably the best one-volume military study.

R. Hutton, *The Royalist War Effort, 1942–6* (1982).

P. R. Newman, *Marston Moor: 2 July 1644: the sources and the site* (Borthwick Papers, No. 53, York, 1978), revises all previous accounts.

——*The Battle of Marston Moor* (Chichester, 1981).

——*Atlas of the English Civil War* (New York, 1985).

J. R. Powell, *The Navy in the English Civil War* (London and Hamden, Conn., 1962).

P. Wenham, *The Great and Close Siege of York 1644* (Kineton, 1970).

A. H. Woolrych, *Battles of the English Civil War* (1961), mainly on Marston Moor, Naseby, and Preston.

P. Young, *Edgehill* (Kineton, 1967).

——*Marston Moor (Kineton, 1970).*

P. Young and R. Holmes, *The English Civil War: A Military History 1642–51* (1974), updating of Burne and Young above: more comprehensive, less incisive.

VIII Regional, county, and city studies (alphabetical by county)

Cambridgeshire: C. Holmes, *The Eastern Association in the English*

Civil War (Cambridge, 1974); F. J. Varley, *Cambridge during the Civil War* (Cambridge, 1935); see also Spufford (VI above).

Cheshire: J. S. Morrill, *Cheshire 1630–1660* (Oxford, 1974); A. M. Johnson, essay in Pennington and Thomas (VI above); R. N. Dore, *The Civil Wars in Cheshire* (Chester, 1968).

Cornwall: M. Coate, *Cornwall in the Great Civil War and Interregnum* (Oxford, 1933; repr. Truro, 1963).

Devon: E. A. Andriette, *Devon and Exeter in the Civil War* (Newton Abbot, 1971); W. B. Stephens, *Seventeenth-Century Exeter* (1958).

Durham: M. James, *Family, Lineage and Civil Society: . . . the Durham Region 1500–1640* (Oxford, 1974).

Essex: see Cambridgeshire above, also Macfarlane, Sharpe, and Wrightson and Levine (VI above). W. Hunt, *The Puritan Moment: The Coming of Revolution in an English County* (Cambridge, Mass. 1983).

Gloucester: art. by P. Clark in P. Clark, A. G. R. Smith, and N. Tyacke (eds.), *The English Commonwealth 1547–1660: Essays presented to J. Hurstfield* (Leicester, 1979).

Huntingdonshire: see Cambridgeshire above.

Kent: A. M. Everitt, *The Community of Kent and the Great Rebellion* (Leicester, 1966); also P. Clark, *English Provincial Society . . . 1500–1640* (Hassocks, Sussex, 1977).

Lancashire: E. Broxap, *Civil War in Lancashire* (Manchester, 1910; repr. 1973); B. G. Blackwood, *The Lancashire Gentry and the Great Rebellion 1640–1660* (Manchester, 1978).

Leicestershire: see Everitt (VI above).

Lincolnshire: C. Holmes, *Seventeenth-Century Lincolnshire* (Lincoln, 1980); see also Cambridgeshire above.

London: See Pearl (VI above), and her chs. in Aylmer (ed.), Lloyd-Jones etc., and Pennington and Thomas (VI above); also arts. by V. Pearl and others in *The Guildhall Review* (1952–73), *Studies in London History* (1973–81) and *The London Journal* (1975–).

Norfolk: see Cambridgeshire above; also R. W. Ketton-Cremer, *Norfolk in the Civil War* (1969); J. T. Evans, *Seventeenth-Century Norwich* (Oxford, 1979).

Northamptonshire: see Everitt (VI above).

Northumberland: R. Howell, *Newcastle-upon-Tyne and the Puritan Revolution* (Oxford, 1967).

Nottinghamshire: A. C. Wood, *Nottinghamshire in the Civil Wars* (Oxford, 1934).

Oxfordshire: F. J. Varley *The Siege of Oxford: Oxford during the Civil War, 1642–1646* (Oxford, 1932).

Somerset: T. G. Barnes, *Somerset 1625–40* (1961); D. Underdown, *Somerset in the Civil War and Interregnum* (Newton Abbot, 1973).

Staffordshire: see Johnson and Vaisey and Pennington and Roots (III above).

Suffolk: see Everitt (III above) and Cambridgeshire above.

Sussex: A. Fletcher, *A County Community in Peace and War: Sussex 1600–1660* (1976).

Warwickshire: Ann Hughes, arts. in *Trans. Roy. Hist. Soc.*, 5th ser. 31 (1981), and *Midland History*, 7 (1982), and *Warwickshire . . . 1640–1660* (forthcoming); P. Styles, *Studies in 17th-century West Midland History* (Kineton, 1978).

Wiltshire: see relevant chapters in Vol. V, pp. 106–10, 132–54 of the *Victoria County History of Wiltshire*.

Worcestershire: see Styles (Warwickshire above).

Yorkshire: J. T. Cliffe, *The Yorkshire Gentry from the Reformation to the Civil War* (1969); chs. in *VCH* of *Yorks*, vols. on Hull and York.

Wales: A. H. Dodd, *Studies in Stuart Wales* (Cardiff, 1952); D. Jenkins, *The Making of a Ruling Class: the Glamorganshire Gentry 1640–1780* (Cambridge, 1983); H. Lloyd, *The Gentry of S. W. Wales, 1540–1640* (1978); J. F. Rees, *Studies in Welsh History* (Cardiff, 1947; repr. 1965); G. Williams (ed.), *Glamorgan County History*, vol. 4, *1536–1770* (1974).

IX Additional articles (with reference nos. from Morrill (I above)

X28 Brenner, *P & P* 58 (1973)
 29 Brewster and Howell, ibid. 46 (1970)
 36 Clifton, ibid, 52 (1971)
 40 Cotterell, *EHR* 83 (1968)
 41 Cotton, *Hist.* 61 (1977)
 42 Crawford, *JBS* 16 (1977)
 47 Davis, *P & P* 70 (1976)
 56 Farnell, *EHR* 82 (1967)
 58 ——*JMH*, 49 (1977)
 64 Foster, *Am. Jnl. Legal Hist.* 21 (1977)
105 Kennedy, *EHR* 77 (1962)
117 Mahony, *HJ* 22 (1979)
138 Pearl, *EHR* 81 (1966)
139 ——*TRHS* 5th ser., 18 (1968)
163 Schwoerer, *JBS* 11 (1971)
167 Snow, *EHR* 74 (1959)
174 Taft, *HLQ* 42 (1979)
180 Underdown, *EHR* 83 (1968)
208 Skinner, *HJ* 8 (1965)
209 ——*HJ* 9 (1966)
292 Vann, *P & P* 43 (1969)
293 White, *Jnl. Ecclesl. Hist.* 17 (1966)

317 Farnell, *EcHR*, 2nd ser., 16 (1963–4)
335 Hoskins, *Agric. Hist. Rev.* 16 (1968)
349 Beier, *P & P* 35 (1966)
367 Everitt, *P & P* 33 (1966)
369 Herlin, *JBS* 18 (1979)
382 Slack, *EcHR* 2nd ser., 27 (1974)
385 Smith, *P & P* 61 (1973)
389 Stone, *P & P* 33 (1966)
393 Thirsk, *Hist* 84 (1969)
402 Wrigley, *P & P* 37 (1967)
410 Forster, *Northern Hist.* 12 (1976)
455 Beckett, *Histl. Studs.* 2 (1959)
461 Lowe, *Irish Histl. Studs.* 14 (1964–5)
464 Percivall-Maxwell, *IHS* 21 (1978)

Index

Fleetwood, Charles, 81, 143, 156, 169, 174, 178, 183–4, 188–9, 191, 194–5, 197
Flintshire, 175
forests, 150
Forth, Patrick Lord Ruthven, Earl of, 47
Four Bills, the, 90
Fowey, 59
Fox, George, 138, 176–7
Foxe, John, 109
France, the French, 6, 105, 148, 150, 167, 175, 183, 186
freeholders, see yeomen
Fuller, Thomas, 105

Galway, county, 38
Gangraena, 66
Gauden John, 140
General Council of the Army, 82–5, 87–9, 95
Geneva, 63
gentry, 41, 66, 117, 156, 189, 202; see also landed classes
George II, 121
Glasgow, 76
Glorious Revolution, the, 203
Gloucester, 50, 52, 83
Gloucestershire, 49–50
Glyn John, 199
Goddard, Jonathan, 184
'Good Old Cause', the, 106, 108, 130, 198
Gordons, 9, 91
Goodwin, John, 67, 141, 179
Goodwin, Thomas, 179
Goring, Sir George, 31, 58, 62, 75
government, the Government, see Commonwealth; Court; Crown; Parliament, Long; Protectorate; State
grand committees, 29, 155, 160, 191
Grand Remonstrance, the, 29–30, 32, 37, 53
Great Council of Peers, 14–15, 39
Great Seal, and Commissioners of, 70, 172
Grenvilles, 51, 62
Grey of Groby, Lord, 99

Habsburgs, the, 186

Hale, Matthew, 153
Hamilton, James, Marquis of, 10, 86, 91, 94, 100, 132, 145
Hammond, Henry, 65
Hampden, John, 13, 19, 33, 39, 48. 52, 63, 106, 184, 204
Hampshire, 49, 52
Hampton Court, 86, 88, 150
Hampton Proposals, 86
Harley, Sir Robert, 111
Harrington, James, and the Harringtonians, 103–4, 192, 194, 198
Harrison, Thomas, 69, 81, 92, 94, 97, 153, 155–6, 159–61, 182, 185, 191
Hartlib, Samuel, 124
harvests, 116, 151
Harvey, William, 107, 128
Hatfield House, 111
Heads of the Proposals, 84–6, 90, 95–6, 133, 140, 155, 164
Henrietta Maria, Queen, 4, 5, 16, 30, 61–2, 69, 76, 78, 93, 105, 141
Henry VIII, 3, 24, 45, 110, 125, 150, 164
Henry, Prince of of Wales, 102; Duke of Gloucester, 163
Hereford, 76
Herefordshire, 110
Herrick, Robert, 108
Hesilrige, Sir Arthur, 33, 73, 98, 148–9, 153, 156, 158, 162, 188, 192, 195–200
Heylyn, Peter, 105
High Church, 3–4, 105
High Commission, Court of, 4; Act against, 18
High Courts of Justice, 98, 100, 135, 185
Highlands and Islands of Scotland, Highlanders, 9, 59, 76, 91, 169
history, writing of, 104–7
Hobbes, Thomas, 103, 120–1, 141
Holborne, Sir Robert, 13
Holland, 45, 63, 151, 166
Holland, Henry Rich, Earl of, 93, 100
Holles, Denzil, 33, 55–6, 80, 82–4, 94, 99, 106, 199–200
Hooke, Robert, 129

Index

270

Naseby, 75, 78, 132, 145
Navigation Act, 151, 202
navy, fleet, naval power, naval war,
37, 61–2, 93, 114, 151, 166, 168,
172, 180–1, 183, 187, 195, 197
Nayler, James, 176–7
Neile, Richard, 4, 102
Netherlands, the, 150, 162, 166, 186
neutrals, neutralism, neutralists, 36,
42–4, 71, 93, 169, 185, 188
Nevile, Henry, 158, 192, 199
New Model, 72–4, 184; see also
Army
Newark, 52
Newbury, 52, 59, 72–3, 78, 132
Newcastle-upon-Tyne, 14, 62, 153
Newcastle, William Cavendish, Earl
(then Marquis, later Duke) of, 51,
57–8, 62
Newcastle Propositions, 79–80, 85,
90, 94, 96
Newport (Isle of Wight), 94–7
newsbooks, 65, 124
Newton, Isaac, 129
Nineteen Propositions, 35–6, 79
No Addresses, vote of, 90, 94, 96
nobility, nobles, see peers
Norfolk, 43
North Council in, 4, 18–19;
propagation of Gospel in, 153
Northamptonshire, 137
Northern Earls, 45
Northumberland, Algernon Percy,
Earl of, 33, 142
Norwich, 45
Nottingham, 47
Nottinghamshire, 49
Nye, Philip, 179

O'Donnell family, 23–4
office-holders, officials, offices, 6,
42, 73, 78, 117, 121–2, 129, 175
O'Neill, Hugh, Earl of Tyrone, 23;
family, 24
Onslow, Sir Richard, 175
Orange, House of, 151, 166; see also
William III
Ordinances, 22, 64, 70, 72, 74, 121,
164–5, 180, 202; see also High
Court; Indemnity; Militia;
Self-Denying

Ormonde, James Butler, Earl (then
Marquis, later Duke) of, 24, 60,
143
Osborne, Dorothy, 158
Other House, the, 180–2, 187
Overton, Richard, 67, 87, 109,
136–7, 142, 171
Owen, John, 179, 184
Oxford, 49, 52–6, 65, 77–9, 83, 110,
112, 129, 137, 179

painting, 112
Palatine, Elector, 33
pamphlets, pamphleteers,
pamphleteering, 65–6, 109, 192,
194, 197–8
Papacy, the, 162
Papists, see Catholics
Pardon Act, 149, 174; pardon, offer
of, 201
Parliament, the two Houses,
parliaments, parliamentay reform,
3–7, 12–13, 43, 82–5, 87–8, 99,
154–7, 166, 169, 180
Parliament: the Barebones (1653),
159–64, 171, 194; the
Cavalier (1661–79), 201; the
Convention (1660), 201; Irish,
25–6; Long (1640–8 and 1660),
15–22, 27–37, 42–3, 48–56, 59,
61–3, 65–6, 69–72, 74, 78–84, 86,
90, 94–6, 99, 101, 104, 110,
113–14, 117, 121–2, 132–3, 150–1,
197–200; the Nominated,
see Barebones
Parliaments: of 1620s, 3, 53, 200; of
1624, 8; of 1626, 39; first
Protectorate (1654–5), 168–70,
172, 182; second Protectorate
(1656–8), 121, 175–82, 188;
Richard Cromwell's (1659), 187–8;
the Rump (1648–53 and 1659–60),
98, 100–1, 112, 135, 147–9, 152,
154–8, 160–2, 164–5, 170–1, 177,
182, 188–92, 194–7, 199; lost
constitutional bill of, 155–7, 164;
Scottish, 8, 11; the Short (1640),
12–14, 17, 101
parliamentarians, 34–6, 38, 40–4, 63,
66, 69, 76–8, 99, 103–4, 109, 114,

123, 127, 129, 131, 134, 142, 169, 196–7, 201
parties, party, 54–6, 63, 74, 80
peers, peerage, nobles, nobility, lords, 14, 21–2, 35–7, 39, 41, 56, 66, 69, 86, 113, 117, 143, 153, 165, 175, 189, 202–3; life peers, 181–2
Pembroke and Montgomery, Philip Herbert, Earl of, 38, 111, 142
Pennines, the, 57
Penruddock, Colonel John, 171, 173
Pepys, Samuel, 112
Personal Rule, the, 3, 7, 12, 31, 34, 40, 43, 93, 99, 118, 152
Perth, 147
Peter, Hugh, 127, 179
Petition of Right, 39, 165
Petty, Maximilian, 87
Petty, William, 124
Phillips, Edward, 104
Physicians, College of, 108, 128
Pickering, Sir Gilbert, 184
Pierrepont, William, 185, 200
'plantation', 23, 144
plots, 54–5, 171
Plots: Army, 21, 40; Popish, 30–1, 61, 104
Plymouth, 59
Pontefract, 94
poor laws and and poor relief, 5, 115, 154
Popery, 4, 118; Popish, see Catholic; Plot
population, 115–17
Portsmouth, 195
Portugal, Portuguese, 168, 187
Prayer Book, Elizabethan, 64; Scottish, 9, 13
prerogative courts, 66; see also High; North; Star
Presbyterians, Presbyterian Church, presbyterianism, 8, 23, 28, 32, 40, 55–6, 62–5, 67, 69, 78, 83–4, 87, 92, 94, 96, 100–1, 118, 124, 131–2, 140–2, 152–3, 169, 185, 188, 192–3, 196, 200
Preston, 93, 132
prices, see inflation
Pride, Colonel Thomas, 97, 204
Pride's Purge, 97–9, 101, 131, 133–4, 197

Prince, the (Prince of Wales) see Charles I; Charles II
Prince, Thomas, 136–7
privateers, 168, 186
Privy Council and Councillors, 5, 6, 9, 16, 18–19, 21–2, 25, 32, 35–6, 38, 40, 53, 70, 78–9, 115, 143
professions, learned, 41, 124–5
Protector see Cromwell
Protectorate, 163–89 passim
Protestants, Protestantism, 4, 24, 30, 46, 60, 62, 64, 68, 119, 123, 125, 166, 185; see also Episcopalians; High Church; Low Church; Puritans; Sects
Protestants, Continental, 37–8, 162, 186
Prynne, William, 4–5, 69
public faith, the, 71, 116
Puritans, Puritanism, 4, 16, 24–31, 39, 46, 61–70, 74, 78, 101–15, 119, 123–9, 134, 138, 146, 153, 179, 185, 196–7, 202–3, 205; see also Baptists; Congegationalists; Presbyterians; Sects
purveyance, 6
Putney Debates, 87–8, 132–3
Pym, John, 13, 20–2, 28, 30, 33, 39–42, 55, 63, 106, 158, 192
Pyne, John, 50

Quakers, Quakerism, 67, 122, 125, 138, 153, 161, 176–7, 180, 193, 195, 198

Rainsborough, Thomas, 69, 81, 87–9, 93–4, 136, 139, 204
Ranters, 67, 135, 137–9, 152, 176
Recruiters, recruiting (of the Commons), 69, 73, 82
reforms, reformation, 118–30, 152–4, 160, 165–6, 174
Reformation, the, 101, 110
regicides, 99–101, 131, 134, 202
religious freedom, see toleration
Remonstrants (Protesters), 92–3, 145–6
Republic, republicans, English, 101–3, 106–7, 112–17, 122, 125–35, 140, 148, 151, 156, 170–1,

176, 182–3, 187–8, 190–1, 193, 195, 198–200, 202–3
Requests, Court of, 19
Restoration, the, 40, 43, 98–9, 104, 106, 110, 117, 121–2, 127, 129, 142, 190, 198, 202–4
Resumption Act (Scottish), 8
revenue, *see* customs; excise; finance; taxation
Reynolds, John, 184
Rich, Robert, 184, *see also* Holland; Warwick
Richelieu, Cardinal, 16
Ripon, Treaty of, 15
Robinson, Henry, 120, 126
Rolle, Henry, 172
Root and Branch, 28–9, 64, 125
Rota Club, 194
Roundheads, 44; *see also* Parliamentarians; Puritans
Royal Society, the, 128–9
royalists, 34, 38, 41–4, 51, 66, 69, 71, 79, 93, 103–5, 109, 117–18, 128–31, 134, 140–6, 149–50, 167–71, 185, 188–9, 192–3, 196, 202; *see also* Cavaliers
Rump, *see* Parliament
Rupert, Prince, 31, 44, 47–9, 52, 54, 57–8, 62–3, 75–6, 93, 140, 148
Russell, *see* Bedford
Ruthven, *see* Forth
Rutland, 43

St James's, 150
St John, Oliver, 13, 21, 33, 39–40, 55, 63, 111, 149, 157–8, 184–5, 194, 199
Safety, Committee of, 53–4, 70, 193
Salisbury, 171, 173
Salisbury, William Cecil, Earl of, 142
Salmasius, 141
Salwey, Richard, 158, 194, 197, 199
San Domingo, 168, 171
Saye and Sele, William Fiennes, Viscount, 33, 39, 40, 53, 75, 142
science, 107–8
Scot, Thomas, 69, 157, 188, 199
Scots, Scottish, 7, 14, 25, 41, 54–64, 67, 70, 77–80, 86, 90–3, 143, 152, 183, 202; *see also* Army; Church; Council; Parliament

Scotland, 8–12, 21, 38, 63, 76, 116, 123, 128, 140, 144–7, 149, 165, 169, 171, 178, 182, 187, 189, 191, 193–4, 202
sculpture, 112–13
Secluded Members, 197–8; *see also* Pride's Purge
Secretary of State, *see* Thurloe; Vane
sects, sectaries (Puritan), 40, 63–4, 66–8, 78, 92, 101, 115, 134, 139, 178, 189
Selby, 57
Selden, John, 199–200
Self-Denial, Self Denying Ordinance, 50, 72–4, 78, 81, 93, 132, 148, 154
senate, 192
Separatists, 5; *see also* Puritans; Sects
Septennial Act, 18
Sexby, Edward, 87–8, 136, 142, 193
sheriffs, 6, 13
ship money, 5–7, 13, 20, 151; Act against, 19
Shropshire, 49
Sidney, Algernon, 158; *see also* Leicester; Lisle
Skippon, Philip, 48, 59, 73, 81
social structure and hierarchy, 31, 113–18, 203
Socinians, 153, 180
Solemn League and Covenant, 54, 67, 74, 81, 132, 140, 146
Somerset, 22, 49–50, 75
Somerset, Robert Ker, Viscount Rochester, later Earl of, 37
Sound, the, 186
Spain, 39, 60, 150, 166–8, 183, 186–7
Spanish War of 1620s, 37; of 1650s, 175–6, 180, 183, 186
Spavin, Robert, 184
Speaker, the, 33, 84, 152
Staffordshire, 49
stage, *see* theatre
Stapleton, Sir Philip, 55
Star Chamber, Court of, 4, 19, 64; Act against, 18
State, the (English State), 36, 64, 66, 90, 104, 108, 114, 117, 120, 122, 151, 161, 176, 187, 203